D1379813

WINNING IN COMMERCIAL REAL ESTATE SALES

An Action Plan for Success

Thomas Arthur Smith

REAL ESTATE EDUCATION COMPANY
a division of Dearborn Financial Publishing, Inc.

While a great deal of care has been taken to provide accurate and current information, the ideas, suggestions, general principals and conclusions presented in this text are subject to local, state and federal laws and regulations, court cases and any revisions of same. The reader is thus urged to consult legal counsel regarding any points of law—this publication should not be used as a substitute for competent legal advice.

Executive Editor: Kathleen A. Welton
Project Editor: Jack L. Kiburz
Interior Design: Mary Kushmir
Cover Design: Sam Concialdi

©1990 by Dearborn Financial Publishing, Inc.

Published by Real Estate Education Company
a division of Dearborn Financial Publishing, Inc.

Printed in the United States of America.

91 92 10 9 8 7 6 5 4 3 2

Library of Congress Cataloging-in-Publication Data

Smith, Thomas Arthur.
  Winning in commercial real estate sales : an action plan for success / Thomas Arthur Smith.
    p.   cm.
  ISBN 0-7931-0008-9
  1. Commercial buildings. 2. Real estate business. 3. Success in business. I. Title.
HD1393.25.S65 1990   90-33092
333.33'873'0688—dc20   CIP

Contents

Exclusive • When an Exclusive Is Not an
Opportunity • Selling a Deal Opportunity and
Making It a Deal • It's Your Deal Opportunity
To Make or Lose So Never Give Away Control;
See Yourself as a Bloodhound and the Deal
Opportunity's Best Friend • Fifteen Surefire
Ways To Lose a Deal Opportunity • On Dealing
with Panic or What To Do When One Side
Wants To Delay, Alter, Rewrite or Renegotiate
at the Eleventh Hour

Preface

After lying on my living-room couch in a catatonic position one evening in the late summer of 1980, I began to question my sanity and my reasons for changing careers at 31 years of age.

Previously, I had completed nine years with Xerox Corporation as a professional selling representative, selling manager and selling training manager, but I found the allure of the ultra-dynamic and high-rolling profession of commercial real estate brokerage too strong to resist. Thus, in May of 1979 I packed up my personal belongings, sold my wonderful home in La Jolla, California, gassed up my 911 Porsche and moved to Phoenix, Arizona, where I joined the ranks of Coldwell Banker Commercial Real Estate Services as a selling agent in the investment division specializing in multifamily properties and sites for development.

Eighteen months later, my extreme discomfort lay in the fact that I had just lost my first major real estate deal opportunity and much to my chagrin was now experiencing the aftershocks of the "blown deal syndrome."

Suddenly, my visions of large commission checks, new cars, an upgraded life-style and immediate professional standing had been annihilated, or so I thought at the time.

Nine years have passed since that day on my couch that fortunately for me have seen many deal opportunities evolve into successful closings and have brought much professional recognition and personal reward.

In writing this book my major motivation is to share the lessons that I have learned from both my own experiences of success and failure in commercial real estate selling and some of those lessons and experiences that have happened in the careers of my peers. All too often, commercial real estate selling agents tend to re-create all the wasteful and nonproductive experiences of those who have preceded them and in the process cost themselves and their organizations hundreds of thousands of dollars in lost revenues, alienated clients, lost deal opportunities and unnecessary selling-agent turnover. While this book is directed toward the commercial real estate selling agent, I believe that many of its principles, concepts and lessons can be applied in the careers of people who literally sell any product or service.

I use the word "selling" in place of the more traditional "sales" when defining real estate agents, their managers and their profession. It seems to me that not enough emphasis has been given to the necessary daily practices that play a part in the development of client relationships and the deal opportunities that they represent; therefore, the word "selling" is more indicative of the acts that lead to a successful deal opportunity closing or "sale."

The vital need for a thoughtful method of selling commercial real estate that can be taught not only to people entering this great profession but to those individuals who have built up varying degrees of tenure and success never has been greater. Far too often, selling agents completely lose their sense of a broad perspective as it relates to the state of their market, the depth of their client relationships, the "makability" of their deal opportunities and their real reason or "purpose" for being in the business. They become so caught up in the vigorous daily grasp for any signs of life within the deal opportunities they pursue that the more meaningful context of their client relationships and overall market strategies often are lost in the shuffle and blur.

A Deal Is Not a Deal
until It Actually Closes

Once again, I use the phrase "deal opportunity" rather than the traditionally used "deal" because I feel that too often selling agents take mental relief and solace in their thoughts about all the "deals" that they have working as if they were somehow more complete or close to closing than they actually are; thus for these purposes the phrase "deal opportunity" will be used to indicate potential deals that are to be developed and closed.

The "Big Bang Theory of Professional Selling Excellence" was based on 19 years of my professional selling, selling management and consulting experience and was greatly fortified by my observations, interviews and perceptions of many other talented professionals with whom I had the good fortune to interact during this period. This theory provides a *consummate mental and physical approach* to the rendering of **preeminent client service** and the attainment of **professional selling excellence.**

In simpler terms, if "Big Bang Selling" (the short form of "The Big Bang Theory of Professional Selling Excellence") is integrated into the values and actions of the selling organization and its selling agents, these entities will lead their industry in every respect by providing the finest service to their clients, their associates and their communities. Furthermore, by setting and achieving a standard of professional selling excellence and responsibility previously unknown as a whole in the commercial real estate brokerage industry, the organization and its agents will realize true greatness within their personal and professional frames of reference.

Acknowledgments

This book is dedicated to all my former peers and competitors at Xerox and Coldwell Banker who taught me the value of intense professional selling competition and the joy in total client service.

I would like to thank the following people for their support and encouragement in my effort to write this book: Peter Bolton, Judy Butterworth, Mark Tanguay, Lee Hanley, Michael Koether, Jeff Kowal, Jim Freeman, Wynn Paoletti, Alanna Mack, David Beck, Pamela Doak, Mike Mueller, Bill Gosnell, Dick Lund, Don Morrow, Bob Crum, Jim Cote, Rosalind Rodriguez, Janell Spetrino, Kay Mersereau and my Aunt Mona.

Introduction

Selling: A presentation and acceptance of ideas based upon a requirement, personal or professional, that is substantiated in knowledge, filled with integrity, pursued with tenacity and rooted in the belief that your thoughts, actions, products and services have merit and benefit for everyone concerned.

As we enter the 1990s, the myriad array of our local, regional and national commercial real estate markets offers a mindboggling context of client relationships and deal opportunities.

Because of the upheaval in the commercial real estate "darling markets" (the Sunbelt and other energy-driven states located in the western half of the United States) caused in large part by deflated energy prices, greatly slowed inmigration, minimal job growth, overbuilding, the Tax Reform Act of 1986 and the well-reported savings-and-loan industry crisis, coupled with the resurgence of the Rustbelt and Eastern seaboard markets, today's commercial real estate selling agent is at the cutting edge of the most challenging yet greatest opportunity for personal and professional success in the history of the commercial real estate brokerage industry.

The ability to grasp this unwieldy selling challenge, however, will not come without a great deal of historical perspective and understanding of how the 1980s has shaped much of the future destiny of deal making in the 1990s.

Like life, professional selling is based on a series of lessons, which, when learned, enable the educated selling agent to move forward successfully. Although this particular text is not meant to be a detailed analysis of the state of the commercial real estate market in the 1980s, a brief review of the major factors that were in play during this period is certainly in order.

Back to the Future

It seems that we are unable to escape the constant attention and the enormity of the current savings-and-loan industry debacle, whether reported in our morning newspapers or on the evening television news. The causes for this sad state of affairs have been widely reported in terms of their negative impact on the taxpaying citizens of the United States. Furthermore, the unscrupulous and at best unethical conduct of many of those individuals who were in charge of their particular savings-and-loan entities also has been exposed in all of its ugly incompetence and greed.

The real lesson for the commercial real estate selling agent seems to have been lost in the shuffle of finger pointing and damage control–oriented public relations. The lesson I am referring to was the ongoing violation of the review and approval process that was incompetently enacted in granting sanction for various real estate loans not only in fraudulently managed financial institutions but in ethically managed entities as well.

This often is known as "Due Diligence" or "The Due Diligence Process" and is defined as "a fair, proper and due degree of care and activity" used to make valid judgments on the relative risks in the lending on any given real estate deal opportunity.

I will use the term "Due Diligence Process" to refer to what should have taken place or should have consistently been implemented by the various lending entities (S&Ls or otherwise) to protect the many depositors and investors in our nation's now panic-stricken lending community and numerous nervous investment institutions.

The lesson is multifaceted; in its simplest context, however, it relates to the question of what were the underlying economic factors that went into the evaluation of granting approval for the necessary financing to bring these "deal opportunities" (development, investment or speculation) to life?

The most fundamental questions seemed to be ignored or brushed over lightly at best: Who will occupy these apartments, office buildings, industrial complexes, retail shopping centers, etc., and at what rental rates will they do so on project completion or deal opportunity closing? Of course, many lenders both in the savings-and-loan industry and in the more traditional banks and institutions were aware of this basic question but relied far too heavily on outside counsel by appraisers, the borrowers themselves, various market consultants or undernourished in-house "expertise."

Because of their reliance on unconfirmed market conditions, overly optimistic pro forma assumptions and sometimes errone-ous market comparables, lenders made many unwise loans on projects that were ill-conceived, improperly planned and wrongly suited for the very market segments in which they were placed.

The one part of the equation that was overlooked consistently was a clear understanding of a market requirement and pres-ence of various potential businesses and bodies to fill these projects. In other words, what were the existing and proposed so-cioeconomic factors that would bring a business and its people to locate or relocate in any given segment of the market and why would that business and its people occupy any given project? If, in fact, a real market for these proposed projects in these particu-lar market segments existed, what was the depth of that market segment and its projects in terms of their abilities to absorb these potential tenants and at what cost to the existing base of developed properties in terms of vacancy impact and rental rate achievement?

The best examples of this lack of thought process are the countless and mindless retail strip and neighborhood shopping centers that were developed without any major anchor tenants. Many developers compounded this situation by building two-story retail structures without anchor tenants in market seg-ments that had never accepted this structural shopping alternative.

Another example of misplaced lending and inappropriate faith in dubious development was illustrated amply in the apartment-development boom in the Sunbelt cities during the 1980s. In their rush to take advantage of the syndication-oriented buyers of the era, many apartment developers con-vinced their lenders of the merits of building literally any type of project in the so-called "can't miss locations." Unfortunately, many of these projects were either overbuilt or underbuilt for their market segments and thus could never hope to achieve the level of rents initially pro formaed to justify either the potential appropriate tenant profile or develop the necessary income stream to adequately service their debt.

Here a Deal, There a Deal, Everywhere a Deal Deal

The third example of *Star Wars* lending was the irresponsible manner in which millions of dollars were lent on highly speculative land investment. At least in the previous examples, the decision making could be justified partially because of the tax-shelter value of these projects. In the case of land lending, this criterion does not hold up. The only justification seemed to be in making loans on parcels based on the erroneous hype of future employment and housing growth and the main justification of the times, "the piece across the street just sold for x; therefore my parcel must be worth at least $x+?$"

Of course, few lenders took the time to understand that the blinding short-term profits from these parcels were in many cases emanating from a type of insider trading among various syndication and land-development entities. Thus, when the reality of the lack of any sound economic base to develop these large parcels within any reasonable and foreseeable future was exposed, the caboose finally joined this mad train of speculation and the chickens, or in this case the land, came home to roost.

Five to nine years later, many of these projects have been returned to the bowels of the lenders from which they originally received life. Unfortunately, the negative impact of this experience only begins here and continues with the overwhelming *"crush-down" effect.*

The "crush-down" effect can best be defined as the limited ability of rental and occupancy rates to move upward because of the expansion and proliferation of either ill-conceived or far-too-similar development. This effect not only crushes rents but also holds down the entire market segment from becoming a vital market area with positive tenant movement and fully leased projects that act in the interests of the entire community.

All Principals Are Not Created Equal

Perhaps in the eyes of our local and national media, all investors, lenders and developers are alike; however, nothing could be further from the truth. The developers, investors and lenders of these various projects who actually understood the economic, professional, competitive and personal profiles of their tenants and market segments generally stayed healthy and continued to survive and in many cases still thrive today. Their impact on their communities and cities is one of positive growth and stimulated economic development. Many credible developers and syndicators, however, took a severe financial beating during the late 1980s because of depressed energy prices, overbuilding and the removal of the tax-shelter value on various projects.

The lesson for the commercial real estate selling agent is to understand the thought process of those investors and developers who build or acquire projects that lease at market or above-market rates and that consistently are well occupied and well conceived not only for today's market but for future markets.

As has been said many times by many people, the business of selling commercial real estate does not involve brain surgery or rocket science, but it does take a keen understanding of who is building, lending, investing and leasing and under what structure and for what purpose.

The commercial broker or agent then must discern which of these entities is acting with a broad as well as a specific understanding of all the relevant economic, political and social factors that will enable these projects and investments to provide positive impetus to the market and to all who inhabit its challenging terrain.

To better understand how financing became so readily available, even for suspect development and investment, and what other factors fueled the go-go commercial real estate markets of the early and mid-1980s, we first must recall some of the changes that took place in the areas of federal tax legislation and savings-and-loan industry regulation.

In 1980, the ceiling for insured deposits in federally chartered S&Ls was increased from $40,000 to $100,000. Through this act, large and small, established and new, ethical and unethical savings-and-loan entities experienced rocket-driven growth.

These increased deposits became the source of funds for home mortgages for which the S&Ls originally had been established; in 1982, however, the Congress relaxed the constraints on S&Ls and permitted them to make loans on all types of commercial real estate ventures, as well as engage in either joint venture with outside parties or direct investment through the counsel of their own internal gurus.

During this same period, the Reagan administration tried to jumpstart the U.S. economy by passing the Economic Recovery Tax Act of 1981 (ERTA). In addition to providing the largest tax cut to date and designed to stimulate the economy, ERTA had its greatest impact on the U.S. commercial real estate market by replacing the system of depreciation, which dated back to 1913, with a new Accelerated Cost Recovery System (ACRS).

In the late 1970s during the Carter administration, rampant inflation had caused a decline in the "real value" of depreciation. As a result of ERTA, commercial real estate properties now could be depreciated over a much shorter time frame and would provide the investors with greatly increased deductions against taxable income. This encouraged additional investment, which, in turn, fueled the construction and service sectors of the national economy.

Thus, in the race to book burgeoning profits and shelter income in the early to mid-1980s, many lending institutions and various investment entities often in the form of private or public syndications gorged themselves in a buying frenzy in many markets and became unwitting partners in the unintentional abuse of the very markets in which they were most heavily invested.

During the early part of the decade, even though no one knew where the markets were heading and no one could foresee the impact that overlending and overbuilding eventually would have on our markets, the long-accepted practice of utilizing prudent decision-making criteria often was abandoned. Commercial real estate deal opportunities were created and approved not only for the demands or user potential of the marketplace, but also for the demands of the myriad of investors who sought to shelter income and reap profits based on the new taxation and lending climates in our country.

Nobody Told Congress:
"Never Change Horses in Midstream"

Cars probably still would be added to this metaphorical great train today if not for the Tax Reform Act of 1986 by which the engine of our conceptual train became very much reengineered. TRA '86 was the most extensive overhaul of the U.S. tax code in almost 40 years, as well as the most fundamental reform of the U.S. tax structure.

The jumpstart that Ronald Reagan had sought and achieved now was deemed not so politically acceptable and this startling legislation was evolved in Reagan's proposal for "revolutionary" reform legislation with the goals of "fairness and simplicity."

I shall leave the argument of whether TRA '86 achieved its goals of fairness and simplicity to much brighter minds, but it nevertheless made history with the breadth of its changes and its impact on existing and proposed players and projects.

While history will judge the overall merits of TRA '86, one thing is certain: The nature, motivation and structure of commercial real estate deal opportunities shall remain changed forever.

As all the elements of TRA '86 and their impact are phased into existing and proposed commercial real estate deals and deal opportunities, we find that the emphasis on and grand benefits of tax shelter now are history. Furthermore, the markets that received new projects with open arms in the name of thoughtless growth are paying the unexpected price of "see-through projects," dashed hopes of easy prosperity, troubled lending institutions and confused but angry citizenry.

What about the lessons for the commercial real estate selling agent? First of all, one must understand the elements of TRA '86 that led to the present state of affairs in both our troubled and our healthy markets:

1. The rules for reporting installment sales changed radically: through these changes a much greater emphasis on all-

cash transactions has taken place and deal structure and financing parameters have changed dramatically.

2. The rules on passive and nonpassive income altered the types of deal opportunities that your clients have come to seek.

3. Accelerated depreciation has been eliminated and after-tax yields must be viewed in the context of the new depreciation schedules, which are 27.5 years for residential properties and 31.5 years on nonresidential properties.

4. The amortization of construction-period interest over ten years no longer applies to real property for interest paid after December 31, 1986. TRA '86 requires that interest incurred in the construction or production of any real property must be capitalized into the cost of the property and depreciated over either 27.5 or 31.5 years.

5. Leasehold improvements no longer can be expensed over the life of the lease. They now must be written off over 31.5 years.

Perhaps these are simple realizations that you grasped immediately on your first exposure to TRA '86 and I certainly hope that is the case. These are, however, just some of the major points or most important lessons to be assimilated.

Deal-Making Ninja

More important is the value and incredible importance of keeping up with the "whys" or motivations taking place in the evolution of deal opportunities every day in our kaleidoscopic markets. You must continually expand your knowledge and act with change and not react to perceived difficulties of newness. Finally, you must form solid, mutually supportive relationships in other professional disciplines, such as accounting, law, title, lending, architecture and planning, to understand alternative perspectives and help you close deal opportunities.

The commercial broker and selling agent par excellence of the 1990s must understand the overall importance of maintaining both macro and micro points of view that will enable him or her to continually find and court success regardless of the state of the market and the various factors that influence its immediate and future vibrancy.

It is my commitment to the reader in the following chapters to provide insights into the wonderful profession of selling that will enable the reader to attain levels of personal and professional achievement previously unknown and unrealized.

My objective is to provide a sound base of education about the joys, strategies, skills and success involved in selling commercial real estate. I hope that this education process inspires the reader to develop an ongoing desire and internal motivation to expand his or her knowledge and skills to bring about win/win deals for everyone.

PART
I

Preparing Yourself
for Success

CHAPTER
1

Winning in Commercial Real Estate Sales: Unraveling Success in Any Market

The current state of various commercial real estate markets offers today's professional broker and selling agent many unique deal opportunities and challenges. The ability to recognize and take advantage of these opportunities depends on the individual's ability to position himself or herself as *the most genuine voice in deal making* in a particular commercial real estate specialty and market segment.

Developing the Most Genuine Voice

The often-overlooked fact is that no one should know more about what is happening in today's marketplace than the commercial broker or agent. As the person in the market every day, you should observe the myriad of deal opportunities, their structure, their financing sources, their specific tenant profiles, the motivations behind their creation and much more.

Only when you are aware of all the significant deal opportunities in their various stages and are at least aware of the pending client requirements within your specialty and areas of expertise, can you begin to consider yourself the most genuine voice of prudent counsel for those who wish to be involved in deal development, investment or utilization of space within your marketplace.

I say "your marketplace" because that is how you must view it. Your personal objective should be to take control of those clients and principals who frequent your arena and to keep abreast of the progress of their movements and decisions. Absolutely no one should know more about your marketplace than you, including real estate lawyers, lenders, market consultants, appraisers and, especially, your competitors. But before you can assume this position of authority, you must learn seven premises that will help you build the appropriate foundation for long-term success.

Very often when selling agents either are beginning in the business or are floundering in their present deal opportunities, they may chase the wrong type of deal possibilities. As tempting as the pursuit of a seemingly easy deal opportunity is with its siren's call of ready commission dollars, this sort of quest often can lead you into the mists of deal mirage. Illogical pursuit of this type will keep you from building the foundation of preplanned activities that ultimately will serve you, your clients and your marketplace in the highest degree.

The following premises are the initial elements of a thought process that always will help you overcome the seductive allure of easy deal making and inappropriate direction.

Premise Number One: The Importance of Charting a Road Map for Success

Before you can become the herald of your marketplace, you must design a road map for success. Simply stated, take the time to establish the relevant mile markers of achievement in the necessary skills and knowledge areas that will make you the most authentic observer of the people and the events that evolve daily in your market and its segments.

Two of the skill categories are *selling* skills (such as empathy and listening, verbal and presentation, relationship and process, closing and control, and tenacity and creativity) and *analytical* skills (such as market segmentation and niche development, deal structure and its rationale, market facilitators or inhibitors and their impact, pro forma acceptance through assumption weighting, and socioeconomic-political influences and their effects).

Another group of mile markers is in the knowledge area. Particular areas of expertise should include an understanding of present-market and market-segment occupancy levels, vacancy levels, rental rates, total square footage by specialty, total number of projects or buildings, profiles of active major and smaller tenants (there is no such thing as a minor tenant), relevant industry influence within a specific market and its segments, actual deal profiles in previous months (including structure and motivations), personal histories and profiles of principals who make the decisions for active and potential client relationships and so on.

One major reason for establishing these mile markers of success is that when you are able to mark them off on your road map, you immediately gain a strong sense of confidence through competence that will lead to a higher level of professionalism and ultimately to *selling excellence*. Furthermore, these professional miles will keep your attitude from wandering into the lost directions of frustration and futility whenever you encounter seemingly irreversible difficulty.

The most important lesson that I can share is that the quality of your professional journey is just as important as your destination. The lesson of the journey and its enjoyment will be, if learned, the enabling factor that will see you through the frustrations, failures, misdirections, misperceptions and erroneous motivations that always will be a part of the commercial real estate selling experience.

Premise Number Two: "Did I Do Everything Possible To Make This Deal Opportunity Succeed?"

You must ask yourself this question at every step of the deal-opportunity development process. Often after a deal opportunity falls through or we lose a client's significant relationship to a competitor, we berate ourselves by saying, "if I woulda, shoulda, coulda," which translated means "if only I had done this or said that, then I would have made this deal." It is important, therefore, that we check the extent not only of our physical but also our mental efforts to determine whether or not we travel that extra mile.

The best way to remember this concept is always to ask yourself, if "based on my greatest awareness, most current information and most creative thoughts, did I, in fact, do everything possible to make this deal opportunity succeed?"

A method of gauging your parameters is to consider your efforts in everything from research to representation. If you can affirm the merits of your endeavor in these two major areas and in everything in between, then for the purposes of long-term and consistent selling success, it makes little difference whether or not that one specific deal opportunity succeeded; if you develop the habit of this type of professional selling checks and balances, you will close more deal opportunities than you ever imagined possible.

Another result of this type of mental process is that you will develop a level of confidence that can withstand the emotional flurries that often occur when a deal opportunity "goes South."

Premise Number Three: Encouraging the "What If?" Question

You cannot pose a more pertinent question, especially when your deal opportunity is at a standstill. As you probably know, there are times in the presentation of a deal opportunity when one of the principals seems totally angry, frustrated, unnerved, irascible and seemingly anxious to dislocate you from your senses. This often occurs when the perplexed negotiator considers you to be something between vegetable, animal or mineral, but he or she is not quite sure because he or she is too confounded by the elements of your deal-opportunity proposal.

I strongly suggest that now is the time to pose the vaunted "what if?" question. It is time for you to inquire about what areas of the proposal are acceptable and why, and what areas of the proposal are unacceptable and why.

The easiest way then to counter the unacceptable area or areas is to pose alternatives, which based on your knowledge of the deal proposal and its relevance to current market reality, might provide an acceptable alternative.

For instance, if I am presenting a retail-lease proposal on a prime location to the developer on behalf of a small shop tenant and that developer rejects my proposal, I must determine why. If the rent offer is unacceptable, I must ask, "what if we move the rate to X, would he then accept my tenant?" At this point, we at least will determine whether or not the rejection is only a matter of rate and not some other factor such as the type of tenant being proposed or the clientele that would be attracted by its presence in the center.

Remember that whether you are involved in a lease negotiation or in an acquisition of an investment property, the decision-making principals will not always lay their cards or, in reality, their thoughts on the table. Therefore the "what if?" question always will enable you to discover the hidden thoughts and motivations of your clients and principals.

Premise Number Four:
Who, What, Where, When, Why and How?

If there is any one situation that causes more frustration to professional selling agents than realizing that they failed "to do everything possible" to make a deal opportunity succeed, it is undoubtedly the eventual and painful blast of awareness that occurs when they realize that they are working on "impossible to make" deal opportunities. Learning the art of "avoiding the great rainbow chase" is one of the most important lessons of Big Bang Selling. Some agents spend their entire careers in confusion and mediocrity because they don't understand why their deal opportunities fail to develop and close.

They never become aware of the doubts that should have sent up red flags regarding, for example, not only the buyer's ability to obtain the required financing but other important matters that can turn into difficult deal points once the opportunity enters escrow. The lesson is always to gain every bit of pertinent information on the front end of the deal opportunity.

Sellers also may fail to share many obstacles or hidden items, such as problems assuming the existing project debt, and thus not conforming to original pro forma assumptions on the buyer's part, or zoning requirements that have not been satisfied. If you can minimize the potential for disastrous unknowns to pop up, then you can better qualify your client relationships and the deal opportunities that they represent.

In the final analysis, commercial real estate selling agents do not get paid just for their creative efforts. We must close our deal opportunities, and by qualifying or screening as many of the relevant deal factors up front before final negotiations, we will realize much more success.

But how do we perform this seemingly obvious task? We must understand deal making in part and in whole and we must never avoid asking pertinent, deal-pointed questions.

At one time or another we all have heard either part or all of the phrase "who, what, where, when, why and how?" Many of us learned this concept as the guiding principle of our junior-high book reports.

If we ask these questions of our clients and principals on both sides of our deal opportunities, we seldom will end up chasing but never quite catching those elusive deal-opportunity rainbows.

We also must question the deal opportunity itself regarding its economic, structural, market and overall potentialities.

To simplify, you must question your deal opportunity principals (clients) about their professional and financial qualifications, what they want to accomplish and what they already have accomplished or previously performed, what their ability is to perform and their expectations of the opportunity, what overall market or its segments are they interested in, what are their corporate/firm, professional and personal motivations for doing so and how do they plan to perform in regard to all pertinent deal-opportunity elements from decision making to signing the necessary documents to closing per contractual or opportunity parameters.

You must develop the habit of mentally formulating the appropriate questions within the context of the "who, what, where, when, why and how?" phrase and your closing ratios and satisfaction level will rise higher than ever before.

Furthermore, you will gain a great deal of insight into many areas of client motivation, expertise, history, challenges and attitudes, which will help you work on those relationships and opportunities that will best benefit all concerned.

Premise Number Five: Energizing a Mission Mentality

A mission is defined as "a particular work or goal that one is or feels destined to do or accomplish; a calling." No one forced you into making the profession of commercial real estate selling your chosen career opportunity.

Few other professions offer the broad range of experiences, relationships and rewards that can be gained if one is successful. Nowhere can one find more individual freedom to pursue his or her professional goals and personal dreams. Although many hear the call and some are chosen, few make or ever realize the necessity to make this profession a personal mission.

The world of professional commercial real estate selling demands that success will not be achieved with integrity or consistency unless its great selling agents first make a commitment to the mission. The mission is multifaceted as we will see later in the context of Big Bang Selling; however, it starts with the awareness and the development of a professional selling mentality that one truly believes he or she is destined to succeed and is willing to work at a continuing series of lessons and goals.

A *mission mentality* involves a mental and physical focus on the successful completion of every step of the deal-opportunity development process. With this mentality, you use a specific method to lead you to a particular result to further your client relationships and deal opportunities. We can call it the *heat-seeking missile approach* to finding the necessary data on anything from your market and its segments to current deal-opportunity strategies and client-relationship evolution.

Begin to see yourself on a mission of success whether you are in your car or in various meetings or engaging in research and related interaction with your associates.

Become acutely aware of how you spend your time in and out of the office. Keep a specific objective in mind for every face-to-face or telephone call that you make.

Never leave your office without being fully prepared for whatever your particular mission happens to be at that time. For instance, if you are about to drive or walk through a particular segment of your market, bring appropriate market data, comp information, a small tape recorder for notes, a list of specific locations or projects to visit and so forth.

Your *mission mentality* will become more energized if you turn off your car radio during your travels and use this free time to refine your thoughts about meeting your goals and objectives. We waste far too much time in our cars listening to music or events on the radio that detract from our primary focus.

Serious intent to succeed is another way to phrase your *mission mentality*, but however it is wrapped, your professional package as a clearly defined selling agent never should waver.

As a matter of perspective, I think you would agree that few fighter pilots, whether in peacetime or wartime, are not constantly aware of their particular missions. Police officers whose very mind-sets sometimes mean the difference between life and death obviously are constantly aware of their missions.

The point is for you to develop and maintain a mental approach that constantly reminds you of the specific reason for any given activity or interaction in which you partake.

In the following chapters, we will look at ways to more clearly define our overall mission in order to preserve our appropriate focus and energy level.

Premise Number Six: Creating a Deal-Opportunity Development Process

One must recognize the critical need to create a deal-opportunity development process and to recognize its value to long-term selling success.

The basic principle to realize is that closed deals result from a series of selling steps that begins with the selection of a specialty within the profession, such as office leasing or acreage selling. Next, gain a broad understanding of your chosen specialty as related to the whole marketplace and then select a specific market segment or segments in which to concentrate.

You must learn about the nature of past, current and proposed deal opportunities that have closed or are in some stage of development. This includes learning about specific price/value relationships, contractual structures, rent and expense levels by specific product type, prices and deal-opportunity structure by parcel, tenant or buyer profiles within your segments, ownership history by specific product or parcel, past and current motivations of key principals and various other elements.

Identify those clients or principals with current and future requirements within your specialty whether or not you have an existing relationship. Then establish face-to-face contact to better understand their requirements and your present abilities to satisfy them.

The exciting part is to enter your market segments to either create or find the appropriate fits for both sides of the deal opportunities. The next step is to gain some degree of control over the client's requirement either to sell, lease or buy and then develop a selling process to market and satisfy these requirements. As we further explore Big Bang Selling, you will be exposed to a more specific selling process.

Your final step is to monitor your progress in matching requirements through specific client meetings and personal review.

Now that you basically understand the development of deal opportunity, you must plan and implement a thought process that enables you to utilize all these premises.

Premise Number Seven: Building-Block Selling or Investing in Success Insurance

In the world of commercial real estate development, you must follow a series of steps or building blocks to ensure the success of a particular development. Successful developers know that their degree of thoroughness in every step of the development process will either aid or damage the potential success of a project. They also know that in addition to control of these steps or building blocks, outside influences and factors exist over which they have no control that can greatly influence the eventual degree or lack thereof of profitable yield. Therefore, smart developers will take into account all the basic premises that we have discussed. They must look at a development from both a macro and a micro point of view and try to minimize all elements of risk.

For example, a retail developer who seeks to build a 250,000-square-foot neighborhood shopping center first would produce an overall plan, including land acquisition, financing, documentation, leasing-phase projections by major and shop tenants, pad (mini site) sales projections, marketing, architectural and engineering plans, construction timetables and property management.

These categories of responsibility are the major building blocks and each is based on smaller building blocks. For example, under the broad heading of financing, the following steps must be satisfied: interim loan agreement, signed loan application, copies of leases, American Land Title Association (ALTA) survey, plat map, pro forma budget, plan and specification approval, Member, Appraisal Institute (MAI) appraisal, budget, site plan, architect's contract, résumé of contractor, permits, demographic package, insurance certificates, description of construction, bonds, development agreement, covenants, conditions and restrictions (CC&Rs), renderings and signed purchase and escrow documents. And this is just one major building block—financing.

You must leave absolutely no block misplaced or improperly set in your building-block selling process. Thus, by constructing a sound mental process through a series of selling premises, you can minimize the chance of controllable mistakes and maximize your chance of constructing a powerful and lasting foundation for long-term Big Bang Selling success.

CHAPTER
2

The Big Bang Theory of Professional Selling Excellence

The essence of the philosophy of the Big Bang Theory of professional selling excellence can best be stated as follows: *to provide the commercial real estate selling agent with **the most genuine voice in deal making** within his or her specialty through a consummate mental and physical approach and methodology. This approach leads toward rendering state-of-the-art client service during the creation and evolution of win/win deals. This methodology distinguishes the selling agent as one who sells with professional excellence and distinction.*

During my years in the commercial real estate brokerage industry, I was amazed that very few of the professional selling agents with whom I came in contact viewed themselves as salesmen. In fact, hardly anyone referred to himself or herself as a real estate salesman or even less as a salesperson.

Everyone, it seemed, liked to think of themselves as brokers or consultants. The word "salesman" seemed to carry a connotation about the individual and his or her profession that was somewhat dubious at best, deceitful at worst and sleazy in between.

Even my edition of Funk and Wagnalls defined "salesmanship" as "the ability or skill in selling" and provided a myriad of subdefinitions of "selling," none of which provided the barest of reasons for any professional selling agent to be proud of his or her profession. To wit, "to deliver, surrender or betray for a price or reward; to sell one's honor." Here's another less-than-inspirational definition: "To cause to accept or approve something; with on: They sold him on the scheme." Then there are the slang definitions: "to betray, joke or swindle." No wonder no one wanted to be called a salesman! In our society in general, I have found that the profession of selling in any industry often is viewed with a skeptical eye by the general public as well as by many of the clients/customers whom we seek to serve.

The key word is "serve" because as the true professional salesman knows he or she is in the business of meeting people's needs by rendering a service and/or providing a product.

The profession of selling, when properly executed, is one of the most honorable, meaningful and vital careers in which anyone can partake. The rewards are unlimited for those who take up its inherent mental and physical challenges.

The profession of selling in the commercial real estate industry is one of the most exciting careers imaginable because of the opportunities to serve others, the potential rewards and recognition and the chance to keep your fingers on the energy and pulse of the cities, markets and communities in which you operate.

The professional selling agent who is in the market every day actually can see why and how economic growth takes place. He or she knows the players and principals who make things happen in terms of economic, political and social vitality. If the selling agent is wise, he or she can treat his or her selling career as a professional scholarship in everything from real estate development to community planning and development. The opportunities are limitless.

Fortunately, my career with Xerox Corporation has given me the proper foundation and understanding about what the profession of selling can genuinely be: a proud and knowledgeable competence in one's professional skills that benefits the customer (client), the organization and the individual.

My Xerox selling training and experience exposed me to the best of the best, and some of the worst, who are involved in the great profession of selling.

Because I always have taken great satisfaction in my ability to compete effectively with the most tenacious, knowledgeable and creative selling minds in the office-products industry, I was not prepared to abandon the dictates of professional selling just because I had entered commercial real estate.

I could see quickly that the need for the professional selling skills and understanding that were part of my daily Xerox experience during the 1970s were as badly needed and as often overlooked in my commercial real estate exposure in the 1980s.

The major theme for the lack of positive identification as a salesman often was stated as, "nobody buys deals by being sold," "as brokers, we don't have to sell anyone" and my favorite, "that Xerox and IBM stuff doesn't work in real estate."

The fact that nothing could be further from the truth seemed of little consequence to many agents until a strange phenomenon began to evolve through the 1980s. Many of the same people who had been exposed to and trained in a meaningful, disciplined and creative selling approach in their previous careers were utilizing many of those skills and methods and finding even greater success in their commercial real estate brokerage careers.

In many cases these same individuals appeared at the very top echelons of performance not only within their own company but within their entire specialty throughout the country.

This message, however, never has been fully translated or received by the upper layers of brokerage company management as it relates to the need for effective and ongoing meaningful selling training for their own individual selling forces.

Traditionally, most men and women who entered the industry discovered it was fraught with a survival-of-the-fittest mentality and thus soon expected little in the way of professional selling training and development. Because that was how it always had been, the various layers of management have seen no need to significantly alter this course.

Many commercial real estate brokerage companies have become successful despite nonexistent or shallow sales training because they hired quality people who somehow figured out how to succeed; therefore, the need to implement effective selling training has not exactly become a vital issue.

As a consequence, the level of professionalism that exists in the industry is as varied as the personalities of the agents and the markets they inhabit. And, unfortunately, so is the satisfaction level of the clients who depend on these same selling agents to render a professional selling service.

In my opinion, the vast majority of agents in the business would like to become more proficient in all the aspects of their profession.

Based on my desire to further educate and support these professionals and thus raise the standards of performance in the commercial real estate selling industry, I have developed *The Big Bang Theory of Professional Selling Excellence.*

I hope that the concepts of this theory will eliminate much of the re-creation process that is reborn every day in commercial real estate brokerage companies throughout the country, a process that has become self-regenerative in its needless unpleasant lessons that sometimes lead to emotional frustration and financial desperation.

Unlike many of the people who manage, control and implement selling training and development in many brokerage companies throughout the country, my experience is not in the education industry but is the result of successfully competing in two of the finest professional selling corporations in American business, Xerox of the 1970s and the commercial division of Coldwell Banker of the 1980s.

Therefore, I would like to offer a unique perspective and a new approach to the survival and prosperity of the professional selling agent in the commercial real estate industry. Additionally, I hope that this book's theory and concepts will support the efforts of those sales trainers and training managers who are trying to find new and more meaningful ways to develop their particular selling forces.

Where Do You Begin?

When you first enter the commercial real estate industry, you can be overwhelmed. The industry is quite active and deals seem to be made everywhere. It all looks so easy! You cannot wait to begin working with your own clients on your own deals. You become so anxious, in fact, that you are willing to pursue the "snipe deals." As you may recall, the only end result of the snipe hunt is not snipe but frustration. You thought you saw one and you were sure that you heard one; however, you always came back empty-handed because no such thing exists.

There are no easy deals, not really, but there is a way to buy yourself a policy of success insurance through what I previously called Big Bang Selling.

In order to avoid the great snipe hunt of the commercial real estate industry, you must understand what you hope to accomplish today, tomorrow and in the future.

In formulating the theory of Big Bang Selling, I am hoping to provide a *consummate mental and physical approach* to the achievement of individual goals and targeted **results**.

Big Bang Selling teaches and promotes excellence in deal making through the successful *understanding, integration and implementation of all deal-opportunity development factors*, which will be discussed in the following chapters.

According to Big Bang Selling, all professional selling begins with an inner core or **purpose**. This *purpose* must be viewed from both a macro (broad) and a micro (finite) perspective that invariably will lead to rendering **preeminent client service** (state-of-the-art client service) and attaining **professional selling excellence**.

In other words, you must set a specific series of goals for every selling call, every client relationship and every selling strategy on the micro level, which will help you provide the finest client service through a broader series of targeted results and goals on the macro level.

As you will discover, *professional selling excellence* will evolve as a result of a joint philosophical and physical approach to everyday selling in your commercial real estate arena, which, in turn, will enable you to render *preeminent client service.*

We find meaning and satisfaction in our lives usually when we realize that we have some important purpose to achieve or discover. This purpose increases the value, joy and peace in our lives and many times results through the love or service that we share with others.

The same is true with professional selling. Personal rewards and professional recognition are wonderful and certainly challenging to attain; as you grow within your profession, however, the greatest meaning will come through the client service you render and through the professional selling excellence you attain.

Big Bang Selling enables you to focus on achieving specific goals and targeted results in all areas of your selling career, which eventually will lead to Big Bang Selling *purpose (preeminent client service and professional selling excellence).*

Big Bang Selling therefore encompasses the value of identifying your professional *purpose;* then it surrounds that purpose with a personal **philosophy** of enhancement; that philosophy is, in turn, surrounded by an everyday selling **process** that works to sustain the philosophy and to achieve the *purpose.* (See Figure 2.1.)

The three major principles of Big Bang Selling serve as the major building blocks that enable you to accomplish every goal and realize every desire for which you set out in the competitive world of commercial real estate selling.

As you might imagine, each of these three major principles contains many concepts. To help you understand the nature of how all the elements of Big Bang Selling work together, I have created a flowchart (see Figure 2.2).

The main point to remember is that your primary goal is to become recognized as *the most genuine voice in deal making within your specialty within your marketplace.* This worthy pursuit eventually will lead you to the Big Bang Selling *purpose.*

"Client service" is a term with many different meanings to many different people. In the case of *preeminent client service,* this means face-to-face, personality-to-personality, charisma-to-charisma (or lack thereof) interpersonal contact. Big Bang Sell-

Figure 2.1   The Big Bang theory of professional selling excellence
or Big Bang Selling.

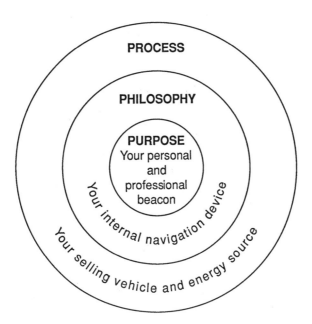

ing postulates that as the combination of your various skills and
areas of knowledge matures, you will get ever closer to rendering
state-of-the-art client service.

Nothing enables you to gain the appropriate knowledge and
skills more rapidly and effectively, however, than being in front
of the individuals who are involved actively in your marketplace
every day. As odd as it may seem, professional selling agents often do not make the necessary amount of face-to-face, ego-to-ego,
presence-to-presence calls that are necessary to achieve *professional selling excellence* that leads or impedes their ability to
provide *preeminent client service.*

I have examined this phenomenon from many points of view. I
have looked at the motivations of selling agents, their initial
training and preparation, the various types of ongoing professional selling development to which they are exposed, the level of
commitment that each has and the relative market segments in
which they work.

Figure 2.2 The Big Bang Selling purpose.

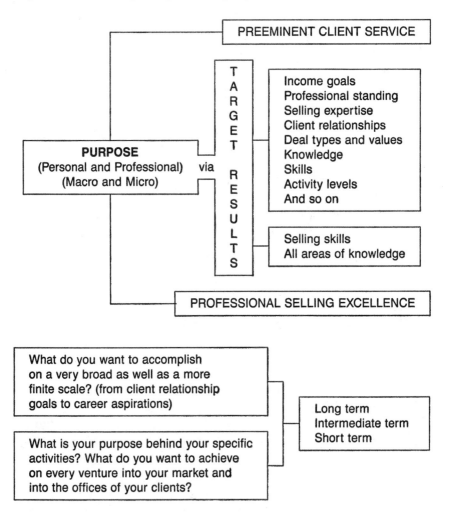

Although my observations would not qualify within any scientific parameters, I am convinced, nevertheless, that the one overriding, most awesome inhibitor of face-to-face selling is **fear**, *coupled with a lack of realistic professional selling training and development.*

You Have Nothing To Fear but Fear Itself!

When it comes to attaining any degree of success in professional selling, it is *fear* that holds us back. *Fear* becomes our own personal "crush-down effect" by sapping our vitality, creativity, competence and competitive spirit. *Fear* rationalizes why we spend so much time in our office "inputting data" or playing "musical desks" with our associates. *Fear* prevents us from making the important calls on those clients with whom we seek to develop relationships and to provide service. *Fear* makes us dread getting up in the morning, going into the office and then actually making the calls.

Sound familiar? Don't be ashamed or embarrassed if this scenario fits, for you are engaged in a battle with one of the most powerful forces in the universe, *fear!*

In order to defeat *fear* and eliminate its destabilizing effects, we first must understand it. In the professional selling world of commercial real estate, it is easy to become intimidated by clients, principals, lawyers, title officers, lenders and those competitors and associates who we feel must possess some special abilities or secrets that to date are unknown to us.

Although nothing could be further from the truth, we often believe that once we discover the secret of selling success in commercial real estate brokerage, all our challenges, frustrations and depression will be overcome instantly.

No special rituals or secrets will help to achieve this success. There are only markets; segments within those markets; principals who inhabit those markets either through ownership, occupancy or various types of speculative and investment activity; historical deals closed and their relative structures; current deal opportunities; socioeconomic factors; and political influences. The perceived secret then lies simply in your ability to gain the appropriate knowledge of and skills in developing your expertise in these areas.

If you study Big Bang Selling with an open and quiet mind, it will provide you with the necessary guidance and insight into capturing this professional success that then will lead you straight to rendering *preeminent client service,* the achievement of *professional selling excellence* and the attainment of every personal/professional *result* (goal) that you can imagine.

The Value of Clarity of Thought and Action

The three major principles of Big Bang Selling work together to help the professional selling agent gain *clarity* in his or her understanding of the broad perspective one must keep to find success in today's complex commercial real estate markets and those unknown future markets.

Because the ability to gain *clarity* is an ongoing process, Big Bang Selling enables the selling agent to continue to evolve and fine-tune the necessary decisions and actions that he or she will need to render *preeminent client service* and achieve *professional selling excellence.*

Purpose at the Core

Let's further examine the three major principles of Big Bang Selling: The inner core of Big Bang Selling postulates that all sales organizations, all professional selling agents and each individual sales call must start with a central *purpose* as their fundamental reason for existing. This *purpose, in turn, will lend focus and direction to every facet of professional selling in commercial real estate.*

Big Bang Selling asserts that the *purpose* behind the professional selling agent and his or her organization always must be to provide *preeminent client service* and to achieve *professional selling excellence.*

Pretargeted results, such as commission dollars, recognition, market share, client penetration levels, professional rank or standing, are not enough to serve as the *purpose* for the professional selling agent engaged in Big Bang Selling. These types of targets are very important, but they are simply a part of the current that swiftly moves the professional selling agent toward his or her real *purpose*.

The commercial broker or agent must understand the value of *purpose* in his or her career and life for it is *purpose* that always will shine brightly and will serve as a beacon of positive direction and focus in the individual and organizational pursuit of greatness.

The manifestation of *purpose* strengthens the element of belief on the selling agent's part because he or she recognizes that by reaching for *professional selling excellence*, one first must provide the finest service to his or her clients in all respects and that as a result of striving to provide this service, the self-oriented goals will become by-products of his or her *purpose*.

In order to achieve the Big Bang Selling *purpose*, the selling agent first must begin to consider the premises of who, what, where, when, why and how as they relate to his or her time, thoughts, actions and commitments. In other words, what do you think about when you are driving alone in your car? Are you considering the *purpose* behind the selling call that you are about to make? Are you reviewing your objectives for that call? Have you defined the level of commitment that you want to gain from the principal with whom you will interact? Do you have the necessary materials (market studies, pro formas, deal-opportunity summaries, pertinent packages of products, personal leave-behind data and so forth) that will further elucidate your point of view?

Far too often, selling agents travel in their markets without any real objective. If your *purpose* is to best serve your clients and would-be clients as well as yourself and your organization, then you must set a series of objectives that will lead to this *purpose*.

Your ability to recall your broad *purpose* and then to translate it into a series of smaller results always will keep you in the middle of the fastest and best-directed current of selling success.

You must realize that *preeminent client service* results not only from your actions but from your thoughts, ideas and attitudes and how they are applied to client requirements.

As your awareness of the value of the Big Bang Selling *purpose* increases, you will find that the real satisfaction in commercial real estate selling comes not only in the professional recognition or personal reward one receives but much more in the service he or she renders. This is further increased as the quality of that service improves through the individual achievement of *professional selling excellence*. As you continually are exposed to and understand all the elements of Big Bang Selling, you will receive a clearer idea of what forms *professional selling excellence*. This understanding will enable you to continue on your journey to becoming *the most genuine voice on deal making within your market and specialty*.

The Inner Ring:
The Philosophy of Big Bang Selling

If *purpose* serves as the beacon of Big Bang Selling, then its *philosophy* (see Figure 2.3) is its on-board gyroscope and internal navigational device. As the ancient mariners would have been lost without their sextants, we professional selling agents easily are lost without some form of mental approach to keep us from deviating from our road map to our Big Bang Selling *purpose*. The essence of this *philosophy* was stated at the beginning of this chapter; however, it is critical to understand that your ability to become *the most genuine voice in deal making within your specialty* is predicated on embracing all the ten tenets of the Big Bang *philosophy*. These ten tenets will be discussed in detail in the following chapters.

The intermediate layer was created to bring wisdom and fortitude to sustain the Big Bang Selling *purpose*.

According to one story, a well-meaning yet overmatched young selling agent thought he was ready to take on the challenges of commercial real estate brokerage. Although he had no professional selling background and little understanding of commercial real estate, he felt up to the task.

His overblown confidence resulted from his misperception of the rigors of the industry. He had seen many friends and acquaintances who had been in the real estate business for a period of two to five years begin to acquire BMWs, new apartments,

Figure 2.3 The essence of the Big Bang Selling philosophy.

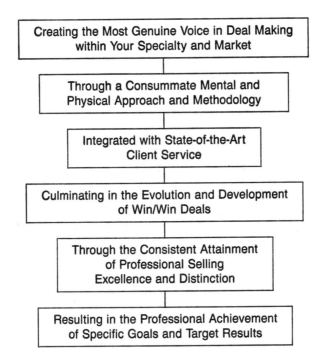

fancy clothing and the like and he thought if they could do it so could he.

Thus with little training he went out on his own to stake his claim to the rewards of selling commercial real estate.

Unknown to him, many of his friends who seemingly had attained easy success either did so through effective up-market timing or luck and thus far had achieved no real lasting success.

The acquaintances whom he viewed from afar not only had a more highly tenured success but also they had great professional selling experience in prior careers.

He soon found out to his great dismay that new cars and fancy clothes did not appear automatically with entrance to the business; he found himself unable to control either real client relationships or makable deal opportunities; he soon became financially overextended and ultimately disappeared somewhere in the West.

If It Were Easy, Everyone Would Be Selling Commercial Real Estate

Far too often, commercial real estate selling agents go riding off into our versions of the West. With little planning, minimal understanding and less perspective, we find ourselves thrashing around, pursuing "deals" to work on, "deals to close" and "deals that will bring us instant gratification." Far too often, as can be expected, we return to our offices feeling about as dismal as the young selling agent.

You were hired to enter or embarked on your own into what seemed to be an exciting and dynamic industry filled with challenge, great reward and unlimited potential. Your peers and managers enticed you with stories of the huge commission dollars that seemed to be "out there for the taking"; they related the major deals that so-and-so just closed; or they continued to point out the additional untapped potential that exists all around you. Yet as you gallop around in your marketplace, you find that the "spoils" and "deals" are not quite so easy to get your arms around, let alone control and close.

It is perhaps fitting at this point to remind you that there is no such thing as having "deals" working, there are only "deal opportunities." Until the "deal" closes, records, occupies and pays, it is only opportunity.

The Big Bang Selling *philosophy* was created in order to find and achieve *purpose* and to act as a mental imaging source for a focused vision and understanding of how to attain your professional and personal *purpose.*

Some of the most fundamental tenets of professional selling excellence often are **missing in understanding, attention and action (MIUAA)** and so many of you and your associates, competitors and colleagues in the business never even realize why you sometimes go dancing in the dark without even the companionship of a horse's sense of direction.

If studied, understood and followed, the Big Bang Selling *philosophy* always will keep you aware of the necessary context of your professional *mission*. Its ten tenets always will serve as navigational devices to keep you from straying too far off track or out of the current of your *purpose*.

Its final effect will be to provide that critical *clarity* that will aid you in your quest to render *preeminent client service*, achieve *professional selling excellence* and attain every goal and targeted *result* that you can possibly imagine.

CHAPTER
3

Knowledge, Relationships and Communication: The Indomitable Triad of the Big Bang Selling Philosophy

The ten tenets of Big Bang Selling and some of their subtenets are presented in Figure 3.1.

Selling begins with the first tenet, **knowledge**. As a professional selling agent in the competitive world of commercial real estate sales, you are completely unarmed and can offer little to prospective clients without it. *Knowledge* enables the professional real estate selling agent to articulate effectively the developmental movement of any specific deal opportunity or market segment.

Knowledge always will defeat **fear** or discomfort in any selling situation and will prevent you from ever being intimidated and ineffective.

Do I Know More?

The professional selling agent always must pose this question to himself or herself: *"Do I know more about this specific deal*

Figure 3.1   The ten tenets of the Big Bang Selling philosophy and some of their key subtenets.

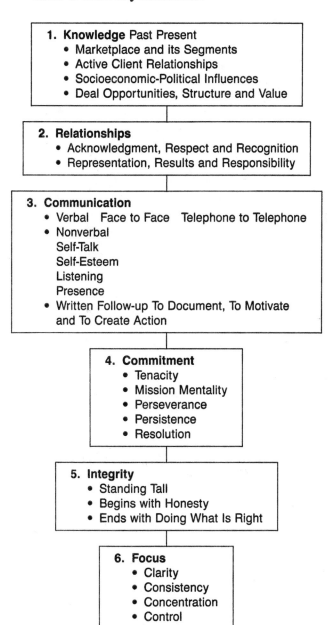

1. **Knowledge** Past Present
   • Marketplace and its Segments
   • Active Client Relationships
   • Socioeconomic-Political Influences
   • Deal Opportunities, Structure and Value

2. **Relationships**
   • Acknowledgment, Respect and Recognition
   • Representation, Results and Responsibility

3. **Communication**
   • Verbal   Face to Face   Telephone to Telephone
   • Nonverbal
   Self-Talk
   Self-Esteem
   Listening
   Presence
   • Written Follow-up To Document, To Motivate and To Create Action

4. **Commitment**
   • Tenacity
   • Mission Mentality
   • Perseverance
   • Persistence
   • Resolution

5. **Integrity**
   • Standing Tall
   • Begins with Honesty
   • Ends with Doing What Is Right

6. **Focus**
   • Clarity
   • Consistency
   • Concentration
   • Control

Figure 3.1 The ten tenets of the Big Bang Selling philosophy and some of their key subtenets (continued).

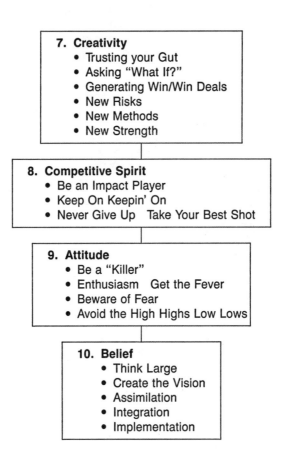

7. **Creativity**
   - Trusting your Gut
   - Asking "What If?"
   - Generating Win/Win Deals
   - New Risks
   - New Methods
   - New Strength

8. **Competitive Spirit**
   - Be an Impact Player
   - Keep On Keepin' On
   - Never Give Up   Take Your Best Shot

9. **Attitude**
   - Be a "Killer"
   - Enthusiasm   Get the Fever
   - Beware of Fear
   - Avoid the High Highs Low Lows

10. **Belief**
   - Think Large
   - Create the Vision
   - Assimilation
   - Integration
   - Implementation

opportunity and all of its evolutionary elements than anyone else?" If the answer is yes, then the selling agent can proceed with competence and confidence that will prevent him or her from ever being intimidated or fearful.

There is no lonelier feeling in the world for the commercial broker than the feeling that springs from the pounding silence that encompasses a meeting room when he or she cannot appropriately answer a critical question involving his or her own deal opportunity and/or market specialty.

No one is fooled when you try to finesse your way around the question or, worse yet, provide an erroneous response. When you find yourself in this compromised position, simply say, "I'm sorry, but I do not know. I will find out immediately following this meeting." There is no shame in not knowing everything, but there is no excuse for not finding out *what you know you do not know!*

Your clients and potential clients will be tolerant for a couple of times perhaps, but time and their patience soon will wear quite thin. Soon a competitor will occupy your place in that client relationship and you will become persona non grata.

No selling agent can know everything immediately, so you must constantly assess where you are in your progression on your road map.

Remember that *fear* is defeated with *knowledge* and with *knowledge* the intimidation factor begins to evaporate. Many of the areas of required learning in commercial real estate were mentioned in the **deal opportunity development process**, but the following is an expanded list of general market and market segment knowledge.

1. Existing square-footage base by specialty (retail, office, industrial, etc.);
2. Historical perspective of rents, expenses, occupancy, tenant profiles and deal structures;
3. Major industries within overall market;
4. Major firms, businesses within those industries;
5. Demographic influences;
6. Political climate (progrowth versus antigrowth influences);
7. Socioeconomic factors;
8. National and regional attitudes and influences on overall market and why;
9. Proposed major events impacting job and population growth;
10. Understanding the attractiveness and benefits for investment and occupancy in general market;
11. Understanding attitudes of major investment groups and employers toward general market;

12. State of local and national lender attitudes toward market;
13. Understanding of federal and state tax legislation and relative market influences;
14. Overall competitive selling (brokerage) presence, marketing strategies and major client relationships; and
15. Basic understanding of market-segment strength by specialty type and reasons therefor.

As mentioned previously, no one can know everything about every element of the overall marketplace; however, by gaining and maintaining an insightful awareness through the preceding areas of general market knowledge, you will be able to listen and to respond intelligently when necessary.

This, of course, is only the beginning, for *professional selling excellence* will come through specialization of commercial real estate type, such as choosing to become the local, regional or national expert on deal making in the office-leasing arena. You further want to specialize in this choice by becoming an expert in any given office-market segment, by developing an understanding of a particular profile of office tenant (i.e., law firms, insurance companies, advertising agencies, etc.), by perhaps choosing tenant representation rather than product (project) representation and so forth.

Once you make these choices, you must gain a firm understanding of the industries within your specialty, not only their particular commercial real estate needs, desires and requirements, but also the dynamics of their industry, its competition (regionally, nationally and internationally), its product types and uses, its customer base and profiles, its competitors and its past, present and future states of health and vitality.

When you choose to specialize by commercial real estate selling type and market segment, you must not forget that there is much more to know about your potential clients than just their commercial real estate requirements.

What should you know about the market segments that you choose? In order to become the most genuine voice in your marketplace and to compete effectively, you specifically must know the following elements of your segment and specialty:

1. Identification and analysis of past, present and proposed deal opportunities and closed deals;
2. Understanding all existing projects in terms of tenant profiles, rent structure, expense exposure, existing debt, current occupancy, ownership, vacancy history, lease profiles, competitive projects and why they are so, fit within the market segment or lack thereof and future outlook for success or failure;
3. Identification of client and nonclient deal closings by specific decision-making principals, deal structure and motivations on both sides (lease and sale);
4. Analysis, review and strategies of all client and nonclient relationships active within your specialty and your segments; and
5. A segmented understanding of deal-opportunity profiles for all existing client and nonclient relationship requirements.

You now understand why you need a general and specific spectrum of *knowledge* that, once learned, will begin to give you a very formidable presence in your marketplace. I also would suggest that you integrate the following understanding.

Why a Deal Opportunity Makes Sense or Works

This involves understanding specific client motivations, operations and idiosyncrasies. Not every client values a deal opportunity or a market segment to the same degree; therefore, you must understand that client's thought process and motivation.

First you must determine how and why the deal opportunity makes sense in traditional terms of market competitiveness, financial solidity, market significance and varied investor attractiveness.

This entails understanding the type of debt that the project will attract, the demand by tenants and investors for this type of project, any unique features and project ambience both in and out of the market segment and your learned understanding of the pro forma and its assumptions in terms of being able to confront and deal with reality in the market.

You also must understand national and regional commercial real estate trends and their spin-off influences on a given market and its segments. Begin to use the who, what, where, when, why and how to identify new industries, businesses and principals who are active in other cities or regions and who you believe might fit in your overall marketplace.

In addition, as you travel and work in your marketplace each day, begin to observe the competitive companies and their people to develop strategies to compete effectively with them in securing control of the most valuable client relationships and the deal opportunities that they represent.

Finally, if you are part of a large organization or a smaller regional or local entity, remember to develop a keen awareness of the organization's management team and its personalities, its selling management and client-relationship management philosophies, its marketing strategies and administrative support mechanisms and the overall competence, involvement and support of the organization's people.

The Major Cornerstone
of Building Block Selling

Not only is *knowledge* the first tenet of the Big Bang *philosophy*, but it is also the cornerstone of Building Block Selling that was discussed earlier as one of the vital premises of success insurance.

The most important lesson to remember is that the quest for and the attainment of *knowledge* always will provide you with strength that comes through the integrity of your knowing. *Knowledge* will provide you with a resounding "yes!" to the question, "Did I do everything possible to make this deal opportunity and client relationship succeed?"

Knowledge, however, is just the first tenet of the *philosophy* that will build your bridge to selling excellence and without working in conjunction with the other nine tenets, it is not enough to enable you to render *preeminent client service* and to achieve *professional selling excellence.*

Relationships:
The Pinnacle of the Triad

It often has been said that the business of commercial real estate is the business of **relationships**. As much as or more than in any other industry, these *relationships* are generally the glue that binds the deal opportunities together and leads them to successful closings.

From the perspective of the commercial real estate selling agent, the myriad of his or her *relationships* quite often is the link to the creative elements that formulate a host of deal opportunities, which, in turn, lead to even more solid client relationships.

You must understand that the *relationships* referred to in the Big Bang Selling *philosophy* expand in many directions. The focal points of these *relationships* should extend beyond just the key decision makers and principals within the firms, businesses, agencies and departments that make up your current and targeted clientele.

Big Bang Selling emphasizes the value of every individual with whom the selling agent interacts whether in client relationship building, deal-opportunity development, support-oriented functions or simply in random happenstance.

You must be aware of and sensitive to the diverse nature, job descriptions and personal challenges of everyone who can influence your professional selling success.

The support staff and receptionist in your office often are the most-abused and least-appreciated people in the organization; yet, unknown to many selling agents, they often are the most vital. The receptionist sets the tone of the organization through his or her verbal interaction with and physical presence toward your clients.

The administrative support staff impacts everything from effectively preparing and turning around your critical documents to ensuring that your commissions are billed, collected and paid properly.

And what about the receptionists and secretaries in your client relationships? How are you interacting with them? What do you know about their satisfaction level within their firm and their overall commitment and contributions to their organization?

Have you ever thought that perhaps you send signals of ambivalence or disrespect to people in your clients' offices whom you consider to hold little professional standing? What about your real feelings toward the second and third layers of decision makers with whom you must first interface?

When you enter a client's or prospective client's office, are the people in that organization genuinely happy to see you? Do they show you more concern, courtesy and interest than they do your competitors?

Are you aware of their personal histories, their professional achievements and goals and their standing within their own firms? If you will look closely, you often will find that these people whom we must learn to treat better often are unrewarded and underappreciated by those in authority within their very own organizations.

I am not suggesting that you embark on a crusade to raise the awareness levels of the relevant principals regarding their inattention to their own employees; however, I am suggesting that these situations create further opportunities to improve or solidify your overall client relationships.

As we all know, the ability to communicate quickly with our client principals often means the difference between gaining deal-opportunity control or losing it to a competitor. Do you believe that a correlation might exist between the quality of your *secondary relationships* (nonprincipal) and your ability to get messages through and returned, timely meetings established and opportunities to present your proposed deals?

Of course there is, and don't think for a minute that the selling agent who is well thought of by more of the people in any given client relationship does not only receive more respect but he or she also gets heard more quickly by the appropriate levels of decision makers.

Please do not confuse the importance of these *secondary rela-tionships* as in any way belittling the value of major principal *re-lationships.* You must understand *the value in charting the development of all types of relationships,* primarily because all people deserve to be considered, and from a vested point of view it makes good selling sense.

Big Bang Selling *relationships* always must be equated with short, intermediate and long-term professional selling efforts and results.

As professional selling agents, we always should aim to *iden-tify, nurture, develop, represent and control* the most active client relationships in deal making within the boundaries of our spe-cialties and marketplace.

The only way to effectively ensure our selling success through the maintenance of long-term client relationships is by provid-ing *preeminent client service.*

The relative incremental deal opportunity that the client rela-tionship represents always must be secondary to the interests of the client relationship. Your focus must be viewed continually as providing service with excellence through an ongoing awareness of the state and nature of specific client-relationship require-ments.

The Three Building Blocks of Relationships

Big Bang Selling *relationships* always begin with three basic ele-ments:

1. *Acknowledgment,*
2. *Respect* and
3. *Recognition.*

Have you ever attended a meeting, an opening or some other professional function where someone you have met on at least three occasions and with whom you hope to "do deals" walks by, his eyes cross your path and he moves on without saying a word? It certainly doesn't feel very good, does it? He hasn't even had the basic courtesy or good manners to acknowledge your presence.

Without knowing, he inadvertently has created a potential feeling of resentment; however, because Big Bang Selling stresses never personalizing slights or rejection, you in an increased state of professional awareness will overcome his rudeness. The lesson to learn is not to create the same problem with people who are entitled to this most basic of courtesies.

The goal of Big Bang Selling is to bring out the best in your human qualities; while it is important to develop intensity and a refined focus, it is just as important to treat all with whom you come in contact with sensitivity and common courtesies.

Acknowledgment is simply nothing more than an expression of goodwill. In fact, according to Big Bang Selling, the substantive *relationship* is one that has goodwill and friendship as parts of its foundation.

In any circumstance when someone whom you recognize appears, always take the time to acknowledge that person's presence and dignity. This goes without saying regarding any meetings within a professional context; however, reach out to those with whom you share any form of association and reinforce your foundation of goodwill.

A function of the Big Bang Selling *relationship* is to seek out and understand the roles that are played by the people with whom you interact. Strive to understand the individual's challenges and performance and then make sure that you *respect* the job well done or the efforts made. You should not give false praise, but you should delight in showing others *respect* for not only their professional standing but for their specific professional commitment.

The ability to lift someone's spirits and to enhance his or her professional effort is best accomplished through appropriate forms of *recognition*. For the major principal, this can be through letters of correspondence from key management personnel in your organization, an invitation to play in some form of sporting tournament, a simple dinner for the principal and his or her spouse or an invitation to speak to an affiliated group of fellow professionals.

Remember, you first must understand the various roles and responsibilities that your principal daily assumes and then understand his or her targets and performance.

I often have thought that the profession of commercial real estate selling is like having a dual major: business developmental studies and the understanding of human behavior.

Our relationships offer us so much if we only are willing to give of ourselves and to become students of our profession.

Let *acknowledgment, respect* and *recognition* formulate how you handle and develop all your relationships. On doing so, you will find that the unlimited personal rewards and professional results will be consistently outstanding.

"What Do You Want and Why Are You Wasting My Time?"

This question, although often unspoken, sometimes seems to fill the meeting room and generally is communicated through the principal's eyes, posture and attitudes.

At times like these we must determine the best ways to navigate through these seemingly difficult client relationships when face to face with the major principal.

Rather than becoming intimidated, now you should "show your stuff." When you are confronted with this type of principal attitude, you are presented with a very short, yet great, window of opportunity. This is your time to perform and to impress on the principal your strong desire to learn about his or her company, its challenges, its competitors, its fit in the industry and his or her role and expectations for success.

You must demonstrate your sincere interest in more than just the deal opportunities that the principal and the company represent. Then you can explore the various requirements and personal preferences within his or her current understanding of the commercial real estate arena.

That old nemesis, *fear*, which I discussed earlier, often rears its ugly head in *relationship* development because we often are afraid to engage certain types of principals. This might stem from a *fear* of an overwhelming personality, an intimidating presence or because of the wealth and size of the organization and the significant deal opportunities that the client relationship, and thus the principal, controls and represents.

Another way of illustrating this point is through a concept that I call *"the dark tunnel principle of successful relationships."* For most people, entering a dark tunnel is a bit frightening because they generally cannot see very well and are unsure of what lies ahead. After they advance a few yards, if their course is true, they begin to detect a small beam of light emanating from the tunnel's end. As their confidence is bolstered, they begin to increase their pace, develop a straighter direction and almost before they know it the tunnel is full of light and they have reached its end.

According to this little metaphor, until we enter the various arenas of client relationships, we cannot engage in the appropriate relationship building steps that will enable us to develop the deal opportunities that they represent. When we do engage in these building steps and begin to defeat *fear,* however, we find that the more service we provide enables us to get to the other side of the client relationship, which further brightens our path toward *preeminent client service* and *professional selling excellence.*

Once you conquer *fear* in client-relationship building and actually begin to develop deal opportunities that lead to successful deal closings, you must remember one major rule:

No One Is Irreplaceable

As wonderful as you may be to that principal for the moment, his or her mind eventually will move on to the next opportunity. Achieving real and lasting client loyalty is like trying to grasp a will-o'-the-wisp. *Loyalty can be earned but never must be assumed.* Most principals would be loathe to admit it, but the "what have you done for me lately?" mentality is more prevalent than not.

Client loyalty and the mutually productive relationship need constant nurturing and attention. The professional selling agent must understand the kaleidoscopic nature of his or her clients' (principals') mentalities.

The demands, requirements and opportunities within the client relationship can change almost daily and often are formed as a result of fluctuating market forces and influences.

This necessitates constant vigilance through face-to-face, ego-to-ego contact in order for you, the Big Bang Selling agent, to keep abreast of pertinent client-relationship and deal-opportunity influences.

Representation, Results and Responsibility (The Three R's of Big Bang Selling)

If *acknowledgment, respect* and *recognition* form the guidance mechanism for Big Bang Selling *relationships,* then the principles of **representation, results** and **responsibility** are the energy sources.

The adage, "If you work for someone, then work for him," directly applies to selling commercial real estate. You must begin to evaluate your performance in these three terms.

Your ability to act consistently in the interests of your client relationships through effective and ethical professional selling conduct will enable you to achieve the desired *results* that create win/win deals and yield the personal rewards that you seek.

In order to provide the appropriate *representation* in your client relationships that will yield the targeted *results,* you consistently must assume a level of **responsibility** *that ensures that you keep abreast of changes in significant market forces, impediments or potential deal-killing factors and undetected market nuances that might yield unique deal opportunities and you must engage in a focused form of vigilance that leads to timely and advisory communication.*

These three principles work together to enable the Big Bang Selling agent to get closer to providing *preeminent client service,* which, in turn, further increases and develops *professional selling excellence.*

"Don't Leave Home Without Them"

One of the most common forms of ignorance that professional selling agents indulge in is their unawareness of their behavior and conduct within the framework of their own office or organization. For some unexplained reason, we seemingly leave our professional selling credentials at the office door and proceed to indulge in the most boorish and outlandish forms of unprofessional conduct.

When we are upset, frustrated or feeling abused, we often take out our negative feeling on our peers, our support staffs and even our managers. Without knowing it, we create an aura of resentment because of insensitivity, which inhibits the wonderful potential that exists for us to enjoy positive and supportive *relationships.*

As mentioned earlier, these people often can play a pivotal role in your success either by supporting you a little harder or by ignoring you a little longer. The results of the latter should be obvious.

We often assume that our managers' and the organization's only purpose is to support our efforts and to enhance our success. If these people do not snap to our pace, we often become sarcastic, cynical and nonsupportive. You must remember that loyalty and support are two-way streets.

Do not assume that your manager loves to sell and thus is capable of providing you with the type of deal opportunity or client-relationship development that you feel he or she should.

As you become more familiar with the strengths of your managers and the organization, you must assume a more active role in supporting their efforts so they more effectively can support your own.

How To Survive and Prosper in the Bull Pen

Entering the sales area, or bull pen as it often is referred to, can be a very intimidating experience. An agent easily can be influenced in a variety of directions in order to "fit in."

You were hired into the organization because your management team felt that you would make a positive contribution and would professionally represent the interests of all the pertinent parties.

This does not mean that you must immediately try to "fit in." The best way to "fit in" is to gain the respect of your associates. You can do this by demonstrating a seriousness of **purpose** that lets everyone know that you intend to spend your time pursuing knowledge, client-relationship service and selling excellence.

Following are a few rules to help you establish your own area of ground without trying to "fit in":

1. Avoid overblown egos, pompous attitudes and immature posturing.
2. Develop a composite role model.
3. Identify and develop relationships with highly motivated and positive peers and associates.
4. Do not be afraid to stand alone when required.
5. Communicate and document all understandings.
6. Listen more than you speak.
7. Support your associates and always keep a confidence, whether told directly or through heresay.
8. Develop and share trust, loyalty and commitment.
9. Resolve or at least attempt to resolve all disputes immediately.
10. Let go of anger and avoid holding grudges.
11. Recognize the value and worth of everyone.

A Final Thought on Relationships

You will find it extremely beneficial to develop *relationships* with affiliated professionals who work in and service the commercial real estate industry. Strive to create mutually beneficial opportunities for these individuals as well as yourself.

The opportunity for learning in related professions is endless and its benefits are unlimited as well. Identify the top professionals and their young associates in real estate law, finance, accounting, title, architecture, city planning, consulting and engineering.

You will be able to provide these individuals with a composite of your observations and experiences and in return seek to find out how their careers and professions impact your existing and targeted client relationships, the local commercial real estate industry, economic development, relevant social issues and our infamous political climates.

If embraced, the Big Bang Selling philosophical tenet of *relationships* will provide you with lifetime experiences of both personal and professional growth that will lead to an ever-enduring form of success.

Communication: The Balancing Act of the Big Bang Triad

More effort is wasted, more emotion is spent and more negative feelings are created because people involved at all levels of deal opportunities are unable to communicate effectively their real meanings, expectations and understandings.

Selling agents in their rush to chase deal opportunities often fail to ask the pertinent questions that are most vital in determining *specific deal-opportunity parameters and structure.*

One of your critical tasks is to avoid assuming what is acceptable to either side of the deal opportunity. Far too often, selling agents chase deal opportunities that are impossible to "put together" because they have not taken the time to ask the who, what, where, when, why and how regarding the motivations, timing, structure and thus the "doability" of any given deal opportunity.

When communicating within any given client relationship, your opportunity and responsibility are to "do everything you can possibly do" to gain an understanding of not only the overall deal structure that the principal expects, but, more specifically, you must define as many deal points as possible within that structure.

Your ability to understand specific deal-opportunity structure and expectation will enable you to articulate effectively and present all important elements of the deal opportunity to the principals on the other side. This will help to ensure that you are taking a specific rather than a general deal opportunity to the marketplace, which will help to prevent a great deal of wasted time for all concerned.

Clarity Makes Things Much Less Fuzzy

As you gain as much *clarity* of the specific deal opportunity as possible as well as the motivations of the client relationship, you should communicate that understanding in verbal and written terms to the relevant principals. Sometimes it is too easy for irresponsible principals to give you false impressions about the nature of the deal structure that they would be willing to accept. Without the proper understanding, you become easily susceptible to chasing the *elusive deal rainbows* that once again can cause you to waste valuable time and energy on *"undoable deal opportunities."*

Sometimes it is extremely easy to lose patience with principals who are consistently elusive regarding the nature of their requirements on either side of any given deal opportunity; therefore, you must develop a strategy for gaining the appropriate understanding.

If you find the principal's expectations are naive or unrealistic in regard to market-based reality, then you must let him or her know in a nonthreatening manner. I have observed too many selling agents whose approach to communicating realistic deal parameters and structures is almost insulting to the client principal.

You must remember that it is a privilege to be in an advisory position with your existing or potential client relationships, a position that requires the human understanding of a psychologist and the skills of a career diplomat.

Your approach to any given communication with your principals always should be *candid yet conciliatory, direct yet considerate* in your quest to gain agreement and understanding, which then will move the deal opportunity toward a successful closing.

How To Effectively Transmit the Intent, Spirit and Particulars of an Offer

If you are like most selling agents, you probably have experienced the disheartening and frightful "drop dead, get out of my face, get out of my office" principal response. This usually occurs when we present some form of offer, counteroffer, contract or lease proposal on a specific deal opportunity that does not live up to that principal's expectation but only serves to raise the principal's blood pressure and pulse rate right off the charts.

You must remember that part of your challenge is to articulate effectively the qualifications and the motivations of the principals and the rationale behind any given offer without fear of principal disgust or retribution. Retribution in these circumstances would be the principal's unwillingness to provide an appropriate response or counteroffer to your proposal.

If you have taken the time to understand the offer in your context of knowledge of the deal opportunity, its market relevance and the nature of the client relationships involved, then you should be able to make your presentation of the offer palatable.

At the point of principal rejection of any offer, you must isolate the specific areas or deal elements that are most unacceptable and then determine why.

The "what if?" question is very appropriate when you are trying to elicit a deal-enhancing response. Never leave a face-to-face principal meeting without a firm understanding of what is or is not acceptable to the client relationship and its principals.

In addition to asking the "what if?" question, you also must cover areas of **high trust**, in which the principal must disclose why he or she can or cannot accept certain elements of your proposal.

These areas would include gaining an understanding of outside influences such as limited or joint-venture partners, existing debt and pro forma influences, current lender relationships, the relative influences and thus potential pressures from nonrelated client holdings or additional deal opportunities in development.

You must remember that the response to any one deal-opportunity proposal often is influenced by the larger context of the overall requirements and goals of the client relationship.

Often, you will receive a response to your proposal or offer that will come in nonquotable terms. Your obligation, then, is to mitigate the harshness, anger or insult of the response in order to make it acceptable enough so the other principal does not take it personally.

Do not forget that you are dealing with human beings and that emotion is a major factor in successful deal making; therefore, you must remove the emotion for the principals and present what is acceptable in terms of who, what, where, when, why and how.

In order to communicate effectively various intentions and understanding between principals, selling agents and all pertinent parties, you obviously must be articulate in all influential deal-opportunity areas. This requirement to be verbally deft, however, also necessitates that the selling agent become a great listener.

The two most important areas involved in Big Bang Selling listening include: *Listening to what people say and listening to what people don't say.* Both are equally important.

When you are bogged down in the netherworld of unrealistic client deal-opportunity expectations, you must inject market and fiscally sound deal-element reality. In other words, you must present valid reasons why the deal works or does not work, what similar deal opportunities have achieved, why under certain terms or areas a specific structure works for that principal and so on.

Obviously, you should be able to listen to what people say, but you must ensure that they are, in fact, heard. By mentally formulating your next question or statement before the principal has completed making his or her point or giving his or her response, you may miss the most important part of the message.

Remember that some principals are not very forthcoming with their feelings and/or attitudes toward you, your client relationships or the particulars of your proposal, presentation or offer. In order to gain the appropriate understanding and achieve the consummate level of communication, therefore, you must listen to the entire message before deciding whether it is too cryptic, needs to be defined further or is complete enough so you can move the deal opportunity forward.

You should take notes during principal dialogues when presenting offers or deal opportunities or in various other forms of communication and interaction. These notes will help you focus on the verbal points of view that the principal makes regarding his or her opinions and attitudes. You then can use your notes to refer to major points that need further explaining and/or emphasis when clarifying your understanding of the principal's perceptions.

The type of communication that motivates selling agents to investigate less-stressful careers is that which takes place when the principal will not respond to anything from the "what if?" question to what time he or she generally arrives at the office.

When you find yourself unable to elicit a clearly understandable verbal response, do not pack up your briefcase and ask the principal to think about what you have said. This critical time requires you to continue to question his or her feeling on the presentation, deal opportunity or offer as a whole and deal with it point by deal point.

Listening to what the principal doesn't say mentally should kick in for you at this point. Take note of any change in the timbre of the principal's voice, take notice of his or her physical posture and what he or she is doing with his or her hands and watch the facial indicators, such as raised eyebrows or tight jaws, for they will tell you just how comfortable the principal feels with you or your information. Observe whether or not the principal engages you in consistent eye contact for this can be a strong indicator of his or her faith or trust in what you, the other principal and this offer actually mean in terms of real value.

Often the evasive or noncommittal principal will clear his or her throat or increase the cadence of verbal response when he or she does not want to respond effectively.

Your challenge is to determine the reasons behind this nonforthright manner. Is it because the principal wants to keep all options open, he or she is not satisfied with some aspect of your presentation or offer, he or she is questioning you or the principal's ability to deliver on the other side or he or she alone cannot make the decision and thus give you a clear response?

Efficient listening demands that you formulate a clear and focused method of questioning in order to hear the thoughts going on inside the principal's mind, whether that message is verbally or physically communicated.

Never leave a meeting with any principal without stating how this particular deal opportunity fits within the realities of the marketplace and how you believe it can fit within the requirements of the client relationships involved. Keep the deal opportunity in a state of continued development by gaining a commitment from the principal regarding the next step, whether this is another scheduled meeting or some other form of follow-up measure.

Agent-to-Agent Communication

Without question, one of the most uncomfortable situations that any selling agent can find himself or herself in is that involving a commission dispute. One agent thinks this, the other agent thinks that and little or no understanding exists about the nature of commissionable or representative positions.

Many agents will avoid at all costs the discomfort of confrontation that often lurks during the deal-opportunity development progression.

They convince themselves that the other parties will eventually do "what's right." Sadly, what seems right for one may seem the opposite for the other. And thus as the deal opportunity streaks toward a closing, the agents apprehensively prepare to march off toward some form of arbitration hearing in order to resolve the dispute.

Bruised feelings and dented egos are the typical results of these resolution forums and often the only thing that is accomplished is a determination of who will receive what in terms of commission dollars.

The lessons to be learned, such as the necessity for agents to communicate their perceptions of deal positions at the very beginning of specific deal opportunities, often are lost in the anger and accusations.

In order to help you avoid this extreme unpleasantness and counterproductive involvement, you should follow these rules for agent-to-agent communication:

1. When you become aware of or involved in any potential client relationship and deal opportunity, open a client-relationship folder or file that indicates all dates, times and contents of your communication and understandings.

2. Detail what is said by specific principals regarding their willingness to work with you and your organization. Document specific deal opportunities and their nature.

3. When bringing in other agents, clearly state your expectations of their involvement. Specify what each of you will do generally and specifically, then write a brief memo to pertinent agents, make sure it is acknowledged and place it in the file.

4. Never avoid a frank discussion when you believe other agents feel that they have a position in your deal opportunity. At the end of this dialogue, write a memo to all concerned that summarizes your position.

5. Develop an ongoing record of all correspondence related to the client relationship and the specific deal opportunity and then place it in the file.

6. If your control is limited within the framework of either the deal opportunity or the client relationship, keep your own quiet counsel.

If you follow these six simple rules for effective communication, you always will be able to avoid the ugly emotion that comes when fighting for your position. Always act rather than react and learn to listen to your inner self regarding your to-date unverified concerns. Although we sometimes act as if we are blindsided by other agents grabbing for a piece of "our deal opportunities," if we are honest with ourselves, chances are we saw this coming for a long time.

CHAPTER
4

Commitment, Integrity and Focus: The Integration of the Mission Mentality

Whenever I reflect on the most outstanding commercial real estate selling agents with whom I either have competed or "done deals" with, the one common trait among their vast array of personalities is the *level of intensity* that they bring to their professional selling careers.

Perseverance, Persistence and Resolution

The refined and sharply honed intensity with which they pursue client service and selling excellence invokes the integration of a *mission mentality* that translates into an indestructible form of professional selling *commitment.*

Their commitment is worn quietly like a badge of honor, which leaves no doubt about the extent of the effort that they are willing to make to accomplish their personal missions and thus achieve professional results.

Commitment involves the physical and mental qualities of **perseverance, persistence** and **resolution.** To be committed, the selling agent must clearly understand the scope of his or her Big Bang Selling **purpose.**

Maintaining an intense level of *commitment* is easier when the selling agent focuses on his or her required **results** and attempts to accomplish those *results* through a disciplined and tenacious professional selling **process.**

This requires a strong sense of dedication and continued mental and physical efforts that easily will yield, through a series of properly executed professional selling missions, the desired *results.*

Commitment is like inwardly possessing some type of internal-combustion mechanism that continually charges the Big Bang Selling agent with positive emotion. *Commitment* is a feeling that you can mentally see your required results and thus combine your mind, body and spirit to reach your required destination of selling success.

Dealing with Rejection and Refusal

The great penalizers or ultimate tests of *commitment* are rejection, refusal, razzing, fatigue, lack of remuneration and sometimes failed short-term results.

Yet every one of these demotivators can be overcome when you can measure your progress on your *road map for Big Bang Selling success.* The critical thing is never to personalize any form of client-relationship or deal-opportunity rejection. Develop the attitude in your client relationships *that your clients are not saying no, you just haven't given them enough reason to say yes.*

When you can view principal disinterest or rejection as a limited awareness on the part of the target client, you can place these potentially debilitating experiences in proper perspective. The cold fact of selling commercial real estate is that before you ever can realize its great rewards, you invariably will first suffer a series of rejections. Whether these rejections will be major or minor impacts on your personal psyche will depend on the perspective in which you place each experience. You must remember that the people with whom you want to work do not know you or your capabilities. In many cases they are not as knowledgeable as you are about your specialty and your areas of market expertise. Your challenge is to view each rejection as moving a step closer to being heard by your target principals.

Always place yourself in the shoes of the people with whom you are trying to work and judge your approach and presentation as if you were calling on yourself. Would your enthusiasm excite you into listening further? Would your articulation of your marketplace motivate you to listen more intently? Would your questions demonstrate a sound understanding of your specialty? Would your appearance inspire professional acceptance and confidence from you as a principal? Remember that the people whom you are calling on may have many other priorities that take up most of their valuable time. So when you finally do get the opportunity to make a presentation, make sure that you take full advantage of the situation.

The lack of interest or the rejection that can be heaped on you from the receptionist to the principal often may be nothing more than their concern about their own deadlines and priorities. Your challenge then is not to view your interactions as a contest in which you either win or lose but as an opportunity to determine what their personal challenges are and to offer constructive alternatives to and empathy with their problems. Whenever you feel defeated, step back and review whether or not you really tried to gain the full attention of your target audience. Don't assume that they never want to speak to you; assume, instead, that the timing just was not proper. Then find a more opportune time to come back and meet in the appropriate forum.

Laughter, Indeed, Is the Best Medicine

As difficult as it may seem to believe, there always will be something to smile about after any sales call, whether the call was a cold call or a preplanned meeting. Think about all that was said and review the perspective of those who said it. Because you are as wonderful as you are and as interested as you are in working with your target principals, this will not be your last opportunity.

Be willing to laugh at your mistakes; just don't repeat them. Try to find the humor in impossible attitudes that you encounter. Treat all difficult personalities with kid gloves. Maybe they just need someone to listen. Maybe they just need your positive presence to get them on track. Remember, in almost every case of rejection that you experience, the individual rejecting or refusing you is not refusing you as an individual but is refusing what he or she perceives you represent. They do not know your purpose or your motivations and intent, so don't assume you are doing something wrong or are inept. Always be willing to propose an alternative time or place to meet with your target principals, stay on track with your call purpose and keep your heart and spirit light.

Be Willing To Stand Apart

At times your *commitment* will keep you apart from your peers and they will not understand or support your strategies and desires. Take strength in the fact that you sometimes must stand alone because you are trying to be innovative in rendering the finest client service that will help you develop the professional selling excellence that is the core of the Big Bang Selling *purpose.*

Integrity Is Not an Ancient Myth

The maintenance and nourishment of your Big Bang Selling *commitment* lies in the **integrity** of your thoughts and actions.

Integrity is not an ancient myth that seemingly has no place in today's fast-paced and sometimes brutal commercial real estate arena. The age-old expression that a person's word is his or her bond never has been more pertinent than in professional selling in your industry. When you present a deal opportunity, make sure that you explain the facts of that opportunity in as honest and knowledgeable a manner as possible. When you say you will perform a specific or general service for a principal, make sure that you do so in a timely and forthright manner. When you agree to participate in some form of professional effort with another selling agent, make sure that you uphold your end of the agreement. When you ask another selling agent to share information, make sure that he or she understands the motivation behind your request to avoid any common pursuits or diverse interests.

*Integrity involves the development of a sound wholeness to your professional selling process that shouts to the world that your efforts can be trusted and that your **purpose** is honorable.*

Integrity means that you employ the necessary physical and mental efforts to properly develop both the client relationship and the deal opportunity. It means not taking shortcuts to get the proper information by relying on secondhand or unconfirmed data.

Integrity enables you to subordinate your personal interests to the long-term interests of the client relationship regardless of its immediate impact on the specific deal opportunity at hand or the commission dollars that are lying in wait.

Integrity means that when you give your word regarding some element in the deal opportunity or client-service process, it can be taken to the mental bank and deposited for peace of mind and for the benefit of all concerned. It means that as your potential for a larger slice of the commission or recognition spoils evolves, you still retain your original deal.

Integrity ensures that the Big Bang Selling agent always strives to provide the most accurate information and analysis on any given deal opportunity for the benefit of the client relationship.

Clarity, Consistency, Concentration and Control

The third part or building block of constructing a *mission mentality* involves your ability to **focus**. Big Bang Selling *focus* will empower **clarity, consistency, concentration** and **control** in the pursuit of your targeted professional results and *purpose.*

If *focus* creates and improves *clarity, consistency, concentration* and *control,* then the lack of clarity fashions *fuzzy selling,* which, in turn, *produces false assumptions and failed client relationships and deal opportunities.*

You must effectively plan, execute and follow up pretargeted client-relationship development strategies that will yield the appropriate deal opportunities in a clear, consistent, concentrated and controlled manner to prevent extraneous activities from blocking your progress.

But your *focus* must extend to the target skills and the knowledge areas to ensure that they are achieved so you can continue down your road to selling success.

Clarity and *concentration* are needed to avoid the *great rainbow chase* whether in client relationships, deal opportunities or peer relationships that you want to develop and nurture. Using consistent and controlled mental and physical approaches to your professional selling career will enhance your ability to maintain your *commitment* and thus the *integrity* of that commitment.

Big Bang Selling *focus* therefore will prevent all outside nonproductive influences from affecting either your mental or physical approach to achieving either professional *results* or your Big Bang *purpose.*

A Final Thought
on Your Mission Mentality

One of the most important lessons to learn about the value that you will receive when selling with a *mission mentality* will be to realize that greatness within your profession only comes through long-term effort and success.

Success comes through a mental approach greatly enhanced by *commitment, integrity* and *focus.* As rapidly as success can embrace you, however, its often fickle behavior can leave you lonely and without a trace of its past presence and grandeur.

As professional selling agents, we continually must remind ourselves that it is our responsibility and a major part of our "selling code of honor" that always must direct us toward the renewal of our *commitment.* We must constantly monitor our level of personal and professional *integrity* and continually review why and where we are *focused.*

No professional selling agent is irreplaceable either to his or her organization, client relationships, peers or deal opportunities. Someone else always will be there to pick up the pace, provide the energy, achieve the results and provide the service if we only momentarily take our eyes off our personal and professional missions.

You never should have to relinquish your positions of strength and success; however, do not forget that the road to Big Bang Selling *purpose* travels through many series of *results* and a continual and evolutionary professional selling effort.

C H A P T E R
5

Attitude, Competitive Spirit and Creativity: Implementing a Tenacious Selling Presence

"If you think you can
or you think you can't,
you're right."—Henry Ford

Attitude determines whether we love to sell or sell to survive. One discussion often heard about *attitude* is in a negative context such as "that principal really has an attitude," which means that the mental and physical postures taken by that person are filled with arrogance, inconsideration and even contempt.

Your ability to ascertain the attitudes of the individuals in your various types of relationships will help you to navigate the challenging waters of professional selling success. As I mentioned in the discussion of "listening to what people don't say," your keen observation skills will enable you to get at the heart of people's attitudes.

As a professional selling agent you must not internalize the negative attitudes of others as bearing some significant appraisal of your knowledge, skills or actions. These negative attitudes, however, should be viewed as a challenge to develop the excellence that you seek in your selling career.

Remember, if you are confident that you know more about a specific deal opportunity or other pertinent data than the other people involved, then you never can be intimidated. Therefore, you should not personalize the lack of professional courtesy from whatever direction it comes.

The lesson to learn from your exposure to these types of attitudes, and there will be many, is that it will further strengthen your personal resolve to provide *preeminent client service* and to achieve *professional selling excellence.*

Demonstrate Confidence, Credence and Compassion

When you can face difficult principal or peer personalities with your own *attitudes* of *confidence, credence* and *compassion,* you are freed from the emotional restraints that result from personalizing the insensitive messages of others.

This newfound strength of *attitude* that is fostered by your *clarity* of *purpose* and supported by the principles of *acknowledgment, respect* and *recognition* for others will help you discover the great joy and contentment that exists in the profession of commercial real estate selling.

When you experience the joy that comes through the satisfaction of selling with an *attitude* of goodwill and service to all, your personal level of *enthusiasm* will take hold of you like a raging fever.

The great thing about Big Bang Selling is that all its principles and elements work together and cross-pollinate to form a very powerful force. When you learn to use this force, the service, excellence and results that you desire will happen beyond your present expectations.

Your *attitude* toward the decisions that you alone can make will determine how you feel about every element of professional selling. You and you alone choose how you feel about everything from cold calling to studying the dynamics of your marketplace. If you choose to see these steps or building blocks as critical components of your selling success, then your *attitude* will support your efforts. If, however, you choose to see these steps as "have to's," then their effects will slow you down emotionally and diffuse your positive charge of energy and *enthusiasm.*

The choice definitely is up to you and you can make this choice much easier when you recognize how Big Bang Selling really works.

Participating in the profession of commercial real estate selling is like taking a ride on the world's most thrilling yet most terrifying colossal roller coaster. While the exhilaration of the steep climb and high highs absolutely fills you with the grandness of professional expectations, suddenly the bottom drops out as you rush toward what seems like certain devastation.

Like the roller coaster, our profession will not let us tunnel into the depths of our disconsolate emotions if we recognize that great client relationships and deal opportunities, as well as their sometimes unfortunate dissolution, inevitably will occur.

Your challenge is to maintain a relatively stable emotional ride that will prevent you from ever experiencing anything akin to my little bout of catatonia.

Through properly qualifying client relationships and specific deal opportunities, you can mitigate unrealistic expectations of success with marginal clientele and opportunities and thus avoid the emotional negative fallout.

Then when you enact all the elements of Big Bang Selling, you can place your lost client relationships and their deal opportunities in the proper context of your professional evolution.

The reason that your *attitude* is so dramatically affected by the high highs and low lows of professional selling is that often you do not have the appropriate amount of backup or additional client relationships and deal opportunities to make up for any one shortfall or failed deal.

When you remind yourself of your professional mission and review your actions to ensure that you are acting with **integrity**, you minimize the emotional or attitudinal energy drain that often is caused by principal or peer misunderstanding because of inadequate communication.

Your *attitude* will determine your physical and verbal response to any type of confrontation. If you know that you are on track and have properly laid your Big Bang foundation, then you can enter any debate on solid ground. Never let yourself get caught up in the emotional turmoil that surrounds such disagreements whether they are over commission understandings, deal positions, responsibilities and so forth.

Just Take a Deep Breath and Giggle

Do not confuse an intense and committed attitude with a tight or tense selling comportment. *Learn to relax.* The preparation that Big Bang Selling requires will provide you with the inner strength so you can effectively *relax*. Channel your enthusiasm into an even clearer *focus*. Use mental visualization to take you through any set of elements of your Big Bang Selling *process*.

Develop an *attitude* that thrives on appearing in front of great client relationships and huge deal opportunities. Learn to mentally prosper on your selling challenges. The larger are the potential *results* of any situation, the more confident your *attitude* should be.

Always try to get all the parties in any dealing, including yourself, to place the emotion off to the side of the table. Avoid entering into a contest of wills or personalities from which no one will emerge truly victorious.

Try to remember that **communication** *should never be entered into as a contest but strictly as a means of arriving at a mutually agreed on end that results in the production of win/win deals.*

The reason that this phrase appears here rather than in the chapter on communication is to further illustrate the manner in which all Big Bang elements work together.

The ability of either positive or negative communication to affect your personal and professional attitude is enormous and you must be ever vigilant of its overall effects and impact.

What To Do When You Feel Like Settling for a Rain Check on a Cup of Coffee

I happened to overhear the conversation of a commercial broker one day when I was making a telephone call while awaiting the departure of my plane from Chicago's O'Hare airport. He was commenting to the person on the other end of his conversation that he had just lost a major deal at the closing table. It seems an argument had occurred over the prorates on an office building deal and both parties had walked out.

The selling agent, who obviously had come to the closing expecting to leave town with a nice commission check, was about to board his flight empty-handed and was completely downcast when I overheard him say, "Right now, I would settle for a rain check on a cup of coffee."

Whether he was able to put his deal opportunity back together again I will never know, but the thing that impressed me was that whoever was on the other end of the telephone line had lent a very sympathetic ear.

The commercial real estate selling world can be filled with frustration, frustration and more frustration for the agents who travel its unforgiving terrain. At times you may consider yourself as Mr. or Ms. Big Bang Selling. Yet despite the fact that you are doing everything correctly, your deal opportunities still are not closing.

At times like these, it is very difficult to maintain a good *attitude*. You may feel like screaming at the world and yelling out the unfairness of your quest and the inequity of your results.

Rather than pontificating your unhappiness or disbelief to the world at large, find someone whom you can trust to listen and to respond. This person may be your spouse, your personal-relationship partner, a friend or even a concerned and caring acquaintance.

This special individual need not know very much about commercial real estate selling but should be a keen observer of human behavior. You may be amazed at how the perceptive and analytical abilities of a person totally removed from the specifics of deal making can offer great insight into your current challenges.

At the beginning and the end of my commercial real estate selling career, I had the good fortune of being able to ask two women whom I was involved with at different times to be my personal sounding boards. Neither understood a great deal about the technical elements of deal making, but each consistently provided much-needed understanding of my frustration, fears and professional challenges. Through their willingness to let me sound off without any type of retributory comments, I was able to articulate my thoughts, which often was all that I needed to do to gain a more healthy and positive understanding of the circumstances.

Believe me, their being there for me was a major contributor to my maintaining a joyful, positive and productive *attitude* that, without a doubt, was a major factor in my professional selling success.

Choose your listening partner with care. Sometimes your spouse may increase the emotional pressure rather than relieve it because he or she is too close to your basic needs for accomplishing your required *results.*

Avoid sharing the particulars of failed deal opportunities with everyone just because you're afraid that your peers will think you are inept if you do not explain what happened.

Most people will offer token degrees of sympathy and seldom little else. You do not need sympathy to refuel your *attitude.* You simply must increase your understanding with the help of one good listener and a qualitative and quantitative review of the actions and events that led to the deal-opportunity explosion.

In my experience nothing impacted my professional selling *attitude* as much as the surge of *energy, excitement and exhilaration* that occurred when identifying the deal opportunity.

When I learned how to recognize a makable deal opportunity, my *attitude* became fortified instantly through the internal mechanisms that told me I was closer to achieving my targeted *results.*

Your ability to grasp a real deal opportunity, which with the proper selling service will expand your client relationships, will improve the quality of your mental outlook and overall performance.

You must learn to literally feel the energy that comes with the discovery of the deal opportunity. This energy will strengthen your **commitment** and refine your *focus* and move you toward client relationships and deal opportunities that will place you at the forefront of your competition.

The famous "thrill of victory" and "agony of defeat" lines used by ABC's "Wide World of Sports" also could have been written about selling commercial real estate.

It's You Against the Market, Your Competitors and Yourself

The difference between tasting the thrill of victory or the agony of defeat often will be founded in your *competitive spirit.* Kirk Gibson (after his bottom-of-the-ninth two-out, three-and-two-count home run to win game 1 in the 1988 World Series) said, "I'm an impact player and I live for these moments, and I don't mind saying so because I love the added pressure to perform."

Big Bang Selling was created for selling agents who already feel this way or who want to feel this way. Selling in the competitive profession of commercial real estate is not for the faint of heart or for those who prefer to "interface" with their telephones or computers rather than meet face-to-face with their principals and peers.

Those who seek greatness in their professional selling careers never can be satisfied simply by being in the profession or a part of a brokerage organization. For those agents, it just is not enough to collect a few commission checks every year and wallow in mediocrity because of *limited knowledge, skills, relationships and activities.*

Big Bang *competitive spirit* propels the selling agent to seek the zenith in all areas of his or her profession. The best illustration of this is the *pride* that he or she takes in knowing more about his or her marketplace and its segments, trends, influences, people, deals and potential.

When I first went to work at Coldwell Banker, I was fortunate enough to be assigned to two top producers, Hank Ragland and Lee Noble. Each was highly tenured and each had a strong track record of success; after a few months, however, I was assigned exclusively to work for and train under Hank.

The thing that I always will remember about Hank besides his consistently finishing in the Coldwell Banker Top Twenty year in and year out was his competitive nature not only in collecting commission checks but in his desire to be the most knowledgeable selling agent in every element of deal making, in his desire to work with and control the finest client relationships and, despite his overall competitiveness, in his *integrity* in never taking a shortcut or surreptitiously using someone else's information for his exclusive gain.

Your *competitive spirit,* however, only can reach into your Big Bang Selling *purpose* when it surrounds every element of your daily activity. *Results,* as I have said before, are great and do play an integral part in your professional evolution; yet they are only one indicator of your progress toward rendering *preeminent client service* and achieving *professional selling excellence.*

Because many of you have yet to achieve the excellence of my former trainer, the question of "how do I compete and win?" begs to be answered.

Like Kirk Gibson, you must strive to be an impact player in your arena. Set your goals and your standards for attaining them as high as you possibly can.

Picture yourself working with the finest, most-active client relationships and providing the service that leads to the development of the most rewarding deal opportunities.

Once you gain the appropriate level of knowledge regarding your market, its principals, deals and deal opportunities, then you can select whom to work with and whom to go after. Let me repeat, *you* select whom to work with and whom to go after.

There is no logical reason why you cannot compete with anyone if you have properly implemented Big Bang Selling. But first you must develop a competitive *attitude* that infuses your human spirit to rise above all others in level of service, degree of excellence and attainment of *results.*

Your challenge is to establish a fierce yet ethical competitive presence that utilizes your will and intensity to outperform all your competitors in and out of your office.

The truly great commercial real estate selling agents love to appear in their client-relationship meetings. They know that they bring something special to that client relationship, which involves a professional approach that few can match.

On the other hand, selling agents who rationalize to themselves or to their managers that they are far too busy to make more calls, offer more presentations or engage in more client travel are fooling only themselves. How can you tell yourself that you enjoy your profession when you let **fear** keep you from face-to-face contact?

Earlier I shared with you the devastation that *fear* can reign on your performance. Now you also must understand how *fear* is the great dampener of your *competitive spirit.*

Think of *fear* as an acronym for F (failing), E (engagement), A (arresting), R (reward). Failing to engage your principal and secondary relationships within the client relationship will arrest the rewards and results that originally motivated you to enter this great profession.

Fear is not always an inhibitor or bad influence on professional selling success. Before I address any group, I always experience a form of *fear* that says don't let these people down and make sure you give them your very best.

When I recall past moments before giving a major listing presentation or articulating the elements of an offer, I also would develop a *fear* that I might not be good enough to achieve my desired *result*.

At the beginning of this book, I said that we must look at this business from a macro and a micro perspective. Thus, our targeted *results* must be understood and sought after not only on an annual or career scale but right down to the individual selling call. Maintaining this micro understanding will keep our *competitive spirit* sharply challenged and honed and our *fear* in perspective.

No matter how competitive you are, there will be times when you do not win. I did not say "when you fail" for in Big Bang Selling failure does not exist because our *purpose,* our **philosophy** and our *process* work together always to overcome any incremental setback and thus defeat our *fear.*

The best way to combat your professional selling *fear* is to think of its universal opposite, **love.** Once again I will share an acronym that will clarify your understanding of the context of *love* within the Big Bang Selling *process.*

Think of the joy and satisfaction that fill you after you outperform a competitor for a listing or for an exclusive representation. Because you are the winner, you can look at all the challenges in a positive context. When you lose, however, and especially when you are not given the chance to be heard, you hope you never experience those feelings again.

When you are competing, which should occur in some form every day of your career, think of L (laughter), O (opportunity), V (vigilance), E (enthusiasm).

The ability to laugh at yourself and with others will keep your heart light and your thoughts focused. The loss of any client relationship or deal opportunity is not the end of your career. Your lips will move tomorrow and your eyes will regain their sparkle, so move on to the next deal opportunity. Recognize that opportunity will appear in many forms and guises throughout your client relationships and in your marketplace. Always remember to watch for new client relationships or deal opportunities. Relate the lost deal opportunity to other relationships to see if there might be a better fit someplace else. Ask yourself who else handles these types of deals. And finally, approach every new relationship and opportunity with great enthusiasm as a result of your Big Bang Selling *attitude.*

Following are some Big Bang Selling rules for developing and maintaining your sense of *competitive spirit:*

1. Establish challenging goals and visions of excellence.
2. Develop a "refuse to lose" mentality.
3. Become the most knowledgeable selling agent in your specialty.
4. Become the most tenacious selling agent in the market.
5. Try to outperform agents in all disciplines and at all companies.
6. Become **the most genuine voice on deal making in your market.**
7. Learn to *love* rather than to *fear.*
8. Don't let lack of tenure or lack of experience deter you.
9. Maximize your time in the marketplace and in front of your clients.
10. Let it always be said of you, "He or she always took his or her best shots."

It Ain't That Tough
To Use Your Smarts

Your originality of thought and execution (a consummate mental and physical approach) in the pursuit of Big Bang Selling is not predetermined genetically. I believe that if you pursue and grasp a clear understanding of the commercial real estate marketplace from past, present and futuristic perspectives, you will place yourself in a position to tap previously unknown wells of *creativity* within you.

By understanding the who, what, where, when, why and how of past and present principal motivations and influences, as well as for the closed deals and existing opportunities, you can use this knowledge of the past to guide you into the realms of what will work and will be created today and tomorrow.

Your willingness to try creative approaches to client-relationship and deal-opportunity development undoubtedly will lead to great and not-so-great results; if viewed simply as another building block in your pursuit of professional selling success, however, the experience will prove quite beneficial.

Being *creative* in thought and action is easy when generated within the context of Big Bang Selling because the selling agent can use his or her grasp of specific areas of knowledge and relationships to create win/win deals.

You first must understand how the *creativity* tenet of Big Bang Selling works. You should view using creative thought and action as a vital link to attaining your targeted or predetermined results.

Utilizing Creativity To Build Client Relationships

Trying to get a firm appointment with a specific principal within a target client relationship often can prove difficult and frustrating. Initially, you must face the first level of screen who generally is the receptionist who wants to know who you are and why you are calling. After getting past the receptionist by showing the proper degree of respect and interest, you now are ready to face the usually formidable presence of the secretary or administrative assistant to your principal.

If you do not handle this situation properly, you might be sentenced to a place in the world's longest queue with perhaps a long shot at a nebulous appointment at some undetermined time in the too-far-distant future.

You should try to build that secondary relationship with this person through a creative approach to your conversation. If your messages to the principal are not getting returned, take the time to review the attitude that you are projecting to his or her staff. The verbal posture that you take with people is more clearly seen than you might realize and the interpretation of your overall attitude and posture will determine how you as a new entity to that client relationship will be judged.

Take the time to employ the three principles of Big Bang relationship development, *acknowledgment, respect* and *recognition,* and use them at every level in your travels to the heart of the client relationship.

It's No Secret Why You Are There

Let the principal's people know why you are calling, what you hope to accomplish and who you are so they will support your efforts to get a face-to-face meeting.

I strongly suggest that you consider your mental and physical approaches to client-relationship development in terms of their creative context. Would you be enthusiastic and excited about listening to you over the telephone or meeting with you face-to-face?

How different and informative are your presentations in explaining why someone should work with you and your organization? Does your approach to marketing the principal's property or representing his or her requirements indicate a dynamic and creative presence and strategy?

When you are not making your targeted appointments via the traditional approach, what are your backup steps? Are you simply accepting at face value the statements of those with whom you do have contact when they say, "We really do not have any real estate needs right now and when we do we use so and so from ABC brokerage services."?

Finding New Strength

Creativity must be nurtured just like anything that you want to develop. *This means taking new risks, trying new methods, seeking new deal opportunities and finding new strength.*

The "what if?" question can serve as your radar device to screen your creative ideas and concepts. Look for the verbal and nonverbal reactions of the principal to gauge whether you are on the mark.

You must infuse your entire approach and implementation to Big Bang Selling with *creativity*. This includes analyzing your present approach not only to client-relationship development but also to deal-opportunity development. How creative are the types of deal opportunities that you bring to your various principals?

Your ability to answer the *"high trust"* questions of the principals who represent the deal opportunities will enable you to take a rifle-shot rather than a shotgun-blast approach to deal making. Sometimes using a creative approach means that you cannot be afraid to look foolish or silly. Recently, a sales manager for a southwestern real estate company told me that during his days of selling commercial real estate, he would go to any ends to develop a relationship with a targeted principal.

On one occasion after making numerous telephone calls without any success, he researched the principal's personal background regarding his work experience, professional affiliations, service organizations, educational background and recreational interests.

He then wrote a very complimentary letter in which he told the principal of his interest in meeting with him, shared with the principal the purpose of the proposed meeting, summarized his own professional background and emphasized his respect for the accomplishments and experiences of the principal.

Next, he found out where the principal parked his car and placed his letter with appropriate support documentation in a plastic bag that he taped to the nameplate/signpost indicating the principal's parking place.

Two days later he received a telephone call requesting that he come in to meet with the principal to discuss his interests; 120 days later he closed a 200,000-square-foot lease with the client relationship.

Doing the creative works. Doing the unusual works.

Until you can assert yourself in some distinctive manner from your competitors, you always will be seen as just another broker or agent.

Another example of a creative approach involved a Chicago selling agent who discovered that a major potential client relationship with whom he had not worked was looking to expand its existing retail locations by an additional 15 stores.

Unable to secure a meeting with the principal supposedly because he always had conducted business with a competitor, the selling agent started dropping in after five o'clock with hopes of seeing the principal in the lobby either coming in or leaving the facility.

After returning three times with no success, he decided to not wait in the lobby but to look for the specific office of the principal.

His aggressiveness was rewarded not only by finding the right office but also the right principal in his office. Although initially taken aback at this somewhat unorthodox approach, the principal was impressed with the selling agent's determination and gave him the opportunity to make what was an extremely creative presentation of the principal's existing locations, competitive presence, proposed locations and recommendations on how to further proceed. It worked! The agent made more than eight lease deals with the client relationship over the next 18 months!

Be Willing To Dare and Try Something New

The most important point of these two stories is that each of these selling agents tried something new. Each trusted his "gut instincts" that his actions would not make matters worse or somehow keep him further away from the client relationship and its deal opportunities.

If you are acting according to the tenets of Big Bang Selling, you never will feel that your more creative approaches are in vain.

The same is just as true when you are trying to meet the client relationship's requirements on either side of a transaction. The more you know about the motivations of all parties concerned, the more you can suggest new and creative approaches to deal structure and results. Learn to network your various relationships to create new deal opportunities.

The selling agent whom I trained under, J. H. Ragland, also was a master at creating deal opportunities. Hank was an apartment specialist and at one point during his career, after surveying the marketplace, he decided that the demand for developable apartment sites would increase tremendously over the next two years. Because he wanted to provide a service to his existing and hopefully new client relationships, he therefore developed the following strategy.

He first met with the heads of planning at the various municipalities to determine their perception of growth corridors, their opinion of preferable areas for new apartment development and their overall level of support for new development and growth.

Because successful apartment development often is contingent on its proximity to employment and shopping outlets, he investigated the planners' attitudes and understandings of the current and proposed development and growth in those areas. He also ascertained the areas in which any rezoning cases might face the most citizen resistance.

After gaining this invaluable insight, he chose a group of specific areas that met his and his client relationships' specific development criteria.

He then contacted various owners of target sites or potential parcels that could be rezoned for more than one use (generally for apartment and retail) and proceeded to make appointments with and give presentations to these owners regarding the value, use and demand for their individual properties.

As might be expected, he received many listings and control of property previously not on the market and placed himself in a dominant position within his specialty.

He then could provide his client relationships with the finest development opportunities in all sectors of the greater metropolitan marketplace.

As an offshoot, he brought in another selling agent who specialized in retail and thus increased his commission opportunities by selling the retail parcels as well.

Creative, of course; thoughtful, certainly; risky, not at all. If no one had purchased any sites, the worst that would have happened would have been a tremendous increase in the agent's overall knowledge base.

Creativity must become a major component of your summary thought process. You must mentally review your macro and micro approaches to client relationships, skill development and all relevant areas of knowledge to ensure that you are not stuck in a rut or employing the same methods and approaches that everyone else is using.

Another method that increases your *creativity* involves keeping an eye on the activities and dynamics of marketplaces that are similar to the one in which you work. For example, if you are an industrial specialist whose focus is on working with distribution-oriented client relationships, then it makes sense to gain an understanding of the dynamics and deal opportunities that are being conducted in other markets where distribution facilities are an important component.

Next, you must identify the entities who are making deals within those markets and contact them to determine what types of deals are being made, for what purposes and with what motivations and if your market and properties might not provide better alternatives.

This certainly is not rocket science, yet I am amazed at how few selling agents look beyond the boundaries of their own marketplaces. Remember you need a macro understanding of the spectrum of your specialty.

Once you understand the necessary information, you can use that knowledge to make new and creative deals by developing new client relationships and their relative deal opportunities.

CHAPTER

6

Belief: The Strength That Comes with Knowing You Can Do It!

We often hear people say, "If only you believe you can do something, you will do it." Although I basically agree with this statement, I have found that when you clearly understand the *constitution of your belief,* you will be able to more quickly accomplish your targeted goals or results.

The tenth tenet of Big Bang Selling, **belief,** therefore might be referred to as the concrete that holds together the entire Big Bang Selling **philosophy**. Your *belief* in your ability to attain your **purpose** brings about the complete integration of the other nine tenets that have been discussed in Chapters three, four and five.

Big Bang Selling *belief* emphasizes that the professional selling agent continually expands the mental image or vision of the boundaries of professional selling excellence and success.

Exploring the Outer Edge

We all probably have heard how test pilots push the outer edge of the envelope in their pursuit to find the limits of the performance capabilities of a new aircraft. You also should strive to push the outer edge of your *professional envelope* as it relates to reaching your *purpose* through the Big Bang Selling approach.

Your *belief* will provide you with the mental vision to see a much larger degree of professional accomplishment and success. Your *belief* will be something that you actually feel inside of you that keeps telling you to go on to pursue the client relationships and deal opportunities that only you believe eventually will provide your targeted *results*.

When others give up on a market segment, a deal opportunity or an unruly principal, your *belief* simply will not allow you to follow suit.

The strength to act in this manner, however, will be correlated directly to how strongly you embrace the tenets of *knowledge, relationships, communication, commitment, integrity, focus, creativity, competitive spirit* and *attitude.*

As I mentioned earlier, the tenets of Big Bang Selling continually will support and stimulate one another to provide you with an *internal mechanism of checks and balances to ensure your professional selling success.*

A strongly fortified system of *belief* will enable you to defeat *fear.* This *belief* will provide you with the strength that prevents you from ever being intimidated in any selling situation because when you are acting within the context of the Big Bang Selling *philosophy* you will develop a heightened state of awareness that your professional conduct and presence are second to none.

It is important to constantly evaluate the who, what, where, when, why and how in three major areas of Big Bang Selling *belief.* First of all, develop mental and physical processes to give yourself a personal *belief* checkup. How are you feeling about yourself regarding your ability to handle any specific client relationship or principal? Ask yourself the questions, "Do I know more about this deal or client than anyone else?" or "Did I do everything I could to make every element of every vital building block expand and succeed?"

Your ability and willingness to constantly nurture your constitution of *belief* will keep you on a fast track toward Big Bang Selling *purpose.*

The second area that you will want to monitor on at least a monthly basis is the client relationships that you are developing and the deal opportunities that you are either controlling or working on.

It is easy to become too narrow-minded about whom we work with and what we work on. Sometimes we are not nearly selective enough regarding the clients or deals that we pursue. You must continually review and ask yourself what are the potential results that either this client relationship or this deal opportunity eventually will yield and, more importantly, at what cost to the potential in similar relationships and opportunities.

Although there always will be enough time to accomplish your goals and results, it is much easier when you treat time like a very valuable commodity. Thus, when you pose the question of potential results and employ the Big Bang makability factor (see *process*), you will get a true feeling for the validity of your *belief* in any given area.

The third area of *belief* rests in the market segments in which you are dwelling and in the creative strategies that you are implementing.

Although your pursuit of clients and deals in specific market segments may appear noble, if these segments either don't fit the client-relationship requirements or the deal opportunities simply are unmakable, then you are acting under a very impaired sense of *belief.* Remember, your *knowledge* tenet will provide you with the proper direction to take as relates to past, present and future client and deal potential in every segment within every specialty of your marketplace. Thus, after weighing the appropriate information, you can properly evaluate the market segments and their potential for your targeted *results.*

The use of effective selling strategies separates the Big Bang Selling agent from the average salesperson. When you are creating unique and effective ways to market your deal opportunities and are monitoring their impact, you will further solidify your professional standing that, in turn, will increase the depth of your *belief.*

When you can articulate your planned and ongoing strategies to your principals in a meaningful and results-oriented manner, then they will harbor no doubts about your capabilities and about their decision to work with you as their selling agent.

The renewed affirmation and construction of your *belief* can be additionally funded by the knowledge that it is your deal opportunity based on your specific client development and marketing strategy. You know that it will be *your efforts* that either will make or break the successful closing and thus your continued enabling strength will come from the quality and analysis of these efforts that, in turn, will fuel your *belief* until each fosters mutual growth and success.

The *belief* that will spring from your progression toward Big Bang Selling *purpose* will serve every element of your professional maturation and its related journey.

The failed-deal opportunity mentioned earlier that fostered my unwillingness to be consoled is a very interesting case study with which I can illustrate many concepts. Although the deal opportunity did in fact fail, I was able to successfully close it with the help and support of another selling agent *three years later.*

The only reason that I eventually made that deal almost four years after my original exposure to the opportunity was because I truly believed it could and, in fact, would eventually sell. My *belief* was predicated on my knowledge of the principals on the selling side of the transaction, their motivations, the current state of the market segment, the existing debt considerations, the availability of new debt, the city planning influences and the motivations of the principals on the buying side of the transaction.

Furthermore, the depth of my client relationship, although fraught with various conflicts and misunderstandings, nevertheless was solid enough to close the deal.

The interesting thing about your *belief* is that the stronger it is toward the client and the deal, the stronger it generally will be returned to you. Your *belief* will create an energy and awareness in which every person involved will be caught up and become committed toward seeing a successful conclusion.

*Make no mistake, you can make the difference in deal making and your **belief** can make the necessary difference in you.*

The Need To Assimilate, Integrate and Implement

The sooner that you decide to **assimilate, integrate** and **implement** the tenets of the Big Bang Selling *philosophy* into the development of a consummate mental and physical approach to your profession, the more tenacious and lasting the constitution of your *belief* will become toward the achievement of your *purpose.*

The powerful value that results in maintaining a strong foundation of *belief* cannot be emphasized enough regarding its positive impact in the profession of commercial real estate selling. You must constantly evaluate it, however, in the macro and micro context of the other nine tenets of the Big Bang Selling *philosophy.*

For example, if you possess every bit of *knowledge* imaginable regarding your specialty and market but lack the **integrity** to properly use this *knowledge* or the **creativity** to devise effective client and deal strategies, the chances that you ever will achieve the Big Bang *purpose* and many of your targeted *results* probably are pretty slim.

Therefore, when you view all nine tenets as working together to form your *belief,* the inherent checks and balances built into the process will keep you on your road to selling success.

One of the best examples of the *assimilation, integration* and *implementation* of the Big Bang Selling *philosophy* was executed by a very close friend of mine who today is the president of the fastest-growing retail-development/brokerage company in the city of Chicago. His name is Mark H. Tanguay, lead partner for Tanguay Burke Stratton.

Mark obviously did not enjoy such a lofty status at the beginning of his commercial real estate career. After leaving Xerox in 1976 and having no success in finding a beginning position in commercial real estate selling in the Southwest, he moved to Chicago and worked as one of the lead selling agents in Coldwell Banker's new venture into the Midwest markets.

After approximately one year of trying to grasp the enormity of the greater Chicago marketplace within his specialty, retail, he acquired the appropriate level of knowledge and set out to specialize in a place called Orland Park. At the time, his sales manager and his peers thought that perhaps he was slightly out of his mind because there had been no significant commercial retail activity in this entire market segment.

What they did not realize was that although Orland Park was a previously underdeveloped retail area, it had been experiencing a significant change in its demographics and the leaders of this new municipality were anxious to bring in various retailers to service their growing community.

Because he appeared in the market every day, my friend was able to use his knowledge of growth trends and political attitudes to demonstrate to potential developers the vast future of this area. With this knowledge he formulated a plan to identify and control the finest land parcels for potential retail development, brought in the appropriate developers to buy the parcels, secured the commitments of major retail grocery chains to act as the anchor tenants for the centers, leased the balance of the shop space, sold the pads and soon became recognized as *the most genuine voice in retail deal making* in *Orland Park, Illinois*.

If this sounds too easy, it was not. I recall having many conversations with him when he was almost totally disconsolate at his inability either to get control of the right land parcels or to convince the development community of the area's potential. He also ran into various levels of local resident opposition and major retailer disbelief and indifference.

He would not be dissuaded, however, because he believed that the area had the potential that would be recognized eventually by the appropriate developers, lenders and retailers. He also believed that quality retail development would provide a great service to the community at large.

He was acting with *purpose* without knowing a specific definition and he was able to achieve his targeted results of commission dollars, market-segment control/expertise and recognized professional standing, as well as having rendered **preeminent client service** and being on his way to achieving a level of **professional selling excellence.**

In fact, he had become a genuine *entity of economic development* through his insatiable desire (**mission mentality**) to observe market trends, then to create appropriate client relationships and finally to control and close specific deal opportunities.

His *commitment* was obvious, his *focus* quite keen, his *creativity* now documented. His *integrity* reigned supreme throughout because he maintained his personal involvement in literally every step of the deal-opportunity process even after he could have relinquished control to the developer, retail clients, lenders and city officials. Instead, he kept involved at every step, learning the building blocks of rezoning, planning, financing, leasing, pad sales and working with the citizenry.

He developed the *attitude* that he was the force behind all of these events, which he was, and that through a fierce *competitive spirit* he could bring all the necessary players together.

Fortunately, he was able to *communicate* his *knowledge* to his target *relationships,* which eventually led to win/win deals for everyone involved. Truly, he is a real-life example of someone who utilized the Big Bang Selling *philosophy* to achieve both his macro- and micro-targeted *results* and *purpose.*

I recently discussed this deal-opportunity development process with him and he is convinced that it was and is his *belief* in himself, in God and in his professional selling process that enabled him to attain the success in Orland Park that has led to even greater success today.

He indeed took advantage of his scholarship in commercial real estate selling.

PART
II

The Building Blocks
of Success

CHAPTER
7

The Professional Selling Process: The Outer Ring of Big Bang Selling

Because Big Bang Selling *purpose* serves as a beacon to guide the professional selling agent toward his or her ultimate goals and its *philosophy* acts as an internal navigational device, the energy source always will be the Big Bang Selling *process*. While it is essential to know and to believe in where you are going within your selling career, you can arrive there a great deal sooner when you can devise and implement a viable method for daily professional progress and achievement.

The best method to achieve both your macro and micro selling goals or target results always will occur through a disciplined and creative daily selling *process*. The Big Bang Selling *process* not only will be your energy source but also will be the vehicle that will transport you to the appropriate *identification, recognition, nurturing* and *control* of those client relationships and deal opportunities that are necessary to attain great success.

I mentioned earlier in this book that one of the lessons that I hope to teach is *avoiding the great rainbow chase*. Far too often, selling agents show up at their office each day with little forethought as to where they subsequently will travel and whom specifically they will call on once they get there. Rather than take a place at the helm of their own destiny, they allow themselves to be blown about at the mercy of the currents of their own markets and local deal-making economies. Thus, when any deal opportunity appears, these nondirected and nonfocused selling agents literally leap at the chance to work on it regardless of its "makability factor." They then compound this mistake by spending most of their time on these pseudo opportunities without understanding whether or not they have a real chance of closing. This mentality also keeps them from performing the more important daily functions of increasing their market knowledge, analyzing, practicing and improving their skills and building the right client relationships that eventually will lead to makable deals.

In order to avoid this errant and frustrating method of selling, you must recognize the need for a professional selling process that includes long-term and short-term planning in regard to market specialization that ultimately will prepare you to become the *most genuine voice in deal making* within your specialty. This cannot be accomplished without a selling process that takes into consideration the ten tenets of the Big Bang Selling *philosophy* and allows you to use them daily to achieve your target results.

The Big Bang Selling *process* will provide a daily reminder of your needed direction for attaining your target results by laying out a focused plan on how you will get there. The development of the consummate mental and physical approach that I mentioned earlier is a result of not only what you think about and plan for in regard to your annual target results but also what you must translate *into every selling call and every trip into your market.*

To clarify, let me say simply that the *Big Bang Selling* process *takes your* purpose *(target results) and translates it into a daily series of actions and events* (see Figure 7.1) that must occur before you can achieve any of your goals, especially *preeminent client service* and *professional selling excellence.* Furthermore, this *process* provides a daily, and even hourly, planning mechanism that when executed and reviewed consistently will provide a focused method of checks and balances to ensure that you are on course to achieve your target results.

Figure 7.1. The Big Bang Selling process: the vehicle to help you arrive in selling purpose.

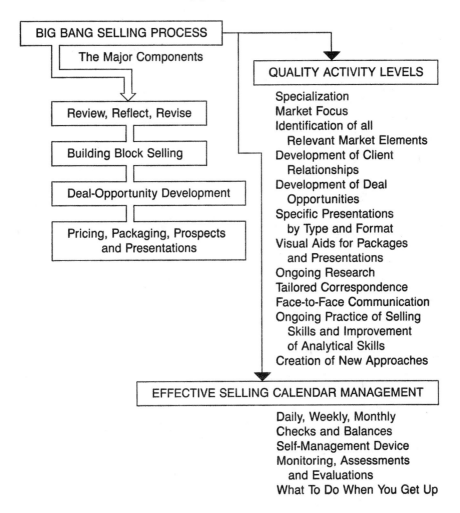

Become Your Own Sales Manager

If you, like most people in the commercial real estate brokerage business, love the independence of both thought and action that you enjoy, chances are that having a manager look over your shoulder ranks one notch below suffering through major gum surgery. Although you should strive to build sound relationships with those in the ranks of management within your organization, never forget that the one sure method for never being intimidated during a one-on-one confrontation rests with your ability to articulate a sound selling process. The axiom that you never can be intimidated in any selling situation if you know more about the situation at hand than anyone else in the meeting could just as easily have been said about meeting with your sales manager. In fact, rather than shy away from meetings with your manager, I suggest that you use these occasions to test and to present your expertise and knowledge within your specialty and target-market segments. I will explain in greater detail the ways to deal with sales managers later on; however, managers often can act as sounding boards for sharing strategies to be implemented in your selling process.

Developing an Awareness
of Deal Closings

If you still prefer to work alone, then let me show you how an effective selling process will enable you to independently manage your own success. Two of the most important things that all effective selling managers must know are their market share of deals actually closing and the clients on both sides of these closings. A manager must know these basics in order to determine if his or her selling agents are involved at any step or building block in the development of these specific deal opportunities and to what degree they have established some form of client relationship.

Without an effective process to identify and chart specific deals and a means for identifying and working with the appropriate client relationships, however, it will be impossible for any sales manager to perform effectively.

This, then, is where I promote you to the rank of professional selling manager—of you. You must constantly be aware of the who, what, where, when, why and how of all deal opportunities and deal closings and the existing and/or potential client relationships that are involved in them. In order to accomplish this task, you *must specialize.* For example, if you are a retail specialist, you might decide to concentrate in two major market segments of your overall market and direct your efforts toward knowing every detail about each neighborhood and strip shopping center located there. This would include being aware of all tenant activity by type, profile, principals, decision-making criteria, specific requirements and so forth.

The Two Major Components
of the Big Bang Selling Process

In order to accomplish this task that will lead you directly to becoming *the most genuine voice in deal making* within your specialty, you must plan and execute your time and activities to yield this invaluable knowledge. The ability to be successful in this vein will spring directly from your willingness to embrace the following two major components of the Big Bang Selling *process:* **quality activity levels** and **effective selling calendar management.**

The most important principle of the Big Bang Selling *process* is that it is always *results oriented and results yielding.* In other words, everything that you do should lead toward achieving your target results. For example, if you want to make five lease deals a month, then every selling call that you make must in some way add progress toward your target results of moving at least five prospective tenants toward occupancy within five specific projects with available and "fittable" space. This fit must be proper in terms of the amount of necessary square footage; an acceptable lease rate, term and structure for all relevant parties; appropriate timing; the proper location; and an acceptable neighboring tenant profile.

If you are now the most amazing commercial-leasing specialist in history and need only to identify five prospective tenants and five projects in order to meet your target results of five signed leases, then chances are you already have a bulletproof selling process and have little need for what follows. If, on the other hand, you struggle to make two lease deals each month and cannot seem to get a handle on where to put your limited number of prospective tenants and do not know why, then you probably are a pretty good candidate for the Big Bang Selling *process.*

What Are Quality Activity Levels?

If we agree that *selling activity might be defined as brisk or vigorous movement or action in the progress of some element of deal-opportunity or client-relationship building,* then I think we are on the right track. Activity is what you as a professional selling agent should be doing at any given time to better serve your clients and fulfill their commercial real estate requirements. Activity includes the things that you do to increase your knowledge of the marketplace, its deal-making process and the players or principals who inhabit it. Activity includes the cold calls that you make to identify prospective tenant (client) requirements and the particular nuances of their companies and industries. Activity includes the number and type of presentations that you create and make to control clients and deal opportunities. Activity includes the schedule of meetings that you hold with city planners, architects, engineers, lenders, accountants and other affiliated professionals to identify new opportunities and to share your knowledge. Activity is the energy and the progress that you make in the growth and achievement of your target results. Activity is the effort that you make to understand the nature and components of other markets and their clients with whom you can create positive relationships to foster your knowledge and/or create new deal opportunities. Activity is reading that further facilitates your understanding of your specialty, your industry and the overall happenings in the country's and world's business. Activity is your personal involvement in your communities in your target charities and service organizations. Activity is also your personal time spent with your family, your friends, your associates and yourself. Activity can, in essence, make you or break you and thus your ability to maximize your most productive types of activity is what the Big Bang Selling *process* is all about.

Your understanding of *quality activity levels* must translate to your ability to perceive how everything you do either supports or detracts from the attainment of your professional and personal target results. When you embrace the ten tenets of the Big Bang *philosophy*, it is critical that you begin to understand how to weave them into your daily, weekly and monthly activity levels.

It is not enough to say that you would like to grow and to continue to increase your knowledge of your market without implementing the appropriate activity to provide you with this knowledge.

For example, although the need is obvious, many selling agents simply do not spend enough time driving through or walking around their territories or areas of specialization. To truly understand a comparable sale or project, it is not enough to review the rents or cost per square foot. You must look at all the factors that create value in the project from the significance of the location, the ambience of the site and project, the tenant profiles, the community in which it resides, the motivations of those who inhabit it, the development of the site plan, the design characteristics and floor plates, proposed floor plans and why this project truly is unique.

Thus, what I am referring to here is the *quality* of the activity. It is not enough to just look at a lot of projects without understanding what to look for and how to look and compare. Remember, Big Bang Selling is a consummate mental and physical approach to your profession and, therefore, you must not only be aware of the amount of your activity but the quality of it.

One more example of *quality activity levels* would be the selling agent who determined that she wanted to become the finest and most successful commercial retail agent in her entire company. The agent developed a selling strategy for gaining the appropriate levels of knowledge and then decided to establish sound client relationships with the most active principals in her market segments. She developed a list of all the major and minor clients who either developed shopping centers or bought them, who purchased existing sites (either zoned or unzoned), who owned centers that needed additional leasing, who had additional pads for sale and who might be interested in selling projects. Finally, she studied the types of centers, locations, tenant profiles, ages, conditions, etc., prior to her first meetings. Then she set out to meet with every major and minor principal within a given time frame that she carefully tracked and planned on her calendar. On all her calls she ran a very specific track regarding her questions, asking not only about the principal's present real estate requirements or whom he or she worked with in brokerage, but also about the principal personally, his or her company and current outlooks and perspectives. Next, she made a carefully planned and meaningful presentation of the state of the retail market in regard to land prices, tenant activities, occupancy and vacancy fluctuations and reasons why, current and future trends and current lenders looking for deals. During the course of her presentations, she made sure that each principal understood her presentation and kept close watch to ensure that she held his or her interest. She also explained her professional qualifications and deal-making history during the course of the presentation. Needless to say, this quality approach paid off because within a short period of time this particular agent became a force in her specialty.

Sometimes You Get Only One Chance

The inescapable lesson here is that you make the most of your time whether you are in front of clients or within the boundaries of your specialized marketplace. Sometimes you only get one chance with a client or deal opportunity *so don't waste it.*

Engaging in *quality activity levels* requires that you always are prepared with the necessary tools and plans to implement predetermined objectives within your area of specialization and its market segments. You consistently must review your objectives for the day, week and month and analyze how these objectives will move you closer to your series of target results or goals. You will be able to continually evolve your selling process as you always try to refine your time-management methods, your presentations and their components, your sensitivity to everyone with whom you come into contact, your understanding of client objectives and requirements and so forth.

The ability to consistently engage in quality activity necessitates that you "think" about what you are doing and why you are doing it every day, before, during and after your day is completed.

Effective Selling Calendar Management

The second component of the Big Bang Selling *process* is **effective selling calendar management**. You must consider your daily planner or time-management device as a selling tool that will yield the most available time in which you can implement results-oriented activities.

The easiest way to begin to effectively use your selling calendar is to refer to it nightly after your day is complete to determine what meetings, calls or travel must be made to keep you on track for your target results whether they are in the client-relationship, deal-opportunity or additional-knowledge areas. Whenever possible, become active in your planning approach and not reactive. Because this business necessitates reacting to an ever-changing set of deal-opportunity influencing circumstances, you must anticipate these necessary actions to keep in control of your time and calendar.

Quality activity levels and *effective selling calendar management* always must begin with your target results during the definition and understanding of your *purpose*. For example, if you set an income goal of $100,000 at the beginning of any given year, you must not proceed without understanding what you will do and who you will do it with on a daily basis. Too often, selling agents go through the year placing their hopes on a handful of deal opportunities without ever gaining any real understanding of their client relationships and the total number of deal opportunities that they represent. They exacerbate this already grim situation by failing to stay on top of all deal influences and generally end up receiving a surprise telephone call telling them that their deal opportunity has fallen through. If they are not following their road maps, chances are they will not meet their income expectations.

Understanding Your Selling Ratios
from an Activity and Numbers Perspective

To truly understand how your activity levels and calendar management work to help you achieve your goals or target results, you must understand your selling ratios. In other words, how many client relationships do you need to generate the necessary deal opportunities that will yield the appropriate number of closed deals that in turn will provide you with a specific income figure? These ratios will be either improved or depleted by your ability to be effective at every step of developing client relationships to get control of their deal opportunities. These selling ratios then will be impacted by the amount of energy or activity that you generate in these deal opportunities. Consider the previous example of the $100,000 income target (see Figure 7.2).

In order to meet your income target of $100,000, you must understand and be able to answer the following questions:

1. What is your average commission yield per closed deal? (Let's assume that it is $5,000 per deal.)
2. How many deal opportunities must you keep active to close the 20 deals that will yield your income goal? (Let's assume 20 opportunities for every closed deal.)
3. How many client relationships do these 20 closed deals necessarily represent and how many client relationships do those 400 deal opportunities represent?
4. How many deal opportunities per day must you develop to stay on track for your gross numbers to ensure or improve your ratios?
5. Let's assume that you actually have 300 days to develop these 400 deal opportunities or 1.33 deal opportunities per day. Now how many calls or meetings do you need daily to yield the 1.33 deal opportunities? (Let's assume ten calls per day.)
6. The next question is where do you find these ten client relationships to call on?

Perhaps now you can see the value of *effective selling calendar management* and *quality activity levels*. Obviously, the more ef-

Figure 7.2.   The Big Bang Selling income graphic: the value of knowing your selling ratios.

Projected target result = $100,000.
Assumptions:
Average commission yield = $5,000;
20 deal opportunities = 1 closed deal.
Thus it will take
400 deal opportunities to yield 20 closed deals that will yield the projected target income result.
20 closed deals @ $5,000 = $100,000.

Your task is to determine how many client relationships you must develop to yield 400 deal opportunities.

Based on an estimated 300 potential selling days, you must create 1.33 deal opportunities each day. If you could improve your selling ratios from 20 deal opportunities for every one deal to ten for one, obviously you would need to create fewer opportunities.

In summary, $100,000 income target = 20 deals = 400 deal opportunities = 1.33 deal opportunities per day.

Now you must determine how many selling calls and presentations you must make daily to create and identify the necessary client relationships and deal opportunities.

If you assume that it takes three to five calls each day to create 1.33 deal opportunities, you can see the value in properly structuring your selling day and the need to make face-to-face calls.

fective you become during your calls and meetings, the more you can impact your positive selling ratios. When you look at your calendar every morning, however, you cannot fool yourself about where you stand regarding your target income or client relationship goals. If, like the calendars of many average selling agents, your calendar shows only five preplanned meetings for the entire week to impact your deal-opportunity development and client relationships, you are not going to stay on track and sustain your necessary selling ratios. Furthermore, as you fall behind in the number of necessary selling calls, the chances are good that you will begin to place your hopes on just a few client relationships and even fewer deal opportunities. And as we have hopefully agreed, this process is just too risky and can lead to gross under-achievement.

Nothing Beats Face-to-Face Principal Contact!

Many selling agents waste too much time! Generally, their morning and early afternoon schedule looks something like this:

8:00–8:15 a.m.   Have a cup of coffee, talk to associates about sports, their love lives, their problem clients or the traffic.

8:15–8:40 a.m.   Straighten desk, read newspaper (local or *Wall Street Journal*), make personal calls, talk to associate in next office or walk across office to joke with friends.

8:41–9:45 a.m.   Review mail, dictate letter from yesterday's meeting, plan current day, make telephone calls for appointments, input into computer, joke around with pals, take up issue with administrative manager.

9:45–10:00 a.m.   Travel to first appointment, get gas on the way.

10:00–11:20 a.m.   Meetings, travel in market, project visitation.

11:21–11:50 a.m.   Travel back to office, get car washed.

11:51–1:15 p.m.   Meet friends, decide where to go for lunch, eat lunch, travel back to office.

1:16–1:35 p.m.   Review telephone messages, check mail, dictate correspondence, review market data.

Sometimes it is necessary to exaggerate a point to make a point. But if you are like the majority of selling agents, you probably have plenty of time in your day to increase the productivity in your minutes, hours and days. Remember, when you must develop any given number of new client relationships and deal opportunities, you can be most successful only when you plan and effectively use your time. Take a look at the amount of time you waste in the office. Just because you are in the office does not mean that you are working hard. In fact, between 8:00 a.m. and

4:00 p.m., you would better serve yourself and your clients if you were in their offices developing your relationships or in your marketplace observing current trends, projects and activities and reviewing present, past and proposed deals.

Review, Reflect and Revise
or How To Stay on Track
in Your Big Bang Selling Process

As I began to think about the lessons I had learned in selling in preparation to write this book, I began to reflect on the effectiveness of many of my selling strategies. I looked at my selling process and how my goals played a part in that process. I looked at how my existing base of client relationships interacted with my ability to develop and service new relationships. And I tried to determine what things truly gave me satisfaction and joy in regard to what I had accomplished. It was a very sobering experience, for many of the things that I had long considered my major motivators were, after a more complete analysis, only secondary motivators.

Never Take for Granted
Your Selling Success

The most striking part of my self-examination, however, was the discovery that during much of my career I was so caught up in the pursuit of deal opportunities in my existing client relationships that at times I ignored one of the most basic lessons that is critical to any professional selling agent's success: I was not consistently seeking relationships with new principals on their entrance into the marketplace nor was I stepping back to view the market from a much broader perspective outside the requirements of my existing client relationships.

The selling principle that I had at times ignored relates to the generation of *quality activity levels* complemented with *effective selling calendar management* and is called the *cookie dough principle of selling*. (See Figure 7.3.) If you can, imagine that all of

Figure 7.3.   The Big Bang Selling principle of making real dough.

CLIENT-RELATIONSHIP DOUGH	=	DEAL OPPORTUNITY	=	DEALS

1	2	3	4	5	6	7	8
A	A	A	A	A	A	A	A
B	B	B	B	B	B	B	B
C	C	C	C	C	C	C	C
D	D	D	D	D	D	D	D
E	E	E	E	E	E	E	E

$= \quad$ 1 2 3 4 5 6 7 8 9 10 $\quad = \quad$ **3.33 DEALS**

Assume these eight client relationships generate 40 deal opportunities (A-E) each year and that your penetration level is 25 percent. If you can close one-third of your deal opportunities, this activity will yield 3.33 deals.

Your ability to increase your overall effectiveness and penetration when working with clients and their deals will determine how you reach your income targets.

your client relationships and their deal opportunities could be kneaded into two sheets of cookie dough. You would see that at any given time you have a fixed potential for perfectly baked cookies. During the baking process, chances are you may lose cookies (clients and deal opportunities) to overheating (inappropriate representation), misshaped or underbaked cookies (competitive pressures) or perhaps because of lack of proper ingredients (poor results and too little responsibility).

To meet your target for the appropriate number and quality of cookies, you obviously must replenish your base of cookie dough. The same is true in terms of your client relationships and their deal opportunities. You cannot afford to miss the chance to add quality clients to your portfolio of relationships and, just as important, you continually must strive to create new deal opportunities within your existing client relationships as well as within your new ones.

I discovered in my reflections that at times I had violated this principle and although I had great success during my brokerage career, my success could have been even greater. I still was uncertain as to how this could have happened and then I discovered that during the latter stages of my career I had not revised my goals, target results and, thus, my *purpose* for being in the business. I want to share this very valuable lesson, so I have created a principle of Big Bang Selling that I refer to as the process of *review, reflect* and *revise.*

During the continuing evolution of your consummate mental and physical approach to selling and/or leasing commercial real estate, you constantly must review the events of your day, week and month. You must examine how the specifics of your daily activities affect the attainment of your target results and goals. In other words, *review* exactly what you did to develop and nurture your clients and their deal opportunities to create win/win deals. Then you must *reflect* on what you have accomplished in the areas of your activity regarding its quantity and quality and determine what you might do differently next time or how you might improve or add to your overall effectiveness and results. The third phase of this principle is the *revise* portion where you make the appropriate corrections in your daily activities and thought processes to meet your macro as well as your micro target results and goals.

For example, in my previously mentioned case, I should have identified my lack of new client relationship activity, made mental notes on how to improve or add to that client activity and then appropriately revised my target results for new client relationships and new deal opportunities. Then I could have used my selling calendar to plan calls on new principals to study their overall makeup and requirements and then devise a strategy of how to work with these principals.

In summary, each day as you plan and preview your next day or the balance of your week, implement the *review, reflect* and *revise* thought process. You will be amazed at the new and effective **results** you soon will achieve. In addition, use your selling calendar as a management tool to guide this process. The more that you focus and concentrate on your marketplace, your client relationships and your makable deal opportunities, the more you will plan and create ways to find success in each of these vital areas. Your calendar will not "lie" to you nor will it ever "mislead" you as to where you stand in the development of these critical areas.

When you first are learning about your marketplace and its principals, use your calendar to focus and direct your efforts. This will prevent you from bouncing around your city in a haphazard and willy-nilly fashion that does nothing but waste valuable time and create needless frustration. Your calendar should be the focal point of your specialization in regard to where you spend your time in your market and how you decide on which segments to make your personal territories.

If the professional selling agent needs a conscience to help gauge his or her efforts and results, it is available in all its honest reality awaiting examination in the selling calendar. Get to know this critical and valuable tool and make it one of your most important allies in pursuing your professional hopes and dreams.

CHAPTER
8

Setting Up for Selling Commercial Real Estate

Whether you reside professionally in an office or a cubicle, or whether you walk to visit your clients and their projects or whether you drive, the manner in which you plan, set up and continually manage your outlets for storing and retrieving information is critical to your overall selling success. You must, of course, understand the relative importance and value of the myriad types of data that you will need to inform and best serve your client relationships, your organization and yourself.

What You See
Is What You Get!

The first step you must take when accessing the support or lack of support given by the organizational format of your office, your cubicle, your briefcase and even your automobile is to evaluate the focus on your client relationships, your current working deal opportunities, your specialty and your marketplace and its segments. I firmly believe that what we focus on eventually will be brought to reality and fruition. If every time you look into your briefcase or cubicle and find chaos, there is a pretty good chance that chaos is what you will realize.

Let's look at the individual office or cubicle that each selling agent inhabits and review what should be in there (see Figure 8.1).

Aerials. Whether posted on the walls or reduced in size and stored within a file, a system of aerials showing your overall marketplace with its segments should be available to view to keep a perspective on how the segments where you specialize and focus relate to the overall picture. Additional aerials should be available showing your focused segments and should include the identity within your specialty of existing projects, projects under construction, proposed sites for new projects, vacant sites (zoned and unzoned) and significant landmarks and roadways.

Each of these categories should be keyed with all pertinent data from ownership to occupancy levels, rental rates to tenant profiles, deal history to socioeconomic-political influences. This data should be kept in market-segment files that are easily accessible and retrievable within the cubicle or office area. Additional aerials from a micro perspective should be available of all your current listings or controlled projects together with a site plan, tenant profiles, demographic characteristics, current debt profiles, deal structure under consideration and so forth. Once again, this information should be kept in files and stored for easy reference. If you have limited room, reduce the aerials and store them in file folders to aid your knowledge of the specific deal opportunity or market segment.

The major point is that the more you visually focus on the projects within your specialized market segments as well as your working deal opportunities, the more you will add to your knowledge and awareness, which will more rapidly lead you to greater clarity, more focused deal-opportunity development and more closed deals.

Site plans, Working Drawings and Floor Plans. I would venture to guess that you could walk into any cubicle or office in your organization and find at least three to five out-of-date sets of plans. The only thing that these oversized space grabbers do is

Figure 8.1. The contents of an individual office or cubicle.

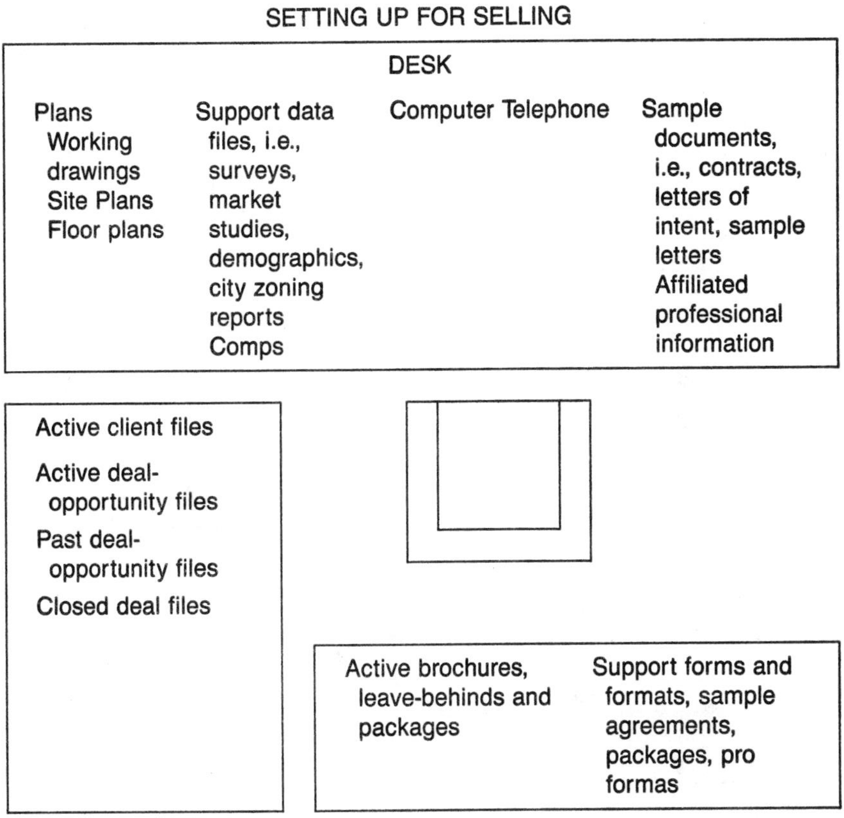

SETTING UP FOR SELLING

DESK			
Plans Working drawings Site Plans Floor plans	Support data files, i.e., surveys, market studies, demographics, city zoning reports Comps	Computer Telephone	Sample documents, i.e., contracts, letters of intent, sample letters Affiliated professional information

Active client files

Active deal-
  opportunity files

Past deal-
  opportunity files

Closed deal files

Active brochures, leave-behinds and packages	Support forms and formats, sample agreements, packages, pro formas

to make someone look busy. You always should have ready access to the plans of the projects and the deal opportunities that you are working on or hope to work on to increase your knowledge and awareness of the development of those who put the project together. By keeping unnecessary plans and drawings around, however, you only create confusion in your cubicle or office.

Brochures, Flyers and Packages. At least one of each of these items must be kept in your deal-opportunity file with a handful available and organized by project and/or client submission. The bulk of these data sources should be stored in a nearby filing or storage area, preferably out of the cubicle or office. Keep this information readily available to facilitate your telephone and intraoffice discussions. When the brochure or flyer is in the development stage, make sure that you are involved in every step of its creation and development. Far too many brochures are created by public-relations or advertising people who seldom know very much about why a particular project is competitive within its market segments. You know what sells and why, so be aware of what a particular brochure or package actually says to the prospective tenant or acquisitions person who actually will review this important information source. Remember, it will take more than a pretty picture to sell or lease your principal's project, so make sure that the brochure sells when you are not around to articulate the project's merits.

When you see especially effective packages on projects or creative brochures, collect them to use as samples to create great marketing sources of your own.

In-baskets and Out-baskets. Two of the biggest misnomers in the commercial real estate office, these trays generally end up being used to store mail of all types, such as old pro formas and packages, one-week-old *Wall Street Journals* and so forth. Try to use either one or two sets of in- and out-baskets for final correspondence awaiting review and signature, cassettes awaiting typing, rough drafts of documents awaiting review and restructuring, current-day memos, current-day mail, memos to associates, commission vouchers to be processed, etc. Take newspapers, magazines and junk mail home for reading and disposal.

The File Drawers. Create file folders for specific types of market data from occupancy reports and surveys on the general market in all specialties to segment files relating to your specialties. Create a report that summarizes much of this data that can be used for your own reference or as part of an information package for your prospective and existing client-relationship principals.

Set up a system of files for sample documents of finished leases, purchase agreements of various structures, letters of intent and sample correspondence to principals, peers, managers and other professionals. Use these documents as effective and professional guidelines to aid you in preparing documents that are pertinent and creative. Do not let yourself fall into using a system of form letters. Your correspondence always should indicate some specific happenstance from the communication to which you are referring. If you indeed are going to "stand out from your competition," begin to do so through the quality of your written communication. The aforementioned samples that you should collect should be outstanding and relevant. As far as using form letters, even after cold calls, think of your reaction when you receive such a letter. Take a risk with your writing and be creative to gain and hold the attention of all with whom you seek to communicate and interact.

Keep a file for architects, engineers, title officers, lawyers, consultants, city planners and anyone else with whom you have or want to establish relationships. Create a file with all relevant municipal data, including the names of current political figures such as city council members, planners, city managers, deputy mayors and their staffs. This also should contain copies of zoning ordinances with general guidelines for development (new and redevelopment) and local newspaper articles concerning all related real estate development issues. Keep a file on national and regional issues related to your specialty and market segments. This file should include articles from local, regional and national real estate magazines and newspapers that specialize in your field. Finally, keep a few blank forms of all types such as commission vouchers, standard lease documents, expense reports, selling calendar fillers, etc. By having them on hand you will save a great deal of time over the course of a year by not having to leave your desk area to procure these forms from a storage area.

The Rolodex. This well-organized and current system for keeping telephone numbers with accurate client-relationship data handy is invaluable. You should organize this information alphabetically either by client-relationship name and/or relevant principals. Data kept on Rolodex cards should be kept to a minimum with ready reference to specific client-relationship, deal-opportunity, tenant or owner files. I also strongly suggest you create an abbreviated form of a portable Rolodex that you can carry as a vital segment of your selling calendar; thus you always could have the names and telephone numbers of your most active client relationships at your fingertips.

The Calendar. I have stressed the value of a selling calendar that you can use to organize and plan your needed activities. Whatever type of selling calendar you use, make sure that it is easily transportable and can be utilized on your desk when you are in your cubicle or office. Avoid using multiple calendars such as a desk calendar, a selling calendar and a calendar at home. Use one selling calendar that can be organized to facilitate all your necessary professional and personal planning. Besides showing each day and month with their respective areas to note appointments and things to do, develop a place within your selling calendar to keep summaries of your current deal opportunities by status and a summary of client-relationship requirements. These two important areas will continue to foster your focus and creativity to meet their particular needs as necessary.

The Desktop Computer. Although I initially did not use computers during my brokerage career, I since have become a strong believer in their amazing capabilities. With the advent of tremendous software capability, you literally can create all the files and information that I have mentioned simply and efficiently through the touch of some keystrokes. A computer is not only a tremendous way to store and call up data, but it is also a great aid in determining various aspects of a deal opportunity's makability. If you have any inclination or ability to use a personal computer, I strongly would recommend that you use the computer as an integral component of your setting up for selling.

Desk Drawers. As obvious as it may seem, you always should keep on hand at least three pencils, pens, felt tips and yellow highlighters to serve as writing tools for various uses. Keep at least two legal pads in your drawer for taking notes in meetings as well as at your desk. A working calculator, a mini-35-mm. camera and a dictating unit also should be handy. Of course, two sizes of paper clips and 10 to 20 empty folders should be available when you need them. At least once every quarter, go through your desk drawers to refile and organize their contents.

Develop a habit of using your camera and dictating device in concert to define more clearly your observations within your marketplace. These two support tools can be invaluable when pointing out competitive strengths between your projects and those of the competition.

The Briefcase. Besides the way you are dressed and your professional attitude and demeanor, nothing will tell your clients more about you than the organization of your briefcase. You should view your briefcase as your traveling office. Your briefcase should be a storage reference point for your support mechanisms for every call that you make. You always should carry a calculator, a dictating device (with two blank tapes), at least two pens and pencils, base market data, legal pads and the specific marketing and information packages relevant to your selling calls. In addition, any brochures or marketing studies that might be important should be a part of your package. The final ingredients in a Big Bang Selling briefcase would be a summary of your professional qualifications, personal and company specialty deal history and some form of leave-behind information package on you, your company, your specialty and your market.

A tool that is being used more and more to add strength and integrity to the selling presentation is the video camera. If you have access to such a device, definitely use it to record your marketplace and its projects. The tapes can highlight your listing presentations and point out your volume of knowledge and understanding of your marketplace and its deal opportunities. Using a video camera is another way to definitely stand out from your competitors and, if used properly, it can make a major difference in the depth and quality of all your presentations. Furthermore, if you were to catalog all the important projects by client relationship, you would have a wonderful means of ready access to show prospective tenants and buyers at first glimpse why that particular deal opportunity should make sense to them.

Both types of cameras can be useful to record the tenancy in any given project that will enable you to develop valid tenant profiles and increase your prospective tenant base for your own controlled projects.

Your Automobile. Keep it clean and use its trunk to store market-data sheets and information, brochures, leave-behind packages, site plans/working drawings on your current project representations and deal opportunities and a camera to record necessary properties and locations.

In summary, remember that a cubicle or office can be either friend or foe, your best support or worst enemy. It can provide or hide time-vital information that if available can make you appear to be either the consummate professional or just another voice of brokerage mediocrity. Strive to keep only relevant and pertinent data available in your cubicle or office but do so in a method that will complement your selling efforts rather than hinder them. Remember, using important market, deal or client data should not require an "expedition" to find it. Three pages of erroneous, out-of-date or irrelevant information can soon become the three-thousand-sheet misinformation behemoth that refuses to leave.

The Deal File:
The Selling Agent's Best Friend
and Most Important Ally

The human memory can be an amazing vehicle for total recall, but in the commercial real estate brokerage business, you are inviting disaster if you depend only on your memory. With deal-opportunity factors and influences changing at will, it can be difficult at times just remembering the context of your most recent conversation let alone remembering what was said three weeks before and by whom. Therefore, develop the habit of keeping a file on every client relationship that you currently either control or share or are developing toward some more significant step. Create a format that includes specific information categories for each one of your client relationships: all principal names, telephone numbers, specific positions in the organization, deal history, existing ownerships, development history, type of business, type of industry, decision-making criteria and profile, major competitors, current- and future-year business plan and goals, support personnel roster, current locations and profiles of support personnel, financing sources and lending relationships, education and family histories of principals, principal job description and professional charter and so forth.

This format serves two primary functions: It gives you a wealth of knowledge and insight into the people and pursuits of the client relationship and it provides you with a consistent track to run on when you are developing your understanding of

the client relationship. Remember, developing a mutually productive business and selling relationship demands more than
knowing a client's commercial real estate requirements.

In regard to the deal-opportunity file, this nugget of information should contain all correspondence, documentation, telephone interaction history, meeting summaries and records of
pertinent outside-person contacts such as with other brokers,
lenders, lawyers, accountants, designers and property managers.
Make sure that every significant factor affecting the various
deal points is summarized by who, what, where, when, why and
how. If you take the time to correspond properly with all pertinent parties from principals to other agents and then document
this correspondence, chances are pretty good that you never will
lose an internal or external commission dispute. Your deal-
opportunity file can play an especially important role when it
comes to making people stand behind their verbal and written
commitments. Do not assume because you act with integrity
that everyone else always will. The chance for others to have an
erroneous recollection or misguided perspective of the deal opportunity during its various stages of development will be diminished greatly when you can produce a specific written
recollection of what actually transpired.

You also should add a summary of all forms of agreed-on support for the deal opportunity and have it acknowledged in writing by the appropriate parties.

Keep your client-relationship files and your deal-opportunity
files in separate cabinets or storage areas with easy access for
you but secured in a confidential manner.

The File as a Prospecting Mechanism

Two friends of mine recently began offering a unique service
within the southwestern commercial real estate markets that
serves as the best prospecting, management-information device
and strategic tool that I have ever seen. Pete Bolton and Chuck
Birkenkamp of Prime Data Services presently are offering their
amazing market analysis in the commercial retail arena. They
have developed a report that breaks down the existing tenant

base in the entire market by category. For instance, they can provide a report that ranges from categories of tenants for appliances and automotive supplies through restaurants, shoes and special-interest stores. They also can point out the existing vacant space in the entire market or by market segment. Furthermore, their report can list such things as every existing competitive retail center within a given radius of any specific site or project. They also can provide a further breakdown in each category, such as appliances ranging from TVs to computers to sewing machines to vacuum cleaners. In each category, they can list the tenants and the numbers and placement of their locations by category type.

The reason that I mention this, besides the fact that their data package is beyond state-of-the-art, is to stress the importance of keeping files by tenant name, type and/or profile in some accessible location. In cases where a computer is not available, list the most active tenants or types of tenants on a document with decision-maker names and telephone numbers. Additionally, it would be helpful to summarize their existing locations. This information should be kept in separate, easily accessible files. Keep specific lease expirations and space requirements in your client-relationship files. You can use these files as a prospect referral list for these tenants to build meetings with them into your daily selling calendar.

By keeping this information so organized in your cubicle or office, you always will have ready access to data by tenant type with specific names to aid you in developing and closing new deal opportunities. This system is applicable regardless of your specialty.

A Last Word on Setting Up

In order to properly set yourself up to sell commercial real estate you must make your mind and body as orderly and complementary to your efforts as an organized desk, cubicle, office and briefcase. You should develop a crisp and professional presence. The people whom you deal with like to see a professional on the other side of the desk. It's great to think of yourself as apart from the crowd by not wanting to be or look like a clone of everyone else in your business, but what I am saying has nothing to do with any specific fashion.

Develop your own style of dress and use it as a complement to providing *preeminent client service*. Ensure that your suits, shirts, sport coats, skirts and blouses are pressed; your shoes highly polished; and your pants neatly creased. Whether you are more Brooks Brothers, Giorgio Armani or Hugo Boss does not really matter. In fact, I encourage you to dress to your own taste, but do be aware of the dress and style of your clientele for whether you agree or not, people generally prefer to deal with selling agents who represent what they believe is an appropriate image of professionalism.

The strength and energy that will come from being totally crisp and organized will provide you with additional power because all these set-up elements will begin working together to help foster a greater intensity and integrity in your total Big Bang Selling effort.

CHAPTER
9

Building Block Selling and the 1-2-3 Make Sense Approach

When I speak of having a *purpose* on a macro and micro scale, I am referring to having a meaningful reason for everything that you do in a professional selling context. That reason or *purpose* on the micro scale (daily appointments and meetings) always should serve to build the foundation toward a greater result on a macro scale. In other words, if you target a specific property that you hope to lease and/or sell to an appropriate tenant and investor, then you first must lay the proper foundation. You can accomplish this through a series of actions (research, meetings, presentations, listings, relationship building, etc.) that leads toward closing the targeted leases or selling the project.

To further your consummate mental approach to selling, think of *each step or action as a building block in your foundation for real estate brokerage success.* (See Figure 9.1.) The higher the quality of your actions, the higher the potential and ratios for your success.

Figure 9.1 Building block selling in the acquisition of knowledge within your specialty and target-market segments.

7. Identification of active lenders within specialty, appraisers, lawyers, accountants and consultants and the development of your outside target relationships.

6. Identification of active client relationships and principals by ownerships, deals (leases), deals (acquisitions), deals (sales), speculation, investment and development entities in same categories.

5. Analysis of historical performance of all target-market segments by product type, occupancy levels, rental and expenses achievements, market demographics, economic-development influences, political attitudes and impact, competitive alternatives, etc.

4. Identification, review and observations of all current deal opportunities.

3. Research and investigation of deal history by specialty vis-a-vis price/value relationships, structures, financing amounts, types and sources, motivations of principals and overall deal structure.

2. Selection of market-segment focus.

1. Identification of target specialty.

The Value of Specialization

The universe of client relationships and deal opportunities in the overall commercial real estate marketplace is immense. Whether you live and work in a throbbing metropolis such as New York, Chicago, Los Angeles, Atlanta or Dallas or whether you practice your profession in a much smaller city and marketplace, you always should specialize in one particular field of commercial real estate. In order to become a force in commercial real estate sales, you must possess the previously mentioned *"most genuine voice."* Because of the multiplicity of the dynamics in each specialty, ranging from unique principal personalities to the varied types of deal structures and alternative projects, it would be almost impossible to know enough about all specialties and thus possess that *most genuine voice.* Therefore, select a specialty in commercial real estate in which you are genuinely interested. Choose an area that currently is very active or that soon will become active because of positive influencing market factors and then select key market segments within that area or specialty that offer the most potential deal opportunities. For instance, if you decide to specialize in the office-leasing specialty, you first might choose to spend most of your time in either landlord or tenant representation. You could do both, but depending on the strength and profile of your marketplace, it might make more sense to choose one or the other. Your next decision is to choose one or more segments of the office marketplace in which to work. For instance, you might have to decide between a downtown high-rise market segment versus a mid- to low-rise suburban market segment. In order to make a rational and strategic decision, you first must understand what segments are most active in leasing and development activity and why. You must determine the motivations for tenant movements and relocations, as well as the prospective target tenants that the active office developers are seeking. Once you make your selection, you must decide on what types of tenants to work with and what developers to seek relationships with based on the quality, marketability and segment profiles of their projects. After you discern what tenants to work with and after you acquire the appropriate knowledge about the projects that would fit their requirements, you are ready to begin developing your brokerage and selling presence in your chosen specialty and its market segments.

Your task is just beginning to bloom because according to your charter, you now must begin to learn about everything that is taking place with those types of tenants (law firms, insurance companies, advertising firms, accountants, etc.). This knowledge includes not only their lease rates, structure, square footage, tenant-improvement allowances, free rent and parking spaces but also the who, what, why, where, when and how behind the motivations and movements of these tenants. A great advantage in specializing by project or tenant type is that you can greatly accelerate the quality and strength of your client relationships. Your clients will realize that you have a specific understanding not only of the marketplace in general but of specific areas—from any given profiles of buildings/projects to the real estate economics to why a particular type of client or tenant is locating in any given segment of the market and, furthermore, why that tenant choses a particular project.

Remember that all the elements and principles of Big Bang Selling work together for you so that in this case your willingness to specialize will enable you to *know more about this given market specialty than anyone else*. This, in turn, will prepare you *to never be intimidated in any selling situation* and always will give you a meaningful track to run on when meeting with principals because you will, indeed, possess the *most genuine voice in deal making in your marketplace*.

Eighty Percent of Success Is "Showing Up"!

Someone once said that "eighty percent of success is showing up" and I always have taken this message to heart. I hope that you will, too, because if you are to grow consistently as a commercial broker or agent and avoid the debilitating effects of **fear**, then you must show up every day either in your marketplace, in the offices of your client relationships or in your own office. You must clearly understand the active client relationships and their principals in terms of the following: who are the developers, the owners/landlords, the property-management entities, the types of tenants, the firms or companies within the types of tenants, the vacant landowners, the local economic policies and attitudes of the municipalities and the existing lending entities. The only way to gain this knowledge, understanding and market perspective is to methodically plan your time to acquire the appropriate experience and awareness. Your planning can be viewed as a series of building blocks that you will construct and lay in your selling foundation for great success.

Getting To Know You,
Getting To Know All about You

If you are a retail specialist and want to learn about the types of tenants within the boundaries of your marketplace, you first must identify the ownerships of all the projects within your market segments. Next, you must visit these projects to ascertain the type of tenant profiles by location within the project, the tenant improvements within the selected space, the store layout, the tenant target-customer profile, the relative vitality of the tenant operation, the quality of its products or services and the attitudes of on-site management and employees. As a selling agent, the quality of the information that you pass on to your prospective clients encompasses many factors. Try to become the eyes and the ears in the marketplace for the owners and tenants within your specialty. Listen and observe how their particular projects or operations are being accepted by their target clients and customers. As a retail specialist, you want to know not only the basic development data about the project (such as total square footage, whether or not the project has anchor tenants, parking ratios, ingress/egress factors, signage, lease expiration and structure and available space), but also you must understand the fundamental marketing reasons why any particular tenant wants to be in that center/project as well as the thought process behind the developer, property manager or owner wanting any particular tenant to be in the center/project.

There is little mystery why some projects are successful and why others are not. Your task is to gain a concrete understanding about the makeup and profile of the tenancy within your project specialty. This includes understanding the tenants' fiscal health, management practices, marketing concepts, target-customer segments, merchandise and service strategies and concepts and viability for additional or transferable locations and outlets.

You can never stop adding on the building blocks to your foundation of selling success.

If you are a retail agent, you must keep abreast of the tenants' customer profiles as they relate to the changes in those tenants' customer base. This, of course, affects the stability and growth potential of the existing or prospective tenants for either expansion or consolidation.

Your building blocks are necessary in every tenet of Big Bang Selling. A retail agent would construct this foundation in at least the **knowledge, relationships** and **communication** tenet areas. Your ability to place yourself in the shoes of the developer/owner or tenant rapidly will increase the strength and durability of your success foundation.

In these areas you must begin to understand the real estate economics of owning or leasing any given deal opportunity. You must learn to develop a pro forma from the owner and the tenant perspectives and because many people place varying degrees of emphasis on different pro forma elements, you must understand these perspectives on an individual client-relationship basis.

Create a financial and economic understanding of development, ownership and tenancy within your given specialty. Ask your principals how they create and value their pro formas and their pro forma elements and what their decision-making criteria are regarding whether or not that principal or client relationship will participate in any given deal opportunity. The more that you can place yourself within the thought process of your principals regarding the nature of their motivations and requirements, the more success you will enjoy. Remember that your **integrity** achievement is in large part based on your ability to present meaningful and relevant deal opportunities to your principals.

Drive, Drive, Drive
and Know When To Get Out
of Your Car To Study

I mentioned earlier that just being in your office does not always mean that you are expending quality efforts. Your willingness to walk and/or drive through your market segments will correlate directly to your ability to gain and absorb relevant market data. From demographics to lease rates to absorption and occupancy, you will more rapidly gain a long-term understanding and perspective about why a deal opportunity works, why a certain owner or developer is successful, why a certain type of project leases more rapidly and why the existence or lack of quality municipal and development planning helps or hinders the value of any commercial real estate deal opportunity.

However, you cannot acquire this wisdom by reading market surveys and consultant reports on your market segments and specialty. You should view these sources of information strictly as guidelines to prioritize your field studies.

When a Comp Is Not a Comp
(Knowing How To Define
the Constitution of Value)

One of the biggest mistakes that the decision makers in the banking and savings-and-loan institutions made during the 1980s was their willingness to accept various types of deals and deal opportunities as comparables. For example, the value of an existing office project in a developed market segment with a tenancy profile of companies on long-term leases (whose owners can point to a long-term relationship and understanding of their particular tenants who enjoy strong fiscal health) cannot be compared to an untested office project in a virtually undeveloped market segment (whose owners are willing to accept shaky tenants with suspect financial resources).

This was exactly the type of comps that were accepted by these lenders when they tried to define the potential value of new projects or new acquisitions and to determine not only whether to accept the loan but what type of loan to value ratios to grant. Many of the projects that were accepted openly by the lending community had merit, but often the lenders were far too aggressive in the amount of financing and thus requisite debt service placed on these speculative and risky projects.

The lesson for the selling agent is to continually increase your understanding and awareness of the rationale and criteria that take place in real estate finance. Your ability to build blocks of quality relationships with lenders, developers and investors will help you gain the necessary insights to better understand the thought process behind one of the keys to real estate ownership longevity—the financing source, structure and amount.

Don't be satisfied with just handling a lease. Try to understand the type of tenants and their prospective customers or clients, the structure of the lease and its effective rate, the motivations behind both the tenants and the landlords for creating this lease, who the competitors of the tenants and the project are and with what degree of strength and why the lenders of the first and/or second deeds of trust decided to make these particular loans in the first place.

When you get out in your car to view a project and its tenants, try to understand the mind-sets and motivations of all who are or were involved in the project's development. From the city's willingness to locate this project in its boundaries to the lender's willingness to lend to the tenants wanting to be located there, hone your understanding in these terms and relate them to a total ambience that the project offers and thus what elements constitute the overall value.

In summary, develop a mental and physical inquiry process of thought and observation that enables you to understand the merits or lack of merits of every project within your specialty and its market segments.

Building Block Selling
in the Client Relationship

Next to the importance of specialization in determining and supporting your professional selling success, your ability to *identify, establish, nurture and control mutually supportive and productive client relationships is essential.* (See Figure 9.2.) It is critical, therefore, for you to understand what existing and potential clients are making deals or creating deal opportunities to buy, sell or lease within your specialty.

The first step is to develop an inventory of ownersnips of all significant projects within the boundaries of your market segments. The next step is to identify the existing tenant base within these projects by business or company type and profile. Now you want to learn which of these projects and tenants offer

Figure 9.2 Building block selling in the client relationship.

21. Gain 100 percent penetration.

20. Repeat the process.

19. Employ loyalty, confidentiality, tenacity, knowledge and can-do spirit.

18. Help principals close deal opportunities.

17. Help put together deal opportunities.

16. Find and present appropriate deal opportunities.

15. Follow up, follow up and follow up some more.

14. Gain commitment to serve the client relationship.

13. Acknowledge the competition and overcome.

12. Identify client/principal price/value expectation.

11. Identify client/principal preferred-deal structure.

10. Clarify current principal requirements and objectives.

9. Identify all partnership structures, decision-making criteria, decision-making process, decision-making authority.

8. Investigate target-client relationship history, principal history, past, present and projected activities.

7. Present your personal and professional credentials and those of your organization/company.

6. State purpose and objectives of each meeting from the beginning.

5. Complete preplanning and preparation; have support materials available.

4. Gain commitment face-to-face with principal.

3. Initiate contact via cold call in person, by letter and/or by telephone.

2. Review and research target-client relationship activities and ownerships as well as presence.

1. Identify all pertinent deal-making client relationships.

the opportunity to create additional leasing and/or sale opportunity through your awareness of the overall leasing and sale activity within your market. Additional areas to identify potential client relationships would be with the owners of vacant parcels of land that either are presently zoned for development within your specialty or perhaps might be zoned appropriately in the future. Then you must prioritize the types of tenants that have been the most active in opening new facilities and begin the necessary stages to build meaningful business and personal relationships with the principals who control these entities.

Depending on the size and activity levels within the ownership, development and leasing entities within your target-market segments and specialty, you must begin to make a professional approach that will result in specific meetings with the various entity principals.

Identifying Key Principals and Their Decision-Making Process

During the course of your investigation of each client relationship, you must determine who makes the decisions regarding deal opportunities. This is one of the most important parts of the initial selling call and can be accomplished in its initial phases simply by asking the receptionist or the first level of contact that you meet on entering the given entity's office.

Front Desk in Selling

When you appear in front of the first level of contact and you do not know who the primary contact is, you must ask the appropriate qualifying questions regarding the decision-making criteria and how they relate to the client requirements. Attempt to build and improve the quality of your overall relationships at every level *from the front desk inward.* At all times you must keep relevant market data at your fingertips about the current sale and lease activity that relates to the potential relationship. After identifying the key principals and establishing the requisite meetings, use the relationship-building inquiries that I discussed under the Big Bang philosophical tenet of *relationships.* Your objective during the first meeting is not to gain a commitment to any given deal opportunity but to discuss whether or not you might build a mutually beneficial relationship with that specific principal and his or her company. This entails appropriately presenting your professional credentials and those of your company as well as learning about and understanding the principal's organization, business challenges, competition and past, present and future commercial real estate requirements.

As the meeting progresses and you decide that you would like to work with this particular client, then you must learn exactly what requirements the client hopes to fulfill and how he or she generally best accomplishes them. Very often at this point you may need to go into the marketplace to try to find an appropriate fit for that potential client/principal and then you must appropriately follow up by communicating your task back to the principal and letting him or her know of your intent to continue to work on his or her behalf.

When you have found what you believe to be an appropriate fit, then you must present your deal opportunities. This is one of the most critical steps in building solid client relationships because it is your first chance to demonstrate that you have been listening to the principal and that you have a real understanding about his or her requirements and perhaps now have found an appropriate fit.

Assuming that you have asked the who, what, where, when, why and how questions and that you are comfortable with this principal's ability and authority to make the necessary decision, you now are ready to present your deal opportunity.

The Value of Precall Planning

The planning and preparation that are necessary to be professionally ready often are taken far too lightly by many selling agents. As I mentioned previously, you must place yourself in the shoes or the chair of the client/principal. In other words, if you were calling on you, would you be impressed by your business attire, your readiness with necessary support information, your ability to articulate the elements of the deal opportunity and why they would fit the client requirements, as well as many other factors from your listening skills to your ability to hear what the principal does not say? Furthermore, would you be impressed by your depth of knowledge as it relates to every factor in and around the deal opportunity? For example, many of the finest selling agents package their deal opportunities to meet the interests and requirements of not only the principal but also the lender or equity partner (in the case of an acquisition).

Assume that you are presenting an office building to an investor who already owns a number of office buildings and has indicated a desire to acquire more. The following information would be needed in part by that investor but eventually would be needed in whole by the lender so be as thorough as possible.

The Elements of Packaging:
A Critical Building Block
to the Client Relationship

Because every agent within your specialty would like to work with the finest and most active client relationships, your ability to distinguish yourself often will be the decisive factor in continuing to build the relationships when many other agents would give up and would not be accepted back even if they didn't. The following elements always should be considered and at some point offered during your client's/principal's decision-making process as to whether or not to proceed toward closing the deal opportunity:

1. Cover letter
   a. Summarizing the deal opportunity and its rationale
   b. Review of client requirements and how deal opportunity would fit
   c. Date and elements of meeting that established this requirement (if appropriate)
2. Existing owner information
   a. Type (individual, corporation, partnership)
   b. Financials if available

    c. Investment and management background
(Depending on your level of control of the deal opportunity, part of this information can be withheld until the deal opportunity becomes an escrow.)

3. Property details
   a. Plot size
   b. Building use
   c. Gross square footage
   d. Net rentable square feet
   e. Street address
   f. Age
   g. Parking spaces
   h. Legal description
   i. Ground lease (if applicable)
   j. Most recent title report
4. Appraisal/property tax bill
5. Rent roll
6. Pro forma
7. Revenue and expense information (at least one year)
8. Tenant profiles
9. Leases of tenants
10. Corporate structure of tenants
11. Area competition of similar properties, present and projected
12. Local economic and demographic factors
13. Local and regional maps
14. Color photographs, your deal opportunity and major competition
15. Management agreements and management background
16. Absorption statistics for your deal opportunity and competition
17. Prospects for the future rents as related to rollover of leases

After you present this depth of information either in whole or at least in some large part, your potential client relationship should vastly improve as your principal sees that you possess the most knowledge not only of this deal opportunity but of the entire market segment in which it is based.

Establishing Yourself
as Being Indispensable to Your Clients

I always have tried to understand just what it is that enables some commercial real estate selling agents to become significant parts of the client relationships that they service—to discover the magic that acts as a linchpin between the principal and the agent that seemingly must always be in place before the principal makes a final decision on any deal opportunity. Whether the agent is involved from a commission standpoint or not, often the principal will seek his or her counsel before moving ahead with the deal. The truly professional agent will offer this counsel for free. In some circles in the commercial real estate industry doing anything for free is anathema. The truly great agents, however, realize that when their client-relationship principals need help, whether in gathering market data to support a lending decision or giving an opinion about the merits of a new client venture, they always will make themselves available.

Simply stated, I am talking about providing service or, in the case of Big Bang Selling, *preeminent client service.* This type of service provides rapid turnaround on requests for information and intense activity when trying to meet a particular requirement and always, always is performed with the highest degree of integrity.

The agent who can establish himself or herself as indispensable to his or her client relationships is one who can lift the entire attitude of the people within the organizations whom he or she works with simply by using the elements of *respect, acknowledgment* and *recognition.* The selling agent deals with his or her mistakes, foul-ups, misstatements and outright blunders by readily admitting when he or she makes a mistake and immediately works to get the right answer or the appropriate information. This agent is indefatigable when it comes to working for the interests of his or her clients' deal opportunities. This agent keeps track of all relevant market trends, deal opportunities and significant tenant and demographic influences, as well as the current state of available financing sources and types. The indispensable agent chooses whom he or she will work with and does not choose to prostitute himself or herself in the market acting in personal interests only. This agent tries to keep the current marketplace in perspective by knowing what has taken place in the past as well as in the present. This agent sees his or her profession as an ongoing professional education with the need to know everything from real estate finance to property-management influences. He or she constantly strives to improve his or her skills and thus his or her ability to adequately and preeminently service his or her clients.

Never, Ever, Shop a Principal's Deal Opportunity

One of the fastest ways to move from the client-relationship penthouse to the outhouse is by trying to sell or lease a property that is owned by one of your clients without either verbal or written permission. Many times agents in their effusiveness to "make a deal" will take a perceived deal opportunity to the general market that might be a prospective player for this opportunity. They in fact do what is called "shop the property" around the market in general and in doing so reduce the potential attractiveness to those entities who might have been real prospects for the deal opportunity. *This is one of the most damaging things that you can do to your clients/principals and their properties.*

The effective selling agent first of all receives the blessings of his or her principals before ever taking a deal opportunity to the market. You must ensure that your marketing effort is focused to specific tenants or buyers for any given property. You must understand why any entity might be a prospective player for any specific deal opportunity by determining the nature and criteria of their real estate requirements.

Some agents compound this error simply by sending out flyers highlighting the elements of the property with little or no understanding about why the principals receiving the flyer might actually be interested in making a deal. Make sure that you never commit the great brokerage sin of "air-drop marketing" with or without the authorization to make a deal on your client's property.

PART

III

Turning Deal Opportunities into Closings

CHAPTER
10

The Deal-Opportunity Development Process and Avoiding the Great Rainbow Chase

According to a quaint old saying, "if it looks like a duck and it quacks like a duck, it's probably no real deal opportunity." Obviously, I changed the latter portion of this saying to suit my point that you must develop the ability to adequately qualify both client relationships/principals and specific deal opportunities. The lament of the failed commercial broker or agent is similar to Marlon Brando's famous quote in the movie, *On the Waterfront,* "I coulda beena contenda." He could have been a contender for selling success if only he had had the courage to turn away from the allure of high-risk and unworthy deal opportunities. But how do you develop deal opportunities that lead to actual deal closings?

First, you must learn to ***recognize, seize, nurture, control*** *and* ***close*** *deal opportunities within the context of your marketplace and specialty.*

The Big Bang Deal Makability Factor

To help you decide what deal opportunities you want to spend the most time on, I have developed an additional tool that will serve you well if you are consistently willing to think before you act. Once you have decided what specialty to perform in, what market segments to work in and what client relationships to become a significant part of, you must choose what deal opportunities to pursue (see Figure 10.1). Even within the best client relationships you can be lured into spending far too much of your time on high-risk and low-yield deals. Therefore you must determine what deal opportunities you need to develop to close an all encompassing win/win deal.

So Many Pretty Deal Opportunities and Oh So Little Time

One of the first things that you learn when you become active in your marketplace and when you actually begin to recognize a deal opportunity that makes sense is that your seemingly profound discovery is hardly unique. You soon discover that your keenest competitors also are aware of the deal opportunity and in most cases have at least one client relationship to present it to for serious consideration and evaluation. Your ability to analyze the merits of any given deal opportunity and to reflect on who might be the most likely candidates is just the first step. *You then must get out the word immediately to your most likely clients/ principals* via the telephone and then follow up with a face-to-face meeting to present the prospective deal. When you consider that each active client relationship within your specialty generally has a fixed number of deals that they can close each year, you will begin to feel the importance of developing a strong sense of urgency when presenting your opportunity.

You carefully must consider what deal opportunities to work on first based on their "makability" whether in a sale or lease context. You then must decide whom the opportunity best fits in regard to your best client relationships and then you must package and present your prospective deal in an exciting,

Figure 10.1 The deal opportunity development process

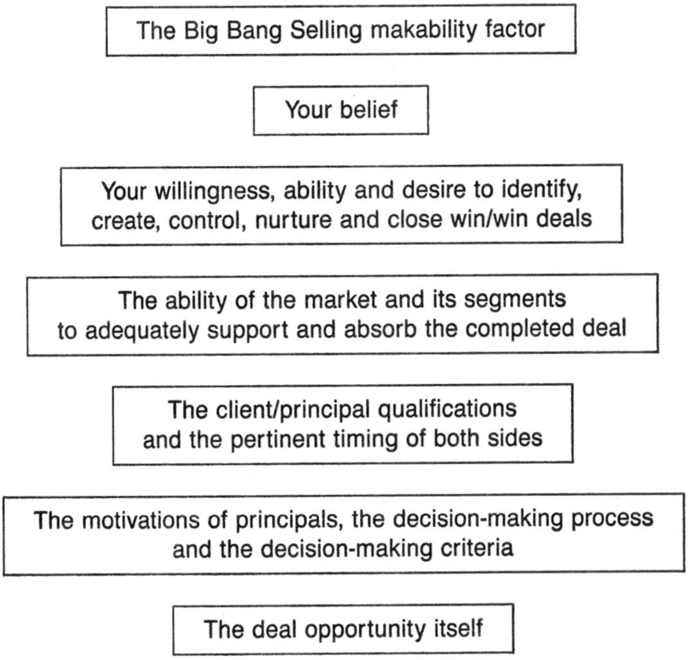

The Big Bang Selling makability factor

Your belief

Your willingness, ability and desire to identify,
create, control, nurture and close win/win deals

The ability of the market and its segments
to adequately support and absorb the completed deal

The client/principal qualifications
and the pertinent timing of both sides

The motivations of principals, the decision-making process
and the decision-making criteria

The deal opportunity itself

informative, meaningful and relevant manner that leads the principal from interest to action.

To help you make these difficult and critical decisions I have developed the Big Bang makability factor that involves five categories for you to consider and evaluate.

1. The Deal Opportunity Itself

The first question you must ask yourself is whether or not this particular deal opportunity will interest a broad sector of principals within its specialty. For instance, if you are considering working on a 75-percent-leased industrial building "for sale" with a variety of tenants all on short-term leases located in a park that is about 20-percent developed with no access to either rail service or adequate highway or air transportation, you probably should choose to spend your time on something else even if the building is priced below the market. This is, of course, unless you know a specific user and/or investor who is looking for this type of deal and who is not concerned about the building's access to transportation. If, however, you discover an industrial building that is 92-percent leased with only three major-credit tenants whose own customers are loyal and fiscally sound, and if this building is located adjacent to a major airport with ready access to rail service and major highways and furthermore is priced and structured to offer a market rate of return, you should proceed because the prospective principals/buyers of this project are broadly based.

The lesson in both of these scenarios dictates that you understand whether or not these buildings are *salable and why*. Thus, you must determine how clients would evaluate this property from a financial point of view, i.e., existing debt, current and proposed expenses, type of leases and quality of tenants, current and future income, present and future returns on investment, age, location, deferred maintenance, taxes and insurance, types of tenant improvements, demand for space within that market segment and proposed construction of similar or competitive projects within that market segment or competing segments. Then you must discern whether the property is of institutional quality/grade or something less than that.

Learn to view and evaluate your deal opportunities in the same manner that an appraiser, a lender, a developer and an investor would. Look at the deal opportunity from yield, market and replacement points of view. Take the time to gather sample appraisals on similar projects within your specialty and learn how to properly evaluate property.

As your expertise grows you will find that all these people will look to you to provide the critical data on potential tenants for rollover rent potentials, realistic and effective lease rates, salable price/value numbers and the impact of current and proposed competitive projects.

Learn to look at a project as a property manager would from the standpoint of the relevant expenses, fixed and variable, needed to keep a project operational and fully leased. Consider the wear and tear of such things as the roofs, the electrical, plumbing, air conditioning and heating systems and so forth.

Just remember that a pretty and shiny building might not be as salable as a more vanilla and functional building. Salability depends not only on the numbers but also on who will occupy these properties and at what rents, as well as on who wants to buy them, for what purpose and at what price.

2. The Motivations, Decision-Making Process and Criteria on Both Sides of the Potential Deal

I once observed a selling agent, who after months and months of working with a particularly difficult principal and owner of a quality 400-unit apartment property located in a great market segment, finally receive an exclusive listing to sell the property. He recognized that the project was incredibly overpriced (a 6.5-percent capitalization rate in at least a 9.0-percent market capitalization rate), but he decided to proceed anyway. He thought that if he could demonstrate to the seller through a series of offers that the market would, indeed, only bring a 9.0-percent cap rate, then the seller eventually would see the errors of his thinking and would capitulate and accept a lower price. Unfortunately for the agent, the seller remained steadfast in his refusal to seriously consider the lower offers, but the agent remained determined. After months of marketing this property to all types of investment entities, the agent brought in an offer at an 8.0-percent cap rate. He was ecstatic because he knew what a stretch this deal would be for the buyer who, faced with the prospect of future flat rents because of overbuilding in that segment, literally could do no better. The agent confidently called the owner, set up a meeting and went to present his winning offer. He encountered his first bit of uncertainty when he entered the meeting room and discovered two other people ready for the meeting besides his seller.

Because his contact, the principal, had encouraged his new offer, he immediately regained his center and began to state his purpose for the meeting and to make his presentation. His heart began to pound and his pulse began to race immediately when the other people were introduced. It seems that his client/ principal had partners whom the agent knew but had never met and they owned a more significant part of the deal opportunity and thus had more say in its sale, which the agent didn't know. He nervously made his presentation and was quite articulate about the state of the marketplace, the significance of the new offer, the history of past offers and the bleak potential for other better offers. When he was finished, he asked for their opinions. The first response came from his contact, who thought the offer was fair; the second response came from the majority partner, who felt the offer was too light. The accountant, who had been listening intently and feverishly working his calculator during the presentation, then spoke. He informed both partners that, based on their relative investment positions in the deal regarding their existing debt, basis and depreciation recapture potential, accepting the offer as structured would not be wise and if they did accept it the impact on their overall financial statements could be quite severe and could negatively affect their existing banking relationships. Needless to say the deal was not made and the agent never did sell the property. But what is the lesson for you, the reader?

The lesson is fourfold:

1. Know why a principal wants to sell a property.
2. Try to understand the financial impact of the deal on all principals on both sides at different achievement levels.
3. Ask to see the partnership agreement to determine the decision-making criteria or authority. If that is not possible, ask your contact about the nature of ownership, who else is involved in the decision making and how the timing takes place. You might encounter decision making through committees of banks or trusts or real estate departments within corporations or pension funds (all of which typically involve a drawn-out decision-making process).
4. Discover and reexamine the who, what, why, where, when and how behind all motivations to sell and buy or lease the property.

The same process would apply to a buyer, landlord or tenant looking to make deals. You must understand their motivations and then must be sure that you are communicating with as high a level of decision-making authority as possible. If this requires going to another city, then do it. Nobody sells like you so don't assume that the essence and particulars of your presentation always will get through to the ultimate decision makers.

3. The Qualifications and Pertinent Timing of the Principals on Both Sides of the Potential Deal

Perhaps you have taken the time to discover that your principals really do want to make a deal and that they in fact do make the decisions; now comes the time when you must examine their qualifications to do so. When I was getting started in brokerage, I met with a fellow from Canada who said he wanted to buy apartment buildings. When I asked what size and price range as well as product profile he was interested in, he said anything from one to ten million dollars. I was pretty naive at this juncture, so I spent days on his behalf before I discovered that he would be lucky to put together a ten-unit deal. This was a good lesson, although I spent weeks initially following up on this meeting, because it taught me to always investigate someone's ability or qualifications to make a significant deal. The following questions should help you measure the ability of any individual, partnership or company to close any deal opportunity:

1. What properties do they presently own?
2. What markets are they in now and why?
3. How do they structure their deals relative to ownership?
4. Who manages their projects and why?
5. What have they developed, built or managed?
6. What are their specific requirements?
7. What are their objectives for this acquisition or location?
8. Who are their financing sources and where are their banking relationships?
9. Would they be willing to share their corporate, partnership and/or personal financial statement with the appropriate parties?

10. What is the personal background and experience of the key partners?

The legitimate principal gladly will answer these questions and when appropriate will provide the necessary financial information. Do not expect a major player to share his or her net worth with you. You must determine his or her willingness to do so, however, because at some point either a principal on the other side of the deal or any involved lenders will ask for this information when necessary.

Timing is everything it often is said to be, so make sure you know when your clients expect to make these deals happen. Determine if the deal opportunity can be structured to facilitate the timing of all the relevant parties. Timing is critical for both sides of the deal and for the deal's evolution.

4. The Ability of the Marketplace To Adequately and Positively Support and Absorb the Potential Deal

This part can be a little tricky because you must understand the niche that the tenant, investor or developer is trying to fill. Remember that not all products and projects are the same even if they are in the same specialty; however, if a market is tremendously overbuilt in one specialty such as office, it would make little sense for someone to buy or build an unleased project unless, of course, he or she had a major user to fill it, was making a tremendous buy or had the appropriate amount and type of financing needed.

On the leasing side of the ledger, if the market is overbuilt, it would bode well for tenants to relocate to newer or better space. Be aware, however, that some tenants might be asking for way too much in terms of free rent and tenant improvements and the owners in the market may not support their requirements. Thus you must understand the tenant's criteria for completing a deal before you spend an inordinate amount of time on his or her behalf.

5. Your Belief Predicated on Your Willingness, Ability and Desire To Effectively Bring the Appropriate Principals Together To Close a Win/Win Deal

Often you may be the only person who believes in the makability of any given deal opportunity. Even though you may be the only one who believes that a tenant actually will come to your city and will occupy the space you represent or who believes that a project for sale makes sense, you should proceed.

Your *belief* does make the difference in your success, but once again remember that this will depend on your willingness to gain the necessary knowledge of why the deal opportunity can be made combined with your ability to articulate to a very specific type of user or investor how everything fits for his or her benefit. Don't be shy about sharing your vision of how any deal opportunity can benefit those to whom you are presenting its merits. *When you truly believe in something, others eventually will share your belief because of your desire and ability to make them see.*

To put the Big Bang Selling makability factor to work for you, determine on a scale of one to five your comfort and serenity in the five previously mentioned areas. If in any area you score less than a three, I suggest that you return to the appropriate principals and satisfy your questions and doubts. If your total score is between 20 and 25, proceed with gusto and close the deal. If your score is between 16 and 19, proceed with caution and appropriately prioritize your other deal opportunities. If your total is between 11 and 15, either go back and fill in the blanks or pass off the opportunity to someone who has fewer deal opportunities and settle for a referral position. If your factor is ten or below, immediately **review, reflect** and **revise** your entire deal-opportunity development process.

As I stated in the beginning, selling commercial real estate does not involve rocket science or brain surgery and obviously neither does this makability factor, but if you pose these questions about every deal opportunity that you pursue, I will guarantee that your success in deal closings will improve dramatically.

Opportunity Really Does Knock, but Sometimes It Just Sounds a Little Different

After training in what was referred to as a "runnership position" for 12 months, I finally found myself on my own with the entire marketplace and all of its unlimited opportunities awaiting my arrival or so I hoped. Three months later with my enthusiasm still quite high and with a draw balance to match, I received a telephone call. It was a Friday afternoon in late August in Phoenix, Arizona. The temperature set a record high of 117 degrees that day. The office was fairly empty because it was about five o'clock and people were on vacations or off to the lakes and mountains to escape the heat.

The caller had a friendly voice and sounded like a good ole boy who probably didn't have anything better to do than to talk to some real estate agent about the apartment market in Phoenix. My first impulse was to kindly thank him for his interest and, because he obviously didn't know how sophisticated I was in the complex world of commercial real estate sales, to refer him to one of our residential offices. Just then, however, I remembered a pact that I had made with myself to always treat unsolicited callers with respect and consideration. This decision had been reinforced after overhearing numerous conversations between various agents and their call-in inquiries.

The conversations from the agents' end tended to be either brief and overly formal at best or extremely rude and inconsiderate at worst. Afterward, the usual banter would occur between the selling agent who received the call and one or more of his or her associates that went something like this: "What a fly that guy was; he was definitely a 'no-clue Lou.' Imagine him or her wasting my time. The nerve of that idiot!"

Fortunately, this attitude was not held by the great majority of selling agents with whom I worked; it always seemed to me, however, that the people who were unwilling to share their valuable time and a little information on the telephone might be doing themselves the greater disservice by not exploring the inquiry further or at least showing a little professional courtesy.

Well, in the case of my caller, after a few simple questions he began to ask for more detailed information about the market. Because the professional selling agent's major asset is his or her knowledge of the marketplace, he or she must be aware of how much time is spent and how much information is given without receiving some form of control or commitment from the person asking for the information. By using common sense and being courteous, you can move from a telephone call to a meeting after further qualifying the caller and his or her company.

After I had been on the telephone listening to and answering questions about the market, I found out that my mystery caller was a major private syndicator who presently owned two shopping centers in the Valley of the Sun (Phoenix) but was quite interested in acquiring high-quality apartment projects or so he said. The fact that he owned commercial property in my marketplace and seemed to be serious, based on his questions, led me to present two properties for his consideration. Because our schedules conflicted, he asked that I deliver the packages on the projects to his hotel that evening so that he could review them during his brief visit. In order to meet his request, I would have to stay at the office until 8:00 p.m. on a Friday evening to put together the packages. At this point I could have said to heck with this guy, I'll just mail them to his office; but something inside told me to follow up quickly.

The weekend went by and I could barely wait until that Monday to call him at his office to see whether he liked the projects. Unfortunately, I could not get through to him nor did he return my call. The same was true on Tuesday, Wednesday, Thursday and Friday and in the following week as well. Yet I persisted, based on his present ownership of commercial properties, his type of business, his knowledge of my specialty and his seemingly keen interest in viewing the projects that weekend, which it turns out he did by himself. After about 11 telephone calls from me, he finally returned my call and the rest is a history of close to $100,000,000 in closed apartment deals.

That man was Spence Clark of Clark Financial Corporation and I eventually joined forces with him and his two outstanding acquisitions people, Drew Pearson and Gordon Oswald, to close deals in Las Vegas, Nevada, and Tucson, Phoenix, Scottsdale and Mesa, Arizona. In addition, we pursued deals together in Houston, Texas; Atlanta, Georgia; and Denver, Colorado.

Our relationships lasted for more than seven years and I handled every apartment deal that they closed in Arizona except for one. I always will be grateful for their loyalty and for the deal opportunities that their client relationship afforded me. One telephone call on a late Friday afternoon from a seemingly unsophisticated person, at least at first, led to many closed deals and many more friends. And it all happened because I was willing to listen to the offbeat knock of big-time commercial real estate deal opportunities and then to act accordingly. So when your telephone rings and you do not know who is calling and are not sure why, give the caller a chance and yourself the opportunity to succeed.

Controlling the Client and the Client Deal Opportunity

Three of the fastest ways to endear yourself to a client/principal are to:

1. Beat your competitors to the best deal opportunities before they are known to the market and give your client/ principal the first chance to make the deal.
2. Ensure deliverability of the deal opportunity.
3. Verify the deal opportunity's accuracy in terms of price, terms, structure and motivations.

These three principles apply whether you are pursuing an acquisition or a lease opportunity. To accomplish all three use your building blocks of client-relationship development and market awareness. In other words, by consistently being in the marketplace and by being aware of market activities vis-à-vis who is "doing" deals and where and why, you will be able to discern potential in your specialty. This process then will allow you to recognize and sometimes even create the deal opportunities that meet the requirements of the client relationship that you are seeking to control.

The best way to control a client relationship is through timely and quality performance. Obviously, an exclusive representation agreement is the tightest and surest way; however, without your continuing ability and willingness to perform the deal-making functions with excellence, those agreements are meaningless and generally can be canceled with short notice.

Every Closed Deal Is Like Yesterday's News

Please don't take this personally, but every time you close a deal with a client, you must start over and prove yourself once again. Clients/principals must see the deal opportunities that fit their particular requirements and when you are unable or unwilling to perform the grunt work (the scavenging around in the market-place, the endless pursuit of seemingly undeliverable deal opportunities, the development and evolutionary meetings for these deal opportunities and/or those "undoable" and unmakable lease deals), then it is time to step aside without a whimper.

You will experience a rude awakening when you discover that client/principal loyalty, regardless of your performance, is as fickle as the most sought-after potential spouse in your town. I have observed the finest selling agents react in horror when they realized that some of their best client relationships were being invaded by inferior talent and, worse yet, that their clients/principals actually were pursuing and making deals with these invaders. Make no mistake, I do believe that when you consistently perform for a client that he or she owes you some loyalty. But if you expect loyalty as a matter of course, even when you continue to perform, you might be setting yourself up for a major emotional fall. This fall, however, often can serve as a strong reminder to raise your level of service and performance to a higher degree.

Client-relationship loyalty can be achieved and, fortunately, I experienced it on many occasions during my brokerage career. The best example is my relationship with Jerry Monkarsh of EJM Development of Santa Monica. Jerry always would repay effort and performance with another great deal opportunity. For me, most of the opportunity came on the sell side of the deal opportunities when he and his brother decided to gradually sell many of their projects in Arizona. Every time that I sold one of his deals, I was rewarded with another fabulous exclusive listing. I should add that my performance was greatly aided by an associate named Justin Lanee who co-listed a great many of EJM's projects. The point is we acted as Jerry's representatives in our specialty. He was a tough negotiator but he always was fair with us and with the people on the other side of the transaction. One of the things I miss most by no longer being in brokerage is my relationship with Jerry, his brother Gene and their entire organization. During the course of my interaction with EJM, I had exclusive control of quality projects and sites for development that were valued at more than $80,000,000.

So you can see that client loyalty is achievable, but I also suffered through the emotional trauma of seeing principals who I thought were locked in with me working with competitive brokers and closing deal opportunities. The fact is this will happen and in the cases when it happened to me, it occurred largely because I took the loyalty for granted or did not uphold or improve my level of service. Clients are not impressed simply by your reputation. They demand performance and excellence every time and all the time. Your willingness to consistently evaluate your efforts and results should prevent you from being surprised. It also makes sense to sit down with your best clients/principals once or twice a year and together evaluate your performance. Invite their comments on how you can improve your overall service to them and to their organizations. Be serious about the process and you will learn not only what they do not like but what you can improve on. This is a great opportunity to update their direction and focus toward new and existing deal opportunities.

The Ever-Elusive Exclusive

Getting exclusive listings and thus control of great deal opportunities never is easy, but often it is a lot easier than meets the eye. Your ability to formulate solid client relationships through the ten tenets of the Big Bang *philosophy* will build the primary foundation for gaining the faith and trust of your clients/principals that will lead to exclusive control of makable deal opportunities. The beginning stages of gaining an exclusive start with your ongoing and timely discussions with your principals at regularly scheduled meetings, lunches or various forms of sports and leisure pursuits. You must be willing to explore client goals and the requirements to achieve those goals and must mutually adjust those goals as the market evolves and changes. You must understand the inventory of real estate projects owned and whether they might be available for sale or lease deal opportunities. You must be willing to analyze these projects to provide your clients with an up-to-date market perspective on their real estate holdings.

When you ascertain that they indeed do want to go to the market with their potential deals, you must create a meaningful exclusive-listing presentation that demonstrates your understanding of the value and the manner in which the opportunity must be structured, priced and taken to market. You must determine what competitive deal opportunities have yielded to their owners, what competitive opportunities will be slated against your client's and how you will specifically market this deal opportunity in terms of a detailed strategy and monitoring system for getting the deal closed. Then you must summarize your past performance both for the client and other clients/principals in similar situations. You also must provide a sample presentation package demonstrating how you would present the deal opportunity to the market and a timetable for a weekly follow-up and review sessions with the client to assess specific degrees of progress. Then you must close your presentation by asking specifically for what you are after, an exclusive listing to represent the client's deal opportunity and his or her company in the marketplace. I will discuss in greater detail additional elements of the professional presentation and package in later chapters.

When an Exclusive Is Not an Opportunity

One of the most damaging things that you can do when pursuing your target results is to take on an undoable deal opportunity with an exclusive listing commitment. Make no mistake, when you agree to accept the exclusive rights to sell someone's real estate, you may as well be taking an oath of allegiance. If you are acting with *integrity*, you must expend a maximum effort to close the potential deal or deals. Therefore, do not take on any type of listings, especially exclusives, without first evaluating their appeal and makability in the marketplace. Like the selling agent who failed to understand all the necessary elements in his ability to sell the apartment building, you might end up trying to sell or lease something that the market either does not want or will not step up to in price because of a lack of either real or perceived value. Because of your commitment to implement the exclusive marketing and selling process, you will have little time to work on other opportunities so be selective in what you choose to go after and list.

Selling a Deal Opportunity and Making It a Deal

At this point it is critical to your success to remind yourself that closing deals is a matter of constructing the necessary building blocks. You must understand the basic structure that is involved in the development of any given deal opportunity to make it a closed deal. Whether you are aiding in the buying, selling or leasing of a deal opportunity, you should proceed in the following manner:

1. *Develop a specific marketing plan that outlines how the property will be sold, acquired or leased.*

2. *Summarize and prioritize all legitimate candidates for the acquisition, sale or lease by category,* i.e., syndicator, institutional investor, individual investor, developer investor, anchor tenant, shop tenant by type, pad user, etc. You must segment your prospective buyers, landlords and tenants because each type, as well as each individual entity, has its unique way of evaluating and weighing that evaluation for potential acquisitions, sales and leases. Once again, you can see the importance of properly qualifying client or potential client relationships in terms of deal-making criteria and decision making.

3. *Create and develop a thoroughly professional marketing package* that provides realistic and relevant data concerning the project, its competition, all of its pro forma elements, its overall market health and specific specialty segment health, its summary of leases and its precise tenant history and accurate tenant profiles. Many owners often will resist your including real or actual financial and debt information in the marketing package; however, if your presentations are focused to real prospects with the interest, motivation, qualifications, timing and need to acquire this type of project, the data will be well received. The most common remark demonstrating your seller's reluctance to provide real data is that "the buyer can wait until we get into escrow before he sees this information." You must make the seller realize that it is pointless to present inflated or misleading pro forma data or financial assumptions. If a price and terms are negotiated based on false numbers, the chances are high that the buyer, on discovering this, certainly will renegotiate at best or "blow" the deal at worst. This approach only causes more problems than it prevents because it erodes all the assumptions from a cost and investment point of view that the buyer makes when he or she initially analyzes the value of the property and whether he or she wants to proceed. One of the most critical tasks that a great selling agent performs, therefore, is to gather real data and to present the property to the marketplace in a focused and meaningful manner. If you experience difficulty with a seller in gaining this type of information, simply ask, if he or she were on the other side of the deal, would he or she want to know as much as possible about the deal before committing time and dollars to its pursuit?

This type of understanding between you and your sellers will evolve only through a firm trust based on the facts that you know what you are doing and that the deal opportunity will not be prostituted and devalued throughout the marketplace. If your seller remains reluctant to disclose financial, maintenance or existing debt issues, I suggest that you reexamine your position and the buyers' positions toward this particular deal opportunity. If you are dealing with sophisticated and serious principals, this information must be disclosed.

Sometimes your marketing effort will involve developing a two-tiered package. The first provides a cursory overview of the property and its influences and the second gives a more detailed and finite view. You and your seller will have to judge who receives what, but if your efforts are focused and you have performed the necessary prequalification, this should be a given.

4. *Seek the opinions and attitudes toward the project from everyone that you present it to* so you can continually update market perspective and perception. Ensure that you constantly review the makability of the deal opportunity from every possible perspective.

5. *Continually update your knowledge of competitive deal opportunities and deal closings.* Compare the relative values to support or adjust your overall strategy and price.

6. *Present your deal opportunity in person,* even when the target principal is located in another city. Sure it costs money to fly to another city, rent a car and visit the prospective buyer/seller/landlord/tenant. If you have identified this potential principal properly, however, this is a great opportunity to develop a new and meaningful client relationship. This also will show both sides of the potential deal that you are very serious in your approach and are willing to leave nothing to chance. When I was working with the Clark people, I always would fly to meet the seller wherever he or she was located. I did not do this simply to impress Spence Clark but to sell my deal opportunity (in this case the offer) myself and if I was unable to convince the potential seller, that my buyer and our offer was the best in the market, I was at least able to ascertain where the deal opportunity could be made. *This is, after all, another major-league responsibility of the great selling agent—determining when, why and how the deal can be made.*

One of the greatest professional salespersons whom I have ever known is William Gosnell. Bill was the first salesman whom I made a cold call with while we were working together at Xerox and it was pretty obvious even then that he had extraordinary talent and energy. Anyway, Bill went on to become the finest and most-productive selling agent in the history of Grubb & Ellis, a major national real estate services firm. Bill is a master at traveling to another city, identifying the major players within his specialty (industrial) and convincing them to come to his market. He seldom fails in his bids to get the top person in the company not only to come to his marketplace but to work exclusively with him and his associates at Grubb & Ellis. Not only is Bill a wizard at creating excitement and belief during his presentations, but he performs afterwards in the interests of his clients. I should add that rumor has it that Bill personally earns in excess of at least one million dollars in commission each year and I am sure that no small part of the reason for his success rests in his willingness to sell face-to-face, regardless of where the other face is located.

7. *Evaluate the level of interest on the part of all the principals to whom you present your deal opportunities.*

Prioritize these interest levels by immediate and future levels of interest. Determine what prospect's timing and ability to perform best suit the objectives of your client relationship on the seller or lessor side of the deal opportunity. Immediately schedule follow-up meetings or visits to the project. Encourage specific offers in the form of the appropriate lease document, purchase contract or letter of intent.

8. *Present all offers as soon as possible,* including those from other agents. When you handle just one side of the deal opportunity, never let anyone else submit your offer.

9. When you have a lease proposal or an offer to purchase but you are not on the listing side of the transaction, *use the time during and after your presentation to ascertain the acceptance level of the other side.* Do everything possible to discover the level of agreement of each deal point of the opportunity. Use the "what if?" question to pose alternatives to various deal points that are unacceptable to the other side. Take your findings back to your principal to revise the offer to best meet the requirements of the other side. This is where your knowledge of the market, as well as your knowledge of your client's/principal's ability and motivation, will enable you to keep the deal opportunity alive. *Refuse to give up on the opportunity when you believe it will benefit your client, that it fits his or her requirements and that its continued evolution will result in a win/win deal.*

It's Your Deal Opportunity To Make or Lose
So Never Give Away Control;
See Yourself as a Bloodhound
and the Deal Opportunity's Best Friend

One of the biggest mistakes that a selling agent can make is to consider his or her job as essentially completed once the deal opportunity goes into escrow. You never must assume that the principals on either side of the deal will ensure that everything happens according to the terms of the pertinent agreement either on schedule or in some cases at all. Hundreds of factors can influence whether or not a deal opportunity closes—anything from the financing portions of the transaction to the tax consequences to the seller entities can blow a deal out of the water. You cannot assume that your clients/principals on either side of the deal necessarily have investigated and approved all elements of the impact of any given deal before it actually is about to close. Your task, therefore, is to view any of your deal opportunities from a very personal point of view and to stay on top of every element in the progression toward closing.

If you were trying to sell a shopping center, for example, had negotiated the price and structure of the deal opportunity and had the appropriate agreements signed, your real responsibility to yourself and the deal opportunity just would be beginning.

This is the time to use "due diligence" to determine whether or not a potential deal actually closes. In the case of the proposed acquisition of the shopping center, the following areas must be reviewed and accepted by the buyer of the project:

1. Lease review
   a. Review by either in-house or outside legal counsel and relevant principals
   b. Verification of rent roll and assumptions
2. Expense analysis
   a. Review of existing service contracts
   b. Review of actual expenses against pro forma assumptions
   c. Estimate and project future expenses
3. Market analysis and study

    a. Analysis of current and future supply of competitive projects and existing and proposed available space

    b. Analysis of current and future demand for existing and proposed acquisition and competitive space

    c. Analysis of existing effective rental rates and lease structures as related to future/projected rental rates and income achievement

4. Title review

    a. Inspection and review of preliminary title report to ensure against adversarial aspects involving exceptions, easements, legal description, existing debt matters, covenants, conditions and restrictions, etc.

    b. Commission or update of an ALTA survey showing all improvements. Review placement of existing improvements as related to their position against property lines to avoid potential encroachment issues

5. Engineering review

    a. Commission a building-condition report to determine relevant and urgent areas of potential deferred maintenance issues, condition of mechanical and structural materials and existence of asbestos

    b. Commission a hazardous-materials report to determine existence or traces of any and all toxic wastes

6. Capital improvement budget

    a. Analyze and quantify the cost of immediate and other necessary repairs or replacements per the findings from the engineering-review process

    b. Analyze and project necessary capital reserves

    c. Develop a timetable and cost projections for all identified capital-improvement items

7. Legal review and compliance verification

    a. Review all relevant zoning regulations to ensure compliance with all existing zoning ordinances

    b. Verify the existence of certificate of occupancy and necessary building permits

    c. Review municipal requirements for development

8. Review of existing and proposed financing

    a. Order MAI appraisal and, if necessary, lender's format of appraisal

  b. Review the quality and stipulations of existing debt
  c. Analyze and project the viability and cost of new amounts and sources of debt

As you now can see, many steps must successfully occur during this review process and at each of these steps the potential for deal disaster looms. If you are to stay in control of your opportunity, you must constantly communicate with the principals on both sides of the transaction to mitigate and resolve all potential problems or "deal breakers." But these are just some of the elements that will affect whether or not that buyer finally decides to close. As this deal moves toward closing, the relevant issues of timing, market fluctuations and much more also can come into play to impact the deal opportunity. Your willingness to understand each of these vital issues will correlate to your never being blindsided by a blown-deal telephone call or message.

In future chapters I will discuss more ways for you to stay in control of your deal opportunities, but for now please let this understanding sink into your thought process for it will pay great dividends on your future prosperity.

Fifteen Surefire Ways To Lose a Deal Opportunity

A selling agent can lose a deal opportunity for many different reasons. Some of these include:

1. Lack of understanding of deal opportunity merits;
2. Lack of understanding of key deal points;
3. Poor communication of principal goals and time frames;
4. Failure to answer the who, what, where, when, why and how;
5. Inability or failure to qualify buyer or seller, tenant or landlord;
6. Inability to articulate principal qualifications, motivations and overall ability to perform;
7. Failure to maintain a personal sense of urgency;
8. Failure to motivate principals to maintain a vital sense of urgency;

9. Failure to keep abreast of due-diligence progression and results;
10. Failure to keep control of deal movement;
11. Failure to maintain the pulse of principal desire in getting deal closed;
12. Letting a competitive deal opportunity cloud the principal's interest in your own;
13. Failure to be involved in all principal-to-principal, principal-with-partner and principal-with-lender meetings concerning your deal opportunity;
14. Letting negative emotion take the place of common sense and the necessary focus on deal opportunity objectives; and
15. Failure to be a bloodhound and the deal opportunity's best friend.

On Dealing with Panic
or What To Do When One Side Wants To Delay,
Alter, Rewrite or Renegotiate at the Eleventh Hour

The ever-changing chorus of negotiating the interim steps of a deal opportunity is something that the active selling agent accepts as a necessary part of win/win deal making. Often during the due-diligence process or at some other point of the latter stages of the deal-opportunity development process, one or more of the relevant parties or players in the transaction will refuse to go further until some significant component of the deal structure and agreement is changed. You must learn to accept this as a matter of course. Some principals will use this as a negotiating ploy to try to grind out a sweeter deal for themselves; some will demand it because of their discoveries during their due-diligence process. However, if you stayed close to the marketplace and competitive deal closings as well as opportunities, know the current state of the financing options and have kept abreast of the motivations and qualifications of the principals on both sides, the chances are good that you can keep your deal opportunity together.

Your first task is to view the requested change regarding its overall impact on the proposed deal. You must understand the rationale of the principal entity who is requesting the change to discover the merits of such a request. If you know it is a boondoggle in its demand and intent, then you must diplomatically say so. If the request is valid, then you must understand how it either adjusts or sustains the original assumptions that were made when both sides agreed to the proposed deal.

Now is the time to refer to the deal-opportunity file, your best ally, to review the initial motivations, assumptions, agreements and expectations on the part of all parties. Refuse to be intimidated into an all-or-nothing proposition. Restate the merits and motivations behind the agreement and once again articulate how this deal opportunity stands up in the winds of the past and present marketplace.

Make sure, however, that you do not make false assumptions regarding these last-hour motivations and actions because at times a principal is forced to improve his or her position to keep the partnership structure intact regarding lenders and investors; thus, your empathy to the needs on both sides of the deal is very critical. Make sure that any of your present or past deal-making successes do not inflate your ego to speak on behalf of all parties until you are sure what all parties will find acceptable. If you stay in control, remain calm and guide your principals toward a state of calm and understanding, chances are quite good that 11th-hour potential fatalities can become healthy, vibrant deal closings.

CHAPTER
11

Pricing, Packaging, Prospects and Presentations

Now that you know the nine broad steps needed to close your deal opportunity, you must examine four major components of those steps, namely, how a deal opportunity is priced and valued (*pricing*); the method, means and format in which the viability of the potential deal is offered (*packaging*); an analysis of the identification and development of the major prospective principals (*prospects*); and the manner in which the deal is physically and verbally presented (*presentations*). These components are essential not only in the selling (*process*) of the deal opportunity but also in its most vital part, the deal closing.

Before any deal opportunity results in a signed lease and occupied space or a signed purchase contract and a closed escrow, many steps (building blocks) must first occur. I will refer to these steps as the *four P's of Big Bang Selling*. Before you can ethically and intelligently take a deal opportunity to the marketplace, you first must ensure that your preparation in establishing and creating as well as directing and implementing the four P's has been thorough and complete (see Figure 11.1).

Figure 11.1 Developing effective selling strategies.

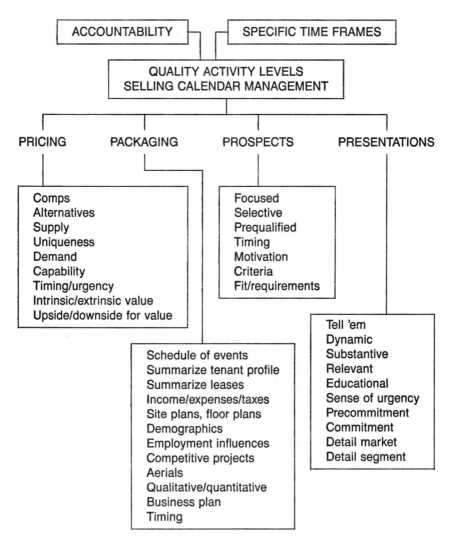

These four important steps to closing deal opportunities best illustrate the necessity for the consummate mental and physical approach that I discussed earlier. The quality you put into developing each of these steps or building blocks depends on and directly affects the other three, thus your ability to eventually close deals. In other words if the pricing on any given potential deal is totally unrealistic from a current or projected future market point of view, your ability to find qualified and motivated prospects will be quite limited or nonexistent. Additionally, if the elements of your marketing package simply highlight the pricing of the deal opportunity, your prospects may not see its overall merits and may opt for some more completely described opportunity. Furthermore, you might offer the most competitively priced deal opportunity packaged with all of the necessary photographs, aerials, market comps, real numbers, etc., and yet, if you present it to the wrong type or an unqualified group of prospects, your chances for selling success again will be limited. And finally, even if your deal opportunity is priced realistically in its market segment, is professionally packaged and is offered to a group of qualified and motivated prospects, you still might not sell the target deal because of an inept, uncreative, inarticulate or bumbling presentation.

The point to remember is that each of these components plays a part in an overall selling strategy that supports your ability to render *preeminent client service* by satisfying your client-relationship/principal requirements.

Accountability and Specific Time Frames in the Action-Oriented Strategy

A professional selling strategy for the success of any deal opportunity within the universe of commercial real estate is lifeless without personal accountability and precise and focused time frames for implementing and monitoring the strategy. Once you take on the challenge of selling or leasing any given deal opportunity, you are accountable for that deal opportunity and no rationalization or lame excuses for poor effort for whatever reason will excuse you from completing the deal. You are accountable; therefore embrace your responsibility and make it work for your benefit by strengthening your *belief* in the deal's makability.

Without establishing specific time frames in which to develop selling strategies and to implement and monitor their components, your priorities are in danger. Set time goals for getting things accomplished to continue building not only your client relationships but all target deal opportunities. For instance, set completion dates for meetings with principals on all key issues; for thoroughly completing the packaging; for organizing by company and principal name and telephone number the telephone contact dates to set up face-to-face meetings for all prospects; and, finally, for determining a deadline by which all prospects will receive key presentations.

The added sense of urgency that comes with committing to time frames will increase your energy and quicken your pace. You will be amazed at the new opportunities that will result from presenting your deal opportunity.

The final part is monitoring, through your prospect client lists and selling calendar, your progress, results and the next follow-up dates.

What's in a Price?

The *pricing* of every deal opportunity must be understood in the context of its overall value both within its own market segment and within the entire local marketplace. You also must understand how this price/value relationship compares with deal opportunities in competitive markets in other cities. When trying to gain a principal's commitment to market a deal opportunity, you always must understand the elements of his or her thought process when he or she sets a price. If you are going to avoid the *great rainbow chase,* you must be fluent in the merits of the price/value deal-opportunity relationship. You both must agree to the who, what, where, when, why and how of pricing that will result in a closed deal. You should be involved in the decision-making process when a client/principal is pricing a deal and you should enlighten him or her about why a given price will or will not sell. You should consider the following when you try to develop, clarify and gain agreement on establishing pricing for any deal opportunity:

1. Current price comparisons with competitive deal opportunities, whether they are projects for lease, sale, acquisition, joint venture, etc.;
2. Current supply of competitive deal opportunities that are either on the market or pending, such as finished projects for sale or lease and those under development toward similar ends;
3. The uniqueness of this deal opportunity in terms of overall value regarding yields, present values, location, ambience, architecture, financing, potential terms, quality and grade of project and the overall market demand for same;
4. Current demand by potential prospect type for this kind of deal opportunity;
5. Current base and diversity of potential prospects;
6. The timing and urgency requirements of both client and prospects;
7. The potential outside influences and factors that may impact the overall value of the deal opportunity; and
8. The potential for building additional value in the deal opportunity after closing.

The most important lessons when pricing any deal opportunity or agreeing to its merits are that you are the one who has to sell it and you are the one who will commit his or her time and effort on its behalf. Obviously, you must believe that "your" deal opportunity will provide the most value and best alternative in its respective marketplace. As I said earlier, you are the one who chooses the client relationships you will work with and develop and thus the value-added deal opportunities that they represent. If you know a deal opportunity is overpriced and overvalued, do not waste your time or your potential clients' time in an ugly pursuit of an unmakable deal.

Packaging for Success

In Chapter 9 I discussed some of the requisite information that should be offered either in whole or in part in the deal opportunity packages that you present to your existing or target clients/ principals. When creating a marketing package and/or brochure to help you develop and close your target deal opportunities, place yourself in the position of the individual to whom your package is being sent. Think about the specific information that this individual needs to determine whether this deal opportunity fits his or her specific and general requirements, whether or not it is in the appropriate market segment, whether it is the best or one of the best locations within its market segment and why this deal opportunity "makes sense today as well as in the future" regarding everything from financial to labor considerations.

For example, in the marketing package and/or brochure of a retail project for lease you obviously would want to:

1. Detail the surrounding market segment;
2. Summarize the existing or proposed tenant profiles;
3. State lease rate ranges and structures;
4. Provide site plan, floor plans, market segment demographics and employment influences;
5. Detail competitive projects and tenants by location, distance, occupancy, lease rates and lease expirations (if known);
6. Provide market segment aerials and project photographs; and
7. Detail signage parameters and benefits and provide CC&Rs, landscaping ambience and parking ratios.

Perhaps the most important element of any marketing package, and one that is most often missing, is a statement of the purpose of the project regarding strategies to keep it fully leased, well managed and growing in value. You should explain the reasoning behind the projected tenant base or validate the existing base.

Some people might argue that this is too much information to share initially with prospects and if you are shotgunning your packages, then I would agree. But I am referring to a selling/ leasing strategy that understands why every type of prospect is receiving the information and how that prospect will benefit your client and his or her project. These same principles hold true for whatever type of project (office, industrial, etc.) that you might be trying to lease with slight modifications for the types of existing or prospective tenants.

Obviously, an industrial tenant will have different motivations and logic for locating in a given market segment and specific project than an office tenant will. These tenants will be influenced by their requirements and how these requirements impact their employees, their customers, their products and their distribution. And do not forget the individual desire of each key principal! Each specialty and its subspecialties, however, always must have specific criteria for every place where they locate. Your willingness to meet face-to-face with the active and existing tenants in your market will help you understand why they are located where they currently are. Then you can determine if they plan to stay, expand, contract or relocate. Given this understanding of your tenant profiles and requirements in your target market segments and specialty, you can tailor any marketing package to be meaningful, distinct and action getting.

In my opinion far too often the selling agent lets some member of a local public-relations firm create his or her project brochures. These brochures tend to be little more than announcements of the project and thus merely inform rather than sell. If you use your brochures simply to provide basic information to real prospects, this approach is adequate; however, these types of brochures and their effects often are negligible. If you have a choice, use the budget dollars for the brochure to create serious packages that will not be mass-marketed but will be *prospect selective and effective.*

Two distinct ways to spend your time include shipping untold numbers of brochures to every prospective tenant in the world with most of the brochures ending up in the round file or selecting a particular category or categories of specific tenant types, identifying the leading candidates by company, establishing face-to-face meetings with the principals of these companies/ firms by type and making your face-to-face presentations.

Your charter is to generate serious interest that will lead to your prospect wanting to visit and pursue your deal opportunity. The worst thing that can happen is that your existing or prospective client/principal will see that you do indeed know the marketplace in much broader terms than the price of lease space in one project. Your ability to professionally and meaningfully package your deal opportunities is one of the key ways in which you distinguish yourself from your competition. Remember, it makes little sense to dance around the lack of merits of any deal opportunities. *The well-versed clients/principals with whom you work or will work have little time to read foolish or incomplete packages. If you want to be taken seriously, you must earn the right. Part of this comes by providing relevant information that supports the efforts of the decision-making process of your client relationships.*

He's a Pepper, She's a Prospect

Wouldn't it be great if, as in the former TV commercial for Dr. Pepper, everyone in the market was a genuine prospect? Who really is a prospect and how do you identify them? And how do you determine if they are genuinely interested in your deal opportunity without wasting a lot of valuable time? Your ability to effectively answer these questions will prevent the *great rainbow chase.*

For our purposes, I am referring to prospects to whom you can take either a lease or an acquisition deal opportunity for serious consideration. Of course, it makes more sense when you firmly control the deal opportunity through some form of listing and/or written agreement. When markets are "hot," many selling agents make many deals without ever having firm control. Therefore, you really must spend your time in the most productive manner possible.

Whether your prospective deal represents either a lease or a sale opportunity, your process for determining prospective players will be relatively similar. You first must understand the deal opportunity from the points of view of the seller and the buyer and, if relevant, from that of the lessor and lessee. This, of course, means understanding how this deal opportunity compares with its competition within its market segment and overall market; understanding the current ownerships of competitive properties both on and off the market; knowing who the tenants are by industry type and company profile; knowing who the active tenants are in the entire market as well as in your segments (by specialty); understanding the current acquisitions market in terms of price, structure and debt, as well as the principals and their companies who are making the deals; and then prioritizing these tenants or owners or those seeking ownership/acquisition by type and time frame (see Effective Selling Calendar Management, p. 91).

After you have identified a relative base of between 25 and 100 potential prospects to sell your deal opportunity, you must set up meetings with the decision-making principals. By this time you should have a good idea of the who, what, where, when, why and how of their individual criteria and decision making so that your challenge at this point is to effectively present and sell your deal opportunity. If some of these prospects have escaped your scrutiny and you have not yet met the principals, the presentation of your new deal opportunity should provide the appropriate forum to begin developing a new client relationship.

Prioritizing your prospects is very important. In terms of a lease opportunity, you should design and procure an agreement from your lessor/client regarding the proposed and target tenant profiles that you want to bring into the project (deal opportunity). You should employ a specific strategy for prospect identification and understand the expectations and time frames of your client/principal. For example, within a downtown, high-rise office marketplace with ready access to the court and judicial system, the offices of state or local government, or perhaps a financial district, your initial prospects would be rather obvious. Law firms specializing in servicing the needs of clients who need access to the courts, seats of government, corporate representation, real estate development representation and so forth, all would be good places to start.

You should prioritize these prospects by examining the lease status of law firms by type, size, expiration date, current configuration, motivations and existing and future requirements. In the cases where you have no such data base, you might prioritize by type of practice, existing presence within the market segment, size of firms and knowledge of decision makers and other criteria.

Other obvious prospective tenants to fill your project would be financial-services firms, advertising firms, corporate offices of major employers, accounting firms and insurance companies. *The key elements are to understand the tenant composition of competitive projects and to identify those existing tenants who would be willing to move and/or expand, and then to identify peer or competitive organizations and companies similar to those existing tenants and prioritize for your deal-opportunity presentation by industry profile and company size.*

One source of your finest prospects results from the expansion of existing tenant facilities or the relocation of another division within the same tenant company (in a lease deal opportunity). Thus, during your client-relationship-building process, make sure that you investigate the company structures and locations of all entities. Try to find out why certain divisions of your tenants are located where they are and if they may be a candidate for relocation. For example, Kraft, Inc., recently located to a 178,000-square-foot distribution center to serve restaurants and institutions in Texas and Arizona. The company then considered a 61,000-square-foot lease to house their food-service information-processing computer. The agents who made the deal probably provided Kraft with a variety of options to better serve their food-services division and thus made these significant leases.

You always should understand the nature of your prospective client relationship's business in terms of all its corporate parts. If its distribution facility already is located here, find out why. Determine the location of its other divisions and their requirements. Know where its sales and marketing operations are located and why. Find out in what types of facilities they are located and why. Then use your knowledge to build higher levels of principal relationships. Creatively compare other companies that have requirements similar to your present prospect. Make it your challenge to gain all its commercial real estate deal opportunities and to act as its eyes and ears in the marketplace.

Scout other cities for prospective client relationships. If you know that your market can offer more value in the appropriate areas that a particular company considers important then set up a meeting and begin to plant the seeds for relocation, one element or division at a time. You must help your principals see your large vision.

Sign Calls, Sign Calls and More Sign Calls, but No Prospects

As most of us know, there is a great difference between being busy and being productive. Because of the limited number of hours you have to actually sell by meeting face-to-face with your prospects, it becomes critical that you learn to effectively utilize your available time. Learn to recognize those people and events that become part of a selling agent's worst nightmare, *the black hole of lost time*, which never can be recaptured in its productive minutes and potential opportunities.

Several types of situations and people will waste every moment of your selling day if you fall into their traps. One of the more notorious types of individuals who will waste your time is the associate who is more interested in discussing his or her personal problems, sports scenarios of all types, interoffice politics and how they keep him or her from being more successful, the reasons that his or her fellow agents are just lucky when they close a deal, his or her glory days in a previous career and as much more drivel as you can imagine. Although it is quite important to build strong and mutually beneficial relationships with peers in and out of the office, you must refuse to waste your time with people whose goals and desires are not the same as yours. It is easy to determine why the consistently successful agents are the leaders year in and year out. When they are in their offices, they focus on their client relationships and their deal opportunities. They have little time for chitchat, gossip and all other forms of mouthomania.

During my first year at Coldwell Banker, it became very clear to me that certain individuals did not like anyone approaching their cubicles or offices unless that person had a serious and meaningful reason for doing so. In fact, it became coolly apparent that if I were to receive any of their valuable time, I had better be prepared with meaningful questions and responses. Were these people being cold or rude? Of course not. They were just using their time effectively and productively. Socially, these people were some of the most gracious and giving individuals whom I have ever known. But the lesson became quite clear to me: Unless you have meaningful business purposes behind most of your interpersonal exchanges during business hours, save your small talk for later. Some of your associates may resent your attitude, but those who share your sense of *purpose* will understand and agree with you.

Unlike the time-wasting individuals whom I previously described who carry on nonselling activities, certain situations and functions that are not related to selling must be performed, such as interoffice and intraoffice research, preparing packages, writing correspondence, filling out deal and commission forms, attending office meetings and, one of the most selectively important, taking incoming telephone calls and selectively returning telephone messages.

When To Research, Package and Follow Up

You should write and conduct research and other forms of in-house investigation before 8:00 a.m. and after 4:00 p.m. The most successful selling agents whom I have observed in companies throughout the United States share this one thread of success: They only perform functions that expand their client relationships and evolve their deal opportunities during prime selling hours. The majority of this activity is in face-to-face principal meetings that create and develop opportunities. Additional elements of their time are spent in driving and walking through their marketplace and examining all the dynamics of their market segments and specialty. If they are not meeting with principals, then they are meeting with real estate lawyers, city planners, architects, lenders and title officers. They spend time before 8:00 a.m. and after 5:00 p.m. performing the necessary in-house research and writing that this business dictates for success. Try to meet with or start a personal discussion with a top selling agent sometime just to test my remarks. You will find that the agent will be willing to do so in all likelihood either over an early breakfast or after 6:00 p.m.

At times, however, you will have to answer your telephone to take incoming calls. You must learn to quickly qualify the caller regarding his or her purpose for calling and then decide whether or not to get back to him or her rather than interrupting your present project. As mentioned earlier, you should treat everyone who calls with respect; however, you must learn to qualify the caller before investing any serious time.

Sign calls that primarily emanate from other brokers and agents are one of the biggest causes of wasted time. Because you have a professional obligation to treat other agents with courtesy and to ensure that your deal opportunity receives the maximum market exposure, working effectively with call-in agents becomes a necessary component in expanding your deal opportunity's prospect base. Therefore, you must decide whether to speak with the agent immediately after you determine his or her reason for calling or whether it might be more productive to set aside a time to return his or her calls and others of the same type. The danger in immediately taking the call rests in the fact that, like their personalities, the talents and knowledge of these call-in agents may be quite varied. At times, however, another agent may have a client, and thus potential prospect, in the car with him or her who needs to immediately know the particulars of your deal opportunity. At this point, you should spend the time and extend the additional courtesy. During this ongoing process of prequalification, you will discover other agents who are serious, well qualified and, although competitors, can work well with you to serve the requirements of both of your client/principal relationships.

You also will receive sign calls from principals who are investigating the terrain of the marketplace on their own and who often would like to have their questions answered immediately. This is the perfect opportunity to expand your deal-opportunity prospect base and perhaps to identify and plant the seeds for a productive client relationship. After you qualify the caller and answer any questions, continue to question his or her qualifications, present ownerships or locations, his or her position or authority and so forth. If you are satisfied that the caller might be a prospective player either for this deal opportunity or for some other yet-to-be-discovered opportunity, try to set up a meeting to help the prospect better understand the nature of the marketplace as it relates to his or her requirements. Remember that call-ins may lead many selling agents who took the time to many great opportunities, but they also may lead others to the black hole of wasted time and effort. *Learn to discern.*

One of the biggest frustrations I experienced during my brokerage years was to receive a call from an agent who represented himself or herself as an experienced commercial salesperson who had a client "looking for deals." Often this agent knew absolutely nothing about his or her client, the client's qualifications to make deals and little or nothing about my specialty and its projects. Needless to say, I quickly learned to qualify these people and if they still wanted to bring their "client" to my deal opportunity, I asked them to bring in the client for a meeting where I made the presentation of the deal opportunity. This often was a good way to ferret out the fishermen from the serious agents.

The Basic Elements of Effective Selling Presentations

Tell 'em What You're Gonna Tell 'em,
Tell 'em and Tell 'em What You Told 'em!

This expression was used on many occasions by Ken Skinner, a Xerox sales manager (and later a successful sales agent for Grubb & Ellis) whom I had contact with during my early years with that company. His point was that a professional selling presentation must contain an introduction that summarizes the content of the presentation, followed by a detailed presentation of the content followed by another summary of what was said and agreed on during the presentation. Although the "tell 'em" concept is presented humorously, it still contains a great deal of truth. I would add, however, the need to listen to the verbal and nonverbal responses of your audience and to ask critical questions to understand the relative enthusiasm for the purpose of your presentation.

It Has To Be Relevant, Substantive and Timely

Relevant, substantive and timely are perhaps the three most important elements in the successful and results-oriented professional selling presentation. You always must present a clearly defined statement of purpose for every presentation that you give. In fact, one of the best ways to begin a presentation is to restate the reason for the meeting and to clarify its purpose. Your selling presentation always should be *relevant* to what you are trying to accomplish in your meeting and the body and support elements of the presentation should be *substantive* enough to answer every potential question that your client/principal might pose. Furthermore, you must ensure that your presentation and its elements are *timely* in relationship to the existing marketplace as well as to your specialty. If you give the presentation after you have ascertained the needs of the client relationship, make certain that you know how the presentation fits the current client requirements.

Relevance

A prospective office tenant who needs to be located in a downtown business district will have little interest in deal opportunities, no matter how wonderful, in the suburbs. Invariably, however, some selling agents will try to sell the outbound location despite the client-relationship requirements. Review your client's/principal's requirements while preparing your presentation and before meeting with a client/principal. You must ensure that what you are selling is *relevant* to a client's/principal's specific requirements. If you are making a presentation on the market in general and are presenting your qualifications and have not yet determined the client requirements, make sure that a significant amount of your time is planned to question the client/principal in all the *relevant* areas. This form of questioning is vital to the initial selling presentation. You should not recommend specific projects or opportunities in this meeting but should gather all the necessary data to find the principal the tightest fit.

The *relevance* of any selling presentation must apply equally to your purpose for being there in the first place as well as to ensure its legitimacy for the prospective client and deal maker.

Substance

One of the more common mistakes of selling agents is to make a presentation, which is initially well received by the principals, and then come up short when they cannot answer specific questions about the deal opportunity. Make sure that your presentation covers in depth everything that the client might ask about the deal opportunity. If your package is complete, most of the potential questions and their answers will be included and awaiting your review. If you are in the introductory meeting and presentation, make sure that you do more than just a hello and give a shallow introduction. It is difficult to get any allotment of time from the movers and shakers in the industry, so value any commitment you get and by all means take full advantage of it. *If questions arise that you cannot answer, admit that you do not know the answers but will find out. Don't try to fool your audience.* Commit to finding the right answer after the meeting, and quickly. Remember, at all times that you and your deal opportunity are competing with many other brokers and agents and their deal opportunities, plus the plethora of direct deals that are conducted strictly between principals. *You must, therefore, treat every meeting and presentation as if it were an audience with the Queen of England or the Pope or both.*

As you probably have experienced when you attempted to purchase an automobile or some piece of high-tech equipment, you had certain questions about the price, financing, engineering of the product, delivery and so forth that had to be answered prior to your making a buying decision. Well, your clients/principals are no different in their needs to understand everything about the deal opportunity. Remember, they will be comparing it to other alternatives; thus your ability to present the entire substance of your potential to perform often will weigh the scale on your side of selling success.

Timing

Your willingness to organize and prioritize quickly your pricing, packaging and prospects will greatly support your selling efforts. As I have intimated, the commercial real estate market changes constantly and is influenced by a myriad of factors. What might appear to be the best deal opportunity today may change in its appeal tomorrow because of factors beyond your control. *The message is never to delay making your presentations.* Use your knowledge of client requirements to lead you to the timely prioritization and execution of your selling presentation.

Some agents delay getting their acts together by taking an ultraaggressive approach to properly preparing and presenting their deal opportunities. Once you realize that the deal-opportunity development process, from identification to closing, can take from 30 days to 30 months and sometimes longer, you will see the need to integrate the phrase "time is of the essence" into your selling process.

Making the Basic Selling Presentation

Your selling presentation generally will be driven by the **responsibility** to put yourself in a position of **representation** to achieve **results**. Therefore, you must be aware of the three most common situations that will require making effective selling presentations:

1. *The first meeting with the principals who represent the deal opportunities for you to take to the marketplace or who might be potential buyers or tenants for new deal opportunities.* This meeting provides the first major impression. The manner in which you present yourself and your qualifications will be scrutinized closely by those with whom you hope to build relationships. Your main purpose in this meeting is to determine whether or not there is a foundation for you to build a quality client relationship. Your direction in this meeting, therefore, is to demonstrate your competence through your knowledge of your marketplace, its segments, its past closed deals and current deal opportunities in all respects, your history and results in the business and the

support that your company or organization brings to the client (if applicable).

Of course, you first must understand the client relationship in every respect from the principals' positions and responsibilities to the nature of their businesses and their challenges, to their commercial real estate requirements. *You always should leave every meeting with a commitment from the principals to another step in the development of the relationship.* You must articulate your knowledge and ask meaningful questions that will begin to build the trust level necessary to actually complete deals together. In fact, at the beginning of your presentation you must let everyone know why you are there (to build a mutually beneficial working relationship to produce win/win deals) and to ask the principals the question, *"If I can demonstrate a significant understanding of the market and your needs, can we proceed to build our relationship and move forward?"* This may sound difficult, but there is no question why you are there in the first place (to render service and to close deals); therefore, be direct in your statement of **purpose** and let the principals know that you are serious.

2. *The initial meeting to present a given deal opportunity to either an existing or potential client/principal.* The presentation of a specific deal opportunity always should occur after you determine the prospect's requirements. You definitely must understand what the prospect likes or does not like about the potential deal and why. At the beginning of your presentation you must ask the prospect the following question, *"If this deal opportunity satisfies all your requirements, will you be prepared to move forward in its pursuit?"* Then during the course of your presentation, you both must agree on the value and benefits of the deal opportunity and how it would satisfy your client's requirements. At the close of the presentation, summarize all the value that you have demonstrated, as well as the agreement that you have gained for this opportunity, and ask for a commitment to prepare the appropriate document demonstrating the principal's intent. If the principal does not agree on some point, you will have the chance to clarify his or her feelings and positions on each deal element.

Big Bang Selling builds on itself; therefore your presentation must methodically make its own case as to its merits in price/value considerations, location, market segment, age, quality, neighbors, demographics, investment potential, market presence, etc. Your presentation must demonstrate why your knowledge of the deal opportunity alternatives is supreme.

Your final step is to ask for and gain the necessary commitment to move forward in the deal opportunity's development.

3. *The meeting with your client/principal, in which you bring either an offer on one deal opportunity or a response from another principal on whose deal opportunity your client made an offer.* Once again, your knowledge of the marketplace, its players, its closed deals and its alternatives will serve you well. If you believe that an opportunity or an offer has merit, then you must present it in a meaningful, relevant and direct manner. Now is the time to use great *tact* in laying out the harsh realities of the current marketplace. You may have to educate your client/principal regarding the merits of either this offer or the one he or she is reviewing on his or her own property. If you understand the current events of the marketplace relating to price/value, past deals, pending deals and current opportunities, you can demonstrate to your principal the overall strength in the offer.

In all these types of selling situations, certain elements appear consistently and should be included as part of your selling presentation:

1. Stating the purpose of the meeting and presentation;
2. Briefly summarizing the professional background and commercial real estate qualifications of the players involved;
3. Investigating your client relationship in terms of its business history and future, its principals and their responsibilities, their current real estate requirements and the decision-making criteria (this can apply in scenarios one and two if you have not already gained this information);
4. Questioning your commitment to move forward if duly interested and satisfied;
5. Presenting the deal opportunity and all its elements;
6. Probing for agreement and interest level;

7. Determining areas of doubt, reluctance, objection and disbelief. (Now is not the time to think everyone is on track
just because they haven't booed you from the meeting room!
Ask the tough questions now because if you are unable to
gain a commitment to the next step of the deal evolution
and do not know why, chances are that as far as that prospect goes, you are a goner.); and
8. Summarizing the value and agreement on all the deal elements; ask questions, remind the principal of his or her
commitment at the outset and ask to move on to the next
step.

Big Bang Selling Tips
for Successful Selling Presentations

Following are several suggestions to successfully sell your presentation:

1. Avoid runaway mouth.
2. Control your fear by preparing and understanding your
deal opportunity and its prospects.
3. Always ask for a precommitment to a next step if you demonstrate enough merit.
4. Maintain physical and verbal control of the presentation
and its elements.
5. Never hand out a copy of your presentation prior to actually giving it.
6. Utilize the appropriate graphics, aerials, photographs,
market studies and all necessary support tools to make
your case and that of your deal opportunity.
7. Ask for and gain agreement to specific deal points and
their value.
8. Never stifle objections for they will appear when you are
not there to clarify them; ask for questions.
9. Be willing to compare the relative merits of your deal opportunity or offer versus other alternatives and be prepared to demonstrate your strength through deal closings
and current opportunities.

10. Summarize the merits of the deal opportunity or offer and repeat how it fits the client requirements.
11. Plainly explain why the deal opportunity makes sense.
12. Ask for the commitment to the next appropriate step.

Perfecting Your Presentation

The more presentations you give, the more relaxed and proficient you will become. *Excellence in the selling presentation comes with experience, creativity, risk taking, knowledge and overcoming fear.* The current makeup of your personality does not matter. Whether you are an extrovert or an introvert, or whether you are an accomplished athlete or seldom indulge in highly competitive activities, makes little difference if you are willing to develop and articulate a meaningful presentation style and content. If you are soft-spoken but are willing to speak with the conviction behind your purpose and are willing to hold your ground when you believe you are right, you will survive. If your personality tendency is to be verbose and somewhat overbearing but you are willing to listen effectively and show the principal the appropriate courtesy and respect, you will survive. *The point is that the quality of the content of your presentation is what is most important.* Your professional selling style, which you should seek to understand and develop, is very important and will help you to build the necessary trust to capture the client relationships and potential deals.

Your clients/principals are human beings, too, and enjoy working with individuals with whom they can establish some meaningful rapport. They most appreciate those agents who professionally prepare and effectively execute the presentation of their materials and information.

Before giving any major presentation, practice giving it in front of a friend. Ask your friend for feedback. Does he or she understand the presentation and all its elements? Is your presentation of the opportunity and of yourself clear and meaningful? Have you built a sound foundation that will lead the principals toward commiting? If a video tape recorder is available, set up the camera and see yourself as others see you. You will be amazed at how much better or worse you will come across at different times in your presentation.

Learn to memorize the important elements of your presentation regarding your market's and its segments' trends and history, significant deals and influences, affiliated lending activity or employment factors and much more. Listen to yourself when you discuss business with friends. Do you sound knowledgeable? Are you really knowledgeable about what is being done and by whom in your specialty? Would you want to meet and work with yourself?

Constantly freshen your presentation format with new concepts and visual aides. Be creative. Watch other presentations and learn their formats. Predetermine the types of hand-out materials that will complement your presentations. *Above all, practice, practice and practice until your presentation becomes as easy as participating in your favorite activity.*

C H A P T E R
12

Using the Telephone as Your Vehicle To Arrive at the Door of Deal Opportunity

Immediate Credibility or Instant Incompetence

The incredible thing about the telephone is that it clearly and without question can translate the professional capabilities and knowledge of any one caller to whoever is seriously listening on the opposite end of the line. Your ability to display a purposeful and focused thought process will become quite apparent to the principal whom you are seeking to meet. You must be aware that your voice transmits much more than just sounds. By distinguishing yourself through your professional competence, you tell the principal that he or she should listen more closely to understand the nature of your call and to determine the value of spending time with your call.

Whether you are calling for the first time to gain an introductory meeting or whether you are calling to update an existing client relationship on the progress of some specific deal opportunity, *the voice that you hear on the other end of the telephone, with all of its varied inflection, emphasis, perplexion, excitement, disappointment, enthusiasm and so forth, is the sound of your client relationship being further established or diminished.* You must visualize the person to whom you are speaking and try to read the signals of acceptance or rejection that are offered through the cadence and pace of your client's dialogue, the clearing of his or her throat and the tone of voice, the irritation or empathy in any responses and his or her overall willingness to listen and respond.

What You Say on the Telephone Cannot Always Be Heard!

To effectively build productive client relationships you must *use the telephone as a wedge not as a crutch.* By this I mean that the telephone provides a way to get on a principal's agenda to develop a deal opportunity. Therefore, use the telephone as part of your *heat-seeking missile mind-set* to direct you into the client's/ principal's office. Your ability to demonstrate your knowledge and commitment to client service and to effectively sell any deal opportunity always can be better accomplished in person; when this is not possible, however, properly using the telephone can support your selling efforts.

One of the greatest values that a telephone provides is that of an information-gathering device. If you are prepared when making the initial contact via the telephone with a target client relationship, you can learn the names and titles of the necessary levels of contact. Never treat the receptionist or the secretary on the receiving end of your call as if he or she just got off the boat. Contrary to misinformed belief, these people play important roles within their organizations. Often their knowledge of the key principals and the focus of their employers is vast and can prove very beneficial if you are willing to show them the proper professional courtesy and consideration (**acknowledgment, respect** and **recognition**).

Do not be evasive about the reason for your call or about what information you need to effectively proceed. Ask for the names of people whom you contact and write them down in your client relationship file. If you have a list of targets to contact in order to ascertain the key players, then take notes of your investigation of the organization and later transfer them to a file. A common mistake made by many selling agents is that once they do reach a decision maker or principal they abuse the opportunity by expecting their target principal to give them as much time as needed to answer their questions. Remember, it is a privilege to have someone take your call to begin with and chances are they would like you to be brief. So use the opportunity to either establish a firm appointment to see the individual in person or to agree on a time when the principal would be willing to spend the appropriate time on the telephone. I cannot express strongly enough, however, that your ability to qualify and create a deal opportunity through face-to-face selling is exponential in its potential when compared to using the telephone.

Many selling agents might disagree, however, for they use the telephone in place of face-to-face meetings to avoid conflict and discomfort when dealing with and developing challenging relationships because of their own *fears*, because they are too lazy to make the effort or because their knowledge base is too limited to make an effective selling presentation.

Tone Is More than What You Hear
When You Pick Up the Receiver

As stated earlier, the art and science of professional selling is a never-ending process in the quest for excellence. You must constantly remind yourself when using the telephone that you are communicating your entire impression to the listener through the manner in which you verbally present yourself as well as through the questions and information that you articulate. Therefore the mood or tone of the conversation is extremely important for through it you will receive the necessary signals that let you know if you are on track. For example, if your listener sounds impatient and overly brief in his or her responses, you should be aware that he or she may be limited for time or may think you are a bozo.

You must listen for the attitudes and emotions that are unquestionably conveyed during every conversation you have. Is the attitude respectful toward you and your information? If not, why not? Do your listeners seem to enjoy speaking with you? Are they willing to share information? Are they willing to give you a firm appointment and thus a chance to seek opportunity? Do not be afraid to question a negative or impatient attitude. Ask for clarification and understanding during your dialogue. Develop the art of seeing over the telephone lines. You can do this through the intensity of your listening and the continued development of your overall listening skills. Make every effort to listen carefully to every response before mentally rushing ahead to pose the next question or to defend your position. Quiet your internal "self talk." Remove any feeling of defensiveness. *Remember that all communication should be entered into as a means to get to a mutually agreed-on end, not as a win/lose proposition; therefore, do not take negative comments or lame responses personally.* Do not ask overly personal questions or "high-trust" types of questions such as what is someone's current net worth. Never try to force your opinions on your listener through either intimidation or with "a pseudo big-time attitude." Chances are your listener will not appreciate this approach very much.

Ring, Ring, Ring,
or Why Won't They Take My Calls?

One of the most frustrating experiences in selling is the seeming inability to get target principals to either take or return your telephone calls. The general tendency is to make two or three calls and if no response is forthcoming, to then give up. In the case where you already have talked to the principal and perhaps have even begun to develop a relationship but you still are not getting your calls returned, you should invoke the process of *review, reflect* and *revise.* Learn to examine the way in which you present yourself and your questions or information over the telephone. If you have not had a serious *purpose* behind your prior calls and did not provide any meaningful service to the target principal, then maybe his or her perception of your professional worthiness is limited. *The proficient use of the telephone must be viewed as another key building block in the development of your client relationships and deal opportunities.*

If you firmly believe that you have **the most genuine voice in deal making in your marketplace within your specialty** or at least are on the road to possessing this voice, then let your tenacity mix in with common sense and keep after the target until you get an audience. When you have exhausted all efforts to reach the principal in his or her office, try to call him or her on his or her mobile telephone.

Recognize that during the development, evolution and closing of key deal opportunities, the telephone is the best way to give and receive time-vital or urgent communication. For those of you who gasped at the thought of calling on someone's car telephone uninvited, let me share this little remembrance. One of my earliest target client relationships was directed toward Lincoln Property Company (LPC). As you may know, Lincoln (not to be confused with Lincoln Savings and Loan) is and has been one of America's most successful commercial real estate full-service development companies for nearly two decades. Although LPC had a reputation for being difficult to work with from a broker's point of view, I was if nothing else determined.

During the pursuit of a luxury garden-apartment deal on behalf of a major client (buyer), I became aware of the attractiveness and viability of an adjacent property. The property happened to be owned by LPC whose managing partner for Arizona and New Mexico was James R. Freeman III, a Harvard MBA with an undergraduate degree in engineering from Georgia Tech, who at the time was not at all seriously interested in selling one of his flagship projects. Unable to get him to commit to selling the project or establishing a firm price if he did, I nevertheless decided to proceed. I knew that my buyer was motivated and I fervently believed that given serious consideration from Jim and his partners we could make a deal. Well, just as I generated an offer from the buyer, I discovered that Jim had left with his family on a two-week vacation to some undisclosed location along the East Coast of the United States. Because I was in Phoenix, this presented a rather interesting challenge. To complicate matters, my buyer also was looking for deal opportunities in other cities through other agents and definitely had a fixed number of deals that he could close because of equity constraints. I also knew that he would be quite disappointed if my offer went without being presented. Somehow, I convinced Jim's secretary of long standing to give me his telephone number at his vacation retreat. Taking a deep breath, I dialed and the telephone was answered by Jim's wife, B.J., who after recovering from her incredulity, proceeded to tell me that Jim was resting on the couch recovering from a broken ankle that he sustained earlier in the day while playing tennis. It was too late to retreat so I asked if she would be kind enough to gingerly hand him the telephone. Thank goodness she did, for Jim was quite gracious in receiving my call until I outlined the parameters of the deal opportunity offering. In fact, after hearing the initial offer of price, I think his ankle started to swell severely. Fortunately, he did respond to my verbal presentation of the offering, asked me to air-express the letter of intent, countered it two days later and within three weeks we entered escrow on a deal opportunity priced at *ten million dollars*. And as one of many of my life's blessings would have it, the deal closed.

That deal led to a tremendous relationship with Jim and many of his outstanding associates and eventually to many exclusive listings on other properties owned and developed by LPC.

The lesson for you is to use the telephone whenever you cannot meet face-to-face, so be prepared with your purpose and let no one or nothing deter you.

Ten Simple Principles for Effective Telephone Selling

The following ten principles should provide you with a methodology for planning and executing effective telephone selling:

1. Establish a purpose behind every call.
2. Organize the necessary information to support the context and purpose of the call. Make sure that support documents, studies, contracts, deal points, ownership data, lease rates, etc., are ready and available as needed.
3. Be aware of your body language and gestures while you are speaking. If you are sloppy and inattentive, your call will be, too; if you are sitting comfortably and are focused, and are speaking clearly with conviction, your call will be well received.
4. Visualize the human being on the other end of the line and extend the proper amount of professional courtesy.

5. State your purpose for calling and get to the point at every contact.
6. When appropriate and practical, always try to confirm a face-to-face meeting with your target principals.
7. Never give up if you have a valid reason for calling.
8. Be willing to bring members of the support staff into your confidence and seek their help in getting to your target.
9. Treat every call with a principal as if it were the initial building block for a tremendous client relationship because it very well could be.
10. Follow up in writing with a summary of the discussion and a confirmation of the next step.

The Body Seems To Fit, but the Head Just Won't Go on Right!

To become proficient and develop excellence in selling on the telephone, you must understand the basic components of the call presentation:

1. Your initial contact with the receptionist or the secretary:
   a. Be effective through courtesy and empathy.
   b. Be willing to listen.
   c. If already known, ask for the target by name.
   d. Ask for the name of the receptionist or the secretary with whom you are speaking.
   e. If unable to get the target, try to engage the receptionist or the secretary in conversation regarding the organization. Be interested but be brief.
   f. Be willing to tell the receptionist or the secretary the purpose for your call. Selling is not meant to be a mystery so be prepared to explain your purpose.
   g. Try to determine if the receptionist or the secretary can set up a meeting or tell you the best time to call.
2. Your first contact with the principal:
   a. State your purpose. In most cases your macro purpose will be to develop a productive client relationship and

your micro purpose will be to get information and an appointment.

b. Be informative, concise and respectful.

c. If given the opportunity, state your professional qualifications briefly and share some relevant market data.

d. Ask for a meeting to determine if you might develop a foundation for working together.

e. Continue to ask for the meeting and offer alternative times and days. Never use "I am going to be in the neighborhood and thought I might drop by." Until you learn to value your time and service, no one else will either.

f. If it becomes impossible to get a meeting, try to get an appointment to spend time on the telephone.

g. If the target states that he or she already has a broker or has no present need, ask to come in anyway because of your willingness to share information on the market. Even though many principals are quite busy, they always like to hear what is going on in the market and in their areas of real estate focus. Be willing to give without getting at all times but especially early in the process. If you truly want to work with this key client relationship, let the principal know that. Share your research on him or her and the company. Become fluent in the client's business and/or type of development. *No competitive brokerage relationship is invulnerable to you when you are acting in the totality of Big Bang Selling.*

3. Closing for the meeting:

a. Summarize your purpose.

b. Offer an alternative choice for a time and place for meeting.

c. If you still cannot get a commitment after offering many alternative reasons for meeting with you, then gracefully wish him or her and the company well, hang up and send a follow-up letter with some small but significant piece of relevant information.

d. Call back one week later to see if he or she enjoyed the material and begin again.

A Time for All Reasons To Make Calls

Set time on your selling calendar each day to return all non-urgent telephone messages. Although the urge to return the calls of people whom you enjoy speaking with will be strong, learn to avoid this nonproductive practice. Use this reserved time to handle broker inquiries and sign calls and to return non-urgent client-relationship calls. Your messages come in during the entire course of the day and as long as you return your calls you will be acting professionally. When working out of the office, which should be most of the time, you should check in at least twice in the morning and twice in the afternoon so that you will not miss any urgent message. If you have a mobile telephone, instruct your receptionist to give out your number to specific principals or callers on an as-needed basis. You will be astonished at the additional amount of time that will free up each day when you place all of your return calls in one time block. Your charter is to appear in front of the client relationships or in your marketplace getting immersed in all that is taking place. By depending on the telephone too much to be your meeting place to sell your deal opportunities and further your relationships, you will be doing yourself a great disservice.

A Final Message on the Telephone

Our telephone-conscious real estate industry offers a glimpse into the psyches of the people who inhabit its challenging arenas. The manner in which a person uses his or her telephone (status, prestige, utility, function, urgency) lends a great deal of insight into the individual's makeup. Learn to listen to what people say when they are not speaking, to their pauses, their tonality, their emotion, their happiness, their tension; you will learn a great deal about their feelings and beliefs toward you and your deal opportunities. Use your telephone to sell when you cannot meet face-to-face or when the urgency of a situation warrants it. Try to see and touch the humanity on the other end of the line. Be forthright, be patient, be tenacious, be brave and be you. (At your best, of course!)

CHAPTER
13

Picking Up the Signs: The Subtle yet Critical Components of Deal-Opportunity Negotiation and Closing

Before presenting any offer to lease, buy or sell a commercial real estate property you first must thoroughly and thoughtfully review its documentation. Make sure that you understand every deal point in terms of its impact on the potential deal as well as its importance to the principal making the demand. Also try to understand the legal components of the document, the manner in which all the legal and deal points are phrased and how they are either advantageous or disadvantageous to each side of the deal opportunity. Make sure that you are aware of all the material facts of the deal opportunity, such as existing debt considerations, structure and soundness of property, toxic-waste considerations and deferred-maintenance and capital-improvement histories, and try to find out what other entities are competing for the same potential deal.

Use a yellow marker to highlight your copy of the offer, letter of intent, lease, contract, etc., prior to making your presentation. Prioritize each deal point (price, terms, free-look period [if applicable], lease concessions, tenant-improvement items, escrow period, move-in and occupancy dates and so forth).

During the presentation of any deal opportunity, never simply hand a copy of the offering document to the principal. You must maintain control of the presentation to articulate all its deal points. If you give a copy of the offer to the principal, he or she immediately may look for the price or rate being offered and if those numbers are unsatisfactory, he or she may dismiss your offer without further consideration. Therefore you must stand your ground and systematically present each point. (I am assuming that the offer has merit in relation to the current market vis-à-vis existing deal-opportunity alternatives and recently closed comparable deals.) Remember your work on the front end of the deal opportunity will make your road to gaining agreement either smooth or rough. If you clearly give an overview of the real value of the deal opportunity to one or both sides at the outset of the preparatory and negotiating process and gain agreement to your proposal, there should be no major surprises from either side. When making your presentation, you must determine how the principal feels about all the elements of the offer so you can make a meaningful counteroffer or regenerate a more acceptable original offer.

You always should get every counteroffer in writing. This will not always be possible, however, if some major deal point is found significantly lacking from the perspective of one side or the other. Then you must ascertain what is acceptable to proceed with the deal opportunity. During this process you must ensure that all principals are aware of your legal or fiduciary responsibilities as they relate to your specific representation. This involves clearly understanding the agency laws and responsibilities within your state. (More will appear on this vital issue in the following chapters.)

You must determine what areas in your existing offers are acceptable and what areas may be totally to mildly rejected. Your ability to ask the "What if?" questions should greatly support your efforts in this critical situation. But to ask the right types of "What if?" questions to develop this opportunity, you must understand what makes sense not only to each principal but to the marketplace in general. Furthermore, because the principals' individual motivations can be quite varied when deciding to make one deal versus another, during your presentation or at some previous meeting with the principals and any other brokers/ agents you must fully determine the width and breadth of their expectations. Your ability to listen after you present each deal element, from the qualifications of your client relationship and its principals to the timing on closing, is one of the most important parts of your role in the deal-opportunity negotiating process. Listening to what principals do and do not say can help you ask the appropriate "What if?" questions. You must be tenacious during this process yet respect the fact that the principal to whom you are making the offer may not want to disclose any more information until one or most of the major deal points are offered in an acceptable manner. This may become quite sticky for the last thing that you want to do is to go back to your offering principal with no new insight into gaining control of and closing that deal opportunity. Therefore you must find some common ground with the receiving principal to keep the momentum going in the development of your deal opportunity.

When another agent is bringing you and your principal an offer on one of your deal opportunities, you should actively respond to the elements of the other side's offer regarding the deal structure, principal qualifications, timing, motivations and overall offer value. Prior to the meeting you should talk to your principal to determine the height of your profile in the negotiation. Your ability to disclose material facts about the deal to clarify or add to the deal opportunity's value will help the other agent meaningfully work with his or her principal.

What To Do When a Principal Flat Out Rejects a Deal-Opportunity Offer Because of Price

I hate to share the vision of the chills that I received when after weeks of working with a qualified buyer, educating him in the market and specific deal opportunities, convincing him to generate a meaningful offer and going to present it to the owner, I had to watch and listen in horror as my offer and its emanator were verbally abused and literally and figuratively tossed into the wastebasket. As a selling agent faced with uncomfortable situations like this, you can either beg for forgiveness and mercy or use the emotion of the moment to your advantage.

Right, you say? Well, if you know that the principal is being unreasonable, then you must make him or her see the quality and overall value of the offer. You can do this by retaking control of the moment: Empathize with the principal's personal involvement with the deal opportunity over a period of time, recognize the current state of the market that perhaps has impacted the value and listen to the principal's rationale for his or her asking price and deal-opportunity parameters. You must get the principal to talk and listen once again. You must sell the merits and elements of the offer from the qualifications of the offering principals to its timing and to its overall value. If you are presenting a low-ball offer and are representing the principal making the offer, then it becomes your mandate to determine "where the deal can be made." In cases where the offer is an extreme low ball, avoid questions about the price and determine the principal's feelings and attitudes about other more acceptable parts of your offer. If you genuinely believe that your principals are motivated and you know the expanse of the parameters they are willing to entertain, then you must convince the other party after his or her rejection that your clients/principals mean no insult but indeed are interested and perhaps will respond to a counteroffer. Always try to get the commitment of a counteroffer. This will narrow the gap of understanding between the principals and the deal opportunity elements.

When you are representing a landlord or seller and are reviewing another broker's or agent's offer, do not be too quick to dismiss the offer, the offering principals or the offer's contents. Remember, these people may not know you or your client. They may not have faith in the abilities of their agent. Their agent may not be capable of providing a realistic overview of the deal opportunity's value. This may be their initial entry into the market and they could be serious but testing the waters. You never know until you ask the appropriate questions.

I have seen too many agents with attitudes of almost unreal disrespect toward other agents and their clients/principals. They act as if they are making the decisions for their principals and often do so without enough principal-to-agent consultation. Your responsibility is to create and/or support a deal opportunity (in this case an offer) that will meet the overall criteria and objectives of your principal. You must explore all aspects of any offer in terms of the qualifications of the principals, the offer price, the offer structure, the alternatives that the offer/principals might be making and what areas might be "soft" or have room for negotiation. Never assume that the other agent really understands the motivations and capabilities of his or her principals. Although it may be sad, it often is true that the agent has not taken the time or does not possess the ability to qualify his or her own principals.

How To Recognize Value and Gain Agreement on the Major Deal Points

Some people believe that there is a difference between selling and negotiating. I am not one of those people. Selling simply means presenting the merits or value of any potential deal in a knowledgeable fashion to gain principal interest and action and result in a win/win deal closing for both sides. The *philosophy* of the Big Bang Selling negotiating process is to support the efforts of your client/principal in meeting his or her overall deal-making objectives. There will be times when you may represent both sides of the deal opportunity, which although potentially a conflict of interest can be done when you disclose your legal position to all relevant parties. In the past this has been a common practice; however, because of some recent trends in litigation, where disgruntled principals are unhappy with the results of their deal making, they and their lawyers, in some cases, are going after the broker and the agent for misrepresentation, malfeasance and anything else they can get their legal arms around.

It is not out of the realm of possibility that your principal hopes to "fleece" everyone with whom he or she makes deals. As we all know, a number of these types of players are in the marketplace. While always respecting and honoring the bounds of your ethical commitment and fiduciary responsibilities, *try to work with client relationships who want to make good deals for themselves but who do not experience cardiac arrest if the other side is satisfied as well.* You must decide about the makeup and character of your target client relationships. The one constant, however, when your principals are being unrealistic, acting unaware, being unethical or just ignorant is that you must set them straight.

I do not mean that you must tell them that they are acting stupid or like crooks. However, if you know that an offer that has been received is of high value and comes from motivated and qualified parties yet your principals will not budge, you must go back and sell them or make them aware of how the offer (point by point) stacks up against its competitors regarding this deal opportunity, offers on competing deal opportunities and similar market deals that have closed.

Once again, you must know what is going on in your market segments and within your specialties to be effective in this pursuit.

Avoiding the "Dead-Shark Syndrome": What To Do When Your Deal Opportunity Begs To Go into Intensive Care

One of the most dangerous things that any selling agent can do is to turn over the balance of the responsibilities of any deal opportunity to the principals once a verbal or nonbinding written agreement is reached between the parties or anytime thereafter but prior to the actual closing. You must remain diligent throughout the entire documentation and due-diligence process. *The potential for a deal opportunity to stall at every level is immense* whether during the offer, counteroffer or counter to the counteroffer or once the agreement becomes a formal document such as a lease, purchase contract or set of escrow instructions. *The critical task during documentation is to ensure that the spirit and intent of the agreement is properly, and without undue burden on either side, legally translated into the content of the document.* This may involve intense negotiation on the part of both sides and their agents. Once again, you must remember that selling is not convincing someone on one side to do something that is without merit, integrity or relevance to the overall worthiness of the deal opportunity. For example, the question of personal guarantees on some parts of the financing arrangements often comes up when negotiating a lease or sale transaction. Some principals on either side will state emphatically, "I never personally guarantee anything." This can become a major deal point and one that easily can blow you and your opportunity out of the water. In these cases, you must make the objecting party (generally the landlord or seller) once again look at the merits of the deal opportunity and weigh whether or not the deal and the responsible parties are of sufficient strength to minimize any perceived risks to an acceptable level.

The request for warranties from the owner of a property (deal opportunity) that is on the market and being negotiated is another example of a major deal point that can become a deal disintegrator. Many principals requesting warranties will insist that if for any reason a space is not ready for occupancy by an agreed-on date then a severe penalty or penalties will incur to the benefit of the tenant or, in the case of a buyer, if some physical component of a property breaks down at some future point then the seller will assume all liability. These are simplifications of very important elements that occur during the negotiating process and that you must continually focus on because they are the issues or deal points that can make a lot of work meaningless and its target results disappear.

Certain stages of deal-opportunity development present minefields of potential problems that must be totally agreed on in intent and statement. When disagreement or misunderstanding appears, you must ensure that the pertinent disagreements or misconceptions are erased and restructured. These development stages include the following:

1. Lease document, construction contracts, property management agreements;
2. Purchase contract;
3. Escrow instructions;
4. Financing agreements and all supporting documents;
5. Promissory notes;
6. Deeds of trust;

7. Guarantees;
8. Bills of sale;
9. Partnership agreements; and
10. Title reports.

In an appendix I will provide some very important checklists to help you stay on top of this challenging paper trail.

Now Is Not the Time To Become a Shrinking Violet or Overly Humble

One time I overheard a friend of mine lamenting a love affair that recently had lost its energy and had dissolved. When I asked him how he managed to remain so calm, he simply stated that "love is like a shark; if it doesn't keep moving, it just dies." In my mind, a client relationship and a deal opportunity are very much like the shark: They must keep moving toward the target results of growth and actual closing. No one should care as much or put in more work and diligence than you when seeing that every component of your deal opportunities is properly satisfied. You cannot count on anyone else—principals, their legal counsel, lenders, etc.—to be as concerned about the success of the deal as you are. Staying on top of every element of a deal is one of the major ways in which you earn your commission and build your professional standing. Perhaps now you will understand the relevance of building relationships with the other people who play the roles of lender, lawyer, accountant, title officer, etc. *Each of these entities plays a vital role in the successful closing of every deal opportunity but with one major difference: They get paid whether or not the deal opportunity actually closes.*

Thus, when you discover any problems with the language of any document, try to determine the purpose and intent of that language. Learn who composed and/or inserted it. Many times, lawyers in their zest to protect their client will write language (legalese) in documents that is impossible for the other side to accept. You must explain to your principals the impact that such language might have on the success of the deal opportunity because of its effect on the other side. At times the other side must include strict language in the various agreements and documents to meet federal or state regulations such as the Securities and Exchange Laws that oversee the protection of various investors. Whatever the case in your particular deal, make sure that both sides are comfortable with all relevant documents, wording and time frames.

Don't Worry, Be Happy

First of all, you are not negotiating nuclear disarmament or the ouster of some Third-World dictator. Relax during these sessions. Stay cool and try to find the eye of the storm if emotions start to get out of hand. You only can do the best that you can do: As long as you can answer the Big Bang premise of "Did I do or say everything I possibly could to make this deal opportunity succeed?", then that's all you can do. Your ability to maintain a strong sense of professional certainty during the negotiating process will lend enthusiasm and confidence in the makability of the deal to all concerned. Always state your purpose during negotiations and stay on course with the presentation. Pick up on signs of disagreement or contempt. Question all areas of doubt or potential misunderstanding. Gain agreement on as many critical points as possible and always, always agree on some pertinent follow-up step or meeting that will continue to move the deal opportunity forward.

At times, after months of negotiation, offers and counteroffers, contracts and escrows on your deal opportunities, you may find yourself with, much to your chagrin, no closings. Many times after all the documents have been approved, *the "Grinch" of due diligence raises its ugly head.* Perhaps some problem with the building and its space arises, perhaps some major issues involving past or needed capital improvements appear, perhaps some changes in the type and availability of pertinent financing occur, perhaps some discovery in the existing leases and tenant base is made, or perhaps one party or the other just changes his or her mind. *Once again, you must maintain a heartbeat when your deal opportunity goes back into intensive care!*

Never Give Up Your Right
To Be Kept Informed of Every
Deal-Opportunity Element
That Affects Its Success for Closing

At times the principals may try to keep you from participating in the daily progress or due-diligence process. Maybe they are secretive or they do not think you need to know. Refuse to accept this posture. Never be satisfied just to be in a deal—be a major part of it! Demonstrate your value to the process through your knowledge and your willingness to support both sides in getting the deal made. Establish relationships with the relevant professionals, such as the lawyers on both sides, the title officer, etc., and communicate with them as needed to move the deal opportunity forward. Remember and recognize that these vital support people also have other clients and other deals on which to work, but insist that your deal opportunity is handled efficiently and properly to meet the time frames, the understandings and the spirit of the agreement. Stay involved because these are just additional building blocks in the overall deal-opportunity development process.

"Don't Worry, You're in the Deal"
and Other Famous Phrases
That Should Make You Nervous

"No problem, I'll take care of you," "the signed document (lease, letter of intent, contract, deed of trust, partnership agreement, etc.) is in the mail," "we might need a few more days" or "I just don't know if there is quite enough juice" are some of the more prevalent phrases that should instantly make your eyes and ears come to immediate attention. Never accept these type of statements without question, clarification and agreement. Unfortunately, you cannot assume that everyone will do "what's right." *You must protect the integrity of the deal opportunity, the position of your client relationship and your very own interest!*
Refuse to let any principals stall or cause unnecessary delay. Refuse to accept trite responses as valid reasons for no action or

incomplete follow-up. Regarding a commission agreement, get it in writing and incorporate the agreement as part of the permanent documents. When one side is not moving quickly enough to meet the agreed-on time parameters or some other major responsibility to the potential deal, get in front of the issues that are causing delay and take the necessary action to put everything back on course.

What about the Need for Closing Skills?

Sophisticated investors, owners, tenants and others can, indeed, be closed on the deal opportunity but not in the more traditional sense of that word. A principal must see the value and opportunity in every deal that you present or help create and thus he or she must be closed on every step. This is why selling in commercial real estate is a building-block process. Principals just do not decide, "OK, I will make this deal," without a great deal of consideration and the combination of many critical components. Perhaps you can close your principals most in the traditional sense when you demonstrate your excellence and they make the commitment to work with you and you present an outstanding, logical and value-based argument on why they should pursue any given deal opportunity. Believe it or not, emotion does play a role in the selection of what deal opportunities a principal will pursue as well as what broker or selling agent he or she will pursue them with. In this sense or context, therefore, you definitely can work on your closing skills. You would, of course, be in the best position to close by consistently demonstrating all the elements of Big Bang Selling and continually asking for various types of commitment to the creation, evolution and closing of deal opportunities that benefit your client relationships, your organization and you.

Deal closings in commercial real estate selling result mostly through the ability to control the finest and most-productive client relationships and the best potential deals in the marketplace in your specialty. You must have the courage to consistently ask for and the tenacity to gain commitments from your existing and target clients/principals to act as their selling agent in the pursuit of their requirements. Your ability to accurately diagnose the marketplace and its pertinent deal opportunities will be your best closing tool. Your ability to integrate the *philosophy* and *process* of Big Bang Selling behind a broad as well as finite sense of *purpose* will enable you to close as needed.

PART
IV

Other Viewpoints in Commercial Sales

CHAPTER
14

Listen to Another Genuine Voice, the Voice of the Client Principal

The very upper echelon of commercial real estate relationships sometimes seems intimidating to many selling agents. The prospect of sitting across the desk from a very successful developer or major tenant principal can cause *fear* and a lack of self-confidence. The fact of the matter is that the most-talented and most-successful principals generally are the most rewarding to work with not only on an incremental basis but especially in an ongoing relationship. The ability to cash in on your scholarship in commercial real estate that I mentioned earlier is never greater than when working with talented principals. When you discover the scope of the client-relationship charter to be consistently prosperous in this business, it really does inspire great respect. Make no mistake in thinking about the ease with which developers, investors, tenants, landlords and others are able to survive and prosper in a very competitive and constantly changing business environment. As I have pointed out in the selling agent's deal-opportunity development process, the very same challenges exist for the client/principal. In fact, the responsibilities and the risks are far greater when you examine the scope of the challenges that your principals face. As some astute observer once said of the business, *"a principal can have years and years of success in developing or investing in various commercial real estate ventures and the rewards will be handsome; however, it only takes one bad deal to put him or her completely out of business!"*

As a selling agent you must weigh your risks through the amount of time that you spend and the effort that you expend in relation to the monetary and relationship rewards that you might receive when successfully performing and closing deal opportunities. Your principals risk a great deal more. When choosing what deal opportunities to pursue and whom to pursue them with, they must weigh what directions will yield the greatest rewards. This is one of the reasons that you must take your responsibilities very seriously when committing to work for any given client relationship/principal. You are risking time spent with them and their deal opportunities; they are risking time and money spent with you and through your ability to successfully perform. They must spend money on their staffs, their facilities, their development ventures and other elements of their fixed monthly overhead costs. *The major reason that principals sometimes are so short-tempered or are seemingly so impatient with selling agents is that the principals' available time represents their ability to create, evolve and close successful deal opportunities.* Therefore, when an unprepared or unknowledgeable selling agent wastes their time on the telephone or in a face-to-face meeting, they are, to say the least, not as happy as a clam.

Your existing and target principals have a huge responsibility to their employees, their lenders, their partners, their families, their local real estate economies and their entire communities. They are men and women of action and creation. They make things happen and they have no time for incompetence or less than maximum effort from those from whom they expect and are entitled to quality performance and results. Your rewards for meeting these expectations are immense not only in monetary and recognition terms but in your opportunities to question these principals regarding their perceptions, capabilities and expectations in the ever-changing world of commercial real estate.

To give you a clearer understanding of the attitudes and expectations of the very finest type of client/principal toward the commercial broker or agent, I recently interviewed a former principal who represented one of my finest client relationships, Lincoln Property Company. The following will provide a little more background on the principal with the formerly broken ankle whom I referred to in a preceding chapter. More important, this information will show the type of personal and professional information that you must learn about your client principals. This is necessary to find additional common ground that will nurture your overall relationship.

Jim Freeman joined Lincoln Property Company in 1974. As Managing Partner of Lincoln's Phoenix office, he is responsible for the selection and development of new apartment projects in Arizona, New Mexico and Southern California. He also handles shopping-center development in the greater Phoenix area. His responsibilities also include the property management of more than 9,000 apartment units in Phoenix, Tempe, Mesa and Tucson, Arizona; Albuquerque, New Mexico; and San Diego, California. Prior to joining LPC, Jim spent four years developing and managing apartment projects in California and throughout portions of the continental northwest. He obtained a mechanical engineering degree from Georgia Tech and a Master of Business Administration at Harvard Business School.

Freeman devotes a great deal of his time to community organizations. He has served as state chairman of the Arizona Multihousing Association and was instrumental in getting rent-control legislation preempted at the state government level. He also was instrumental in getting a renter property-tax deduction through the legislature. Jim is a past chairman of Junior Achievement and is a past president of the Arizona Harvard Business School Club as well as former president of the Phoenix Housing Commission. He currently serves on the boards of the Phoenix Symphony Orchestra, the Phoenix Community Alliance, the Phoenix Chamber of Commerce and the Phoenix Metropolitan Housing Study Committee. Furthermore, Jim was chairman of the Phoenix Chamber of Commerce's Air Quality Task Force and has been involved in such diverse projects as the study for alternatives to finance downtown redevelopment to an investigation of an effective means to reorganize county government.

The list of Jim Freeman's outstanding credentials does not stop here; however, I think you get the point that I am trying to make. If a selling agent is trying to work with Lincoln Property Company or some similar client relationship, he or she will have the chance to work with principals who truly are involved in every aspect of their communities, who are at the forefront in shaping their community's future and who definitely see their personal and professional *purpose* in both macro and micro points of view. You should establish your target client/principal relationships with people such as these to accelerate your evolution toward professional selling excellence.

During the course of a two-hour interview, Jim made the following comments on the current state of the brokerage community, the roles and responsibilities of the selling agents and what he thought was important for every agent to be successful. The following comments are a composite of that interview:

Smith: What is your overall impression of the brokerage community?

Freeman: It seems to vary from city to city, ranging from excellent brokers and agents to those who have difficulty returning a telephone call. In some of the cities where we are active, the tendency is for more principal-to-principal deals.

Smith: How would you describe a professional broker and selling agent? What are the elements in making one so?

Freeman: Several things, the first of which certainly is knowledge. The agent absolutely must know the product. Obviously, other things also are important, such as the agent's understanding of the other elements of the deal opportunity and its players. From my perspective, however, as a user of a brokerage service I want the individual to know the product, not only the physical aspects, that is how many acres are included and whether or not it is served by utilities (in the case of a site for acquisition), and all of the primary things that any developer must know to proceed, but also he or she should know about control and its availability and also something about what motivates the seller. I must know these things to decide about whether or not I should spend my time on this particular opportunity. This becomes more and more important in tighter and more difficult markets. In Southern California, for example, it is absolutely essential. I'm just as interested in whether or not a property actually is deliverable as in whether or not it actually is a good site. So often a property is not even remotely deliverable either because of a nonmotivated or impossible seller or because of very tight state and local regulatory conditions; therefore I depend on the broker or agent to inform me if deliverability is even possible. In summary, then, you must know the terms of deliverability from the seller's standpoint and just as important what the regulatory people will allow us to do with it in cities where such answers might be readily available. In an incredibly complex market, such as Southern California, the process of answering these questions becomes much more drawn out. Although we hope that the broker might clarify these questions, we, of course, ultimately must answer our questions ourselves. In the simpler areas of development, however, we expect the broker to provide answers to these vital questions.

Smith: Can you recall any specific situations where you depended on a broker to provide you with critical information and because of the inaccuracy of the data, you ended up wasting a lot of valuable time?

Freeman: Hmm, well nothing comes to mind immediately, but, of course, we all probably have been handed the wrong map by a broker a time or two and temporarily have found ourselves arriving at the wrong destination. But one of the things that you do after you have been in this business awhile, or in any business that relies on skilled salespeople to make it work, you learn fairly quickly about who to trust and who not to trust. And the result is that rather than taking a chance on someone who might be a competent professional, you tend to ignore the ones whom you are not sure you can trust. I would like to respond further on another element of what makes a good broker or selling agent in addition to knowledge that helps to inspire trust and that is what I call the necessity for *understanding the value of careful talk and careful conversation.* Loose talk from a broker will quickly turn off a thinking developer or seller. If someone gives answers that they know are not accurate or if they think the answers might be accurate and they can cover themselves later, you will quickly figure this out and you will not want to work with that person again. I think that in any business, talking loosely and irresponsibly or gossiping about some pertinent matter of business that the agent has been exposed to is very dangerous.

Smith: This brings up an area of vital importance and that is the level of and establishment of trust between the agent and the client/principal. What are the elements of trust that should be an automatic given between your agent and broker and you?

Freeman: When a broker who you know will answer any question honestly even to say he or she does not know, then you tend to trust him or her. Obviously, there are other elements to trust. For instance, you want to ensure that they keep your information confidential and that there are not going to be other obvious things that are breaches of trust. *To be able to trust, that is to rely on, what they tell you is true and their own integrity in not attempting to blow smoke and to snow you is crucial.* One of the things that I must admit that I did not fully realize ten years or so ago is the utter importance of having one, two or three selling agents whom you have total confidence in who will work for you and your interests and not be out there dealing with anybody who walks in the door. It's just crucial.

Smith: That brings up an interesting question and one that seems to stymie many new selling agents. If I happen to be new in the business yet want very much to work with Lincoln Property Company, how do I establish a relationship in light of those with whom you already are working? As you may know, one of the most difficult objections that a new selling agent must overcome is that of finally reaching the principal and hearing him or her say, "We already work with so and so from ABC Brokerage or we presently do not have any requirements but when we do we work with so and so." As someone new who believes that he or she has credibility and can be trusted, how does he or she then proceed to work with you and LPC?

Freeman: It can be done but it takes time. The most important thing, of course, is to not make a mistake by saying something that you do not know. As a young or new selling agent, you will have the opportunities to contact your target principals whether with LPC or anyone else; however, just make sure that every time you speak, it is a quality communication. Do not shotgun. Do not send 15 packages if you do not know what that principal needs. Do whatever research it takes to be accurate. Talk with everyone you can inside and outside of the target organization who might know something about the requirement of that company. Stay with it and be tenacious and you eventually will find out what a Lincoln Property Company or a Koll Company might need at that time. Then if you find just one of the answers or deal opportunities to fit a specific need, try to get a face-to-face meeting with the principal. If that fails, send the opportunity anyway even if it is through the mail. If, whenever you communicate with a principal, you have something of quality to say, you will find that very soon he or she will give you a meaningful chance. Then you will become one of those selling agents on whom the principal will come to rely.

Smith: How do they do that then?

Freeman: What you do not do is bombard principals with meaningless telephone messages or irrelevant packages and letters. You do send them one or two forms of communications each month that are good. You make sure that the things that you have to sell are what they want to buy. Later on, you can become somewhat more relaxed and come into a meeting with a deal opportunity that they might want to take a chance on because of some currently undisclosed value. But initially your deal opportunity has to be on target.

Smith: Let us assume for a moment that the selling agent doesn't have a clue about your requirements but still wants to meet with you.

Freeman: They have to find out. They have to find out what your requirements are.

Smith: But that's why they want to meet with you in the first place.

Freeman (laughter): Well, they have to find out by doing some digging. By talking to coworkers or other professionals in the business. By visiting our projects and by talking to the planners in the cities where we develop. Find out what deals we have closed and who was involved and then go meet with these key people—perhaps a seller or a buyer or even an architect who might have designed our projects. Just know enough about us, because in any large and active marketplace there are just too many brokers and agents for a principal to meet with everyone in a first or exploratory meeting.

Smith: What is the most creative approach that a selling agent has taken to get a first meeting with you?

Freeman: Hmm, unfortunately, it is easier to remember those types of things in the negative. For example, I have a couple of selling agents now who are trying their best, I guess, to work with me and if they would only do what I have been saying, show me only things that I am interested in, they soon would find success. You know, on further consideration, that it really is not that difficult to get the first meeting with me; in fact, I'll meet with almost anyone, providing that the individual effectively communicates in writing to me why he or she wants to meet with me and why he or she would appreciate 15 minutes of my time. I will take those kinds of meetings; if, however, after that meeting I decide that the person was not organized and his or her presentation was helter-skelter, then I'll write him or her off. I don't think that I am that unusual in this respect because it's my impression that most principals will give somebody a chance to find out what they are all about and if you will use that well and you don't have something to sell that day, other than yourself, you just have to say, "I am good at this business and these are my qualifications and here is my approach and if you will just give me some idea of what you need, I will come back with some good things." Then when you come back with those good things or deal opportunities, just come back with one or maybe two things, not ten. If you show the principal a smorgasbord of deal opportunities, you might just confuse him or her and lose the emphasis on your best potential deal.

Smith: What should the elements of that presentation be?

Freeman: It should be accurate, succinct and as thorough as possible. Make it organized and specific. Don't call someone over the telephone and tell him or her that you have a site at Thirty-Second Street and something and suggest that he or she take a look at it sometime. As amazing as it may sound, in 1989 in at least half of the selling-agent calls that I get, the agent still tries to sell me on a site or some other deal opportunity but has no marketing package or presentation. Yet they still ask me to look at such and such and I find their conduct incredible. Have your presentation in writing and make sure it is clear and understandable.

Smith: How does a selling agent actually get you to look at the site or deal opportunity?

Freeman: I prefer to visit the site initially by myself and then the agent must follow up diligently by telephone to gauge my response and to determine the next step.

Smith: Large development entities, such as Lincoln Property Company, have a reputation, nationally, as being difficult for a broker or selling agent to establish an ongoing relationship with. Is there a corporate mentality toward the brokerage industry and if so, what is the overall policy?

Freeman: Not really. Each of the partners who is responsible for any given area or areas of responsibility pretty much decides for himself or herself regarding the extent of his or her involvement with or need to use the brokerage community. The thing that I always must go back to is knowledge. The selling agent who even when he or she does not have a specific deal opportunity to present is nevertheless willing to share market studies that are targeted in nature is very much appreciated. I consider it an integral part of providing a good service. I am not referring to the macro-market studies that Coldwell Banker or Grubb & Ellis puts out. These are nice, but they alone will not interest a principal in working with that brokerage company. I look to work with someone who knows the areas that I am interested in because I already own a property there and now am looking for someone who will send me unsolicited a study of, say, the six nearest competitive projects to my own as to up-to-date market data and activity. This means receiving information with great detail that is accurate. Believe me, this agent will get my attention because he or she is, in fact, helping me to more effectively do my job.

Smith: What other types of information do you enjoy seeing in these types of unsolicited presentations?

Freeman: In our business, the apartment business, this includes square footages, rents, vacancies, tenant traffic and where it is coming from, amenities and how they are received in the market and so forth. In addition, it is nice to see some qualitative comment about the properties or projects contained in the survey. We also are interested in knowing how others receive us and our properties. Certainly, the agent who specializes in apartments or any other segment of real estate is qualified to shop and investigate the manner in which we are running our properties and to share with us how the market is receiving them. We do not want someone to be negative about our competitors; in fact, you are better off pointing out the good things that make us compete more keenly.

Smith: Where is commercial real estate brokerage heading?

Freeman: I think that the outstanding brokerage firms and the outstanding agents will continue to do well. There is such a great disparity between the minority of agents who sell with excellence and those who do much less, however, that the tendency might be more direct, principal-to-principal dealings.

Smith: What steps should the agent take in the negotiating process when he or she is representing you on a specific deal opportunity?

Freeman: I think that a broker who really is good, who has the ability to communicate well and is willing to spend the time and do the homework to understand the deal opportunity, should be involved in every single step of the sale transaction. He or she should stay in communication with both parties almost daily and attempt to be present at every meeting. He or she should attend the meeting with the principal and the engineers, the lawyers, the lenders and, when appropriate, the other partners. The awareness and understanding that result because of this involvement enable the agent to soften the difficult discussions that sometimes occur with the other side of any transaction as a result of unforeseen circumstances or unwelcome changes. The best example I can think of is the mortgage broker with whom we now have completed six or seven financings who did not allow a meeting to take place between the principals without his attendance and involvement. This was true no matter how brief the meeting and no matter where, geographically, the meeting took place. Because the broker was in New York, the lender was in Texas and we were based in Arizona, you can imagine who flew the furthest. But I was so impressed by the broker's commitment as was the other side (in this case the lender) because we both knew that he understood what was going on based not only on his attendance at meetings but also on his corresponding follow-up letters. During this communication he would summarize the areas of disagreement or concern, perhaps in some regard to prepayment penalties, and would offer very constructive alternatives. Now a selling agent doesn't necessarily have to offer suggestions to solve problems during a negotiation but doing so might very well help. I really believe that a selling agent who is good can gain the respect of both sides and be there in the middle at all times.

Smith: Now that the agent or broker is communicating with you on a daily basis, what sort of information should you receive?

Freeman: I should receive, and this is one of my pet peeves, messages from brokers that are meaningful. A principal should receive a message almost every day regarding the status of his or her deal opportunity. This does not have to be "call me at your first opportunity," so that the principal has to call the broker and needlessly waste time. To spend time on the telephone with a broker or agent or to play telephone tag to get a small piece of information is nonsense. A small piece of pertinent information can be invaluable in keeping the principal mentally attuned as to where the deal opportunity sits. Something as small as a message that says "I tried to reach Mr. Jones this morning and he is out of town until tomorrow" will at least let me know where the other side is and might be quite helpful. This type of communication enables me to let my partners know what is going on and why and further demonstrates that I am on top of every detail. Brokers and agents can help to support the principals in their deal opportunities by keeping everyone informed and crisply accurate.

Smith: Anything else the broker or selling agent can do?

Freeman: Yes. He or she can play the role of the psychologist by making each side feel good about the deal points that they are winning or have agreed are important. This becomes quite important when the agent must gain agreement from both sides on financial, structural or emotional deal points.

Smith: Agency issues seem to be coming more prevalent today. The courts seem to be saying that a broker cannot legally represent both sides of a transaction. What are your thoughts on the responsibilities of the brokers and agents with whom you work?

Freeman: Clearly, we must all recognize that the person paying the commission is entitled to the fiduciary or legal representation. When an agent is working on our behalf even though the other side might be paying the commission, however, we expect that broker or agent to acknowledge to all concerned parties exactly whom he or she represents.

Smith: What about the case where a seller is paying the commission and the broker is representing you in a purchase as the buyer?

Freeman: I'm still not quite sure what the courts will decide in the final analysis of this important issue, but if we are working with a broker or agent and have had an ongoing relationship, we hope that after disclosing his or her representation to the appropriate parties (in this case the seller) that he or she will provide us with the necessary insight and strategies as to how to make the best deal for us. Of course, it becomes necessary for that seller to recognize the various broker-client relationships and representations to know what or what not to disclose in front of our agent or broker.

Smith: How much are you willing to disclose about the economics of any potential deal and the whys or why nots of the makability of the opportunity?

Freeman: I think it is important that the selling agent understand the economics of the deal opportunity to effectively present why we can or cannot go to a certain price. This strategy can be effective; however, in some markets the sellers who have a product that is very much in demand are not terribly concerned about my economics on their deal opportunity. Therefore, if I am unable to achieve my optimum price, a decision must be made as to whether or not to proceed.

Smith: Jim, there are many times when I hear from the female selling agents in the business who are upset at their inability to build more solid client relationships predicated on personal as well as professional interaction. The difficulty for many rests in the age-old challenges of the hint of or bent toward some sexual connotation that makes the agent quite uncomfortable. How can this type of challenge be overcome?

Freeman: One answer is through other types of professional/ social types of activities such as city affairs, social clubs and the like in which the target principal is involved. Get involved in similar activities. I can think of a couple of female agents whom we do business with that I also interact with in the political process and in city activities and I must say that this helps build a more meaningful relationship.

Smith: How can a selling agent get inside of your thought process to really understand your motivations on a specific deal opportunity as related to tax consequences, partnership attitudes and influences, decision-making criteria and so forth?

Freeman: Hmm. It just takes time. After developing sufficient trust this will come to bear; however, many principals, myself included, are offended by a selling agent asking overly personal questions just to understand us better when the groundwork has not been done and the time has not been spent before. A smart selling agent will know when to back off. You know, I mentioned earlier that the finest type of selling agent is one who attends every meeting. I must say that this only applies in the cases where the principals want the agent there because they believe his or her presence is a positive influence and no one attending will be offended by the broker's or agent's presence. Sometimes I just do not want the person there for other nonpersonal reasons and feel I can be more effective on my own.

Smith: How does a selling agent turn your attitude around if you feel his or her presence in meetings is more of a hindrance than a help?

Freeman: Time. If an agent perceives that he or she has made a major faux pas and the principal does not want to listen to his or her advice, the agent must make sure that the next time he or she interfaces with the principal that the agent is fully prepared and his or her communication is quality. It might be that the agent did nothing wrong or inept but that the principal just does not care for the agent or maybe got up on the wrong side of the bed. In those cases, the agent must back off until a more appropriate time appears. Stand in the background until the wound heals and continue to read the principal's attitudes.

Smith: What advice do you have for the selling agent starting out in today's complex and fluid markets?

Freeman: First of all, specialize. Don't try to generalize. Choose an element and know it very well. Try to make your deals in that sector.

Smith: How should that agent choose his or her client relationships?

Freeman: Well it's easy to say that he or she should choose those relationships that will yield the best results over a long period of time; however, those tend to be the slowest in actually yielding immediate commission dollars. So you initially need to establish a mix of those deal opportunities and client relationships that will yield your micro-target results more quickly together with those that will yield your macro results as well.

Smith: How can the brokerage community protect itself against the advent of and the momentum toward more principal-to-principal deals?

Freeman: That raises an issue not in direct answer to that question. The people who are the controllers of money who are crucial to us as well as to those in the brokerage business invariably come from large organizations with heavy institutional types of mentalities. This tells us a great deal about how anyone of us who wants to stay active in this business needs to prepare himself or herself to work with those organizations that control the money. First of all this means better, more thorough and more professional presentations, particularly written presentations. This means dressing better and being in the right kinds of places that will attract the attention of bankers, life-insurance executives and pension-fund managers because these are the types of folks who will make the decision about where the money will be invested. These people are well-educated MBAs, college graduates with finance-oriented backgrounds who are impressed with and respond well to people who show thorough knowledge of their subject and express themselves well, particularly in writing.

Smith: How then does the selling agent translate this to his or her advantage? What you are saying is that these people basically want to work with people in their own image.

Freeman: That's correct. I do not like to overuse the word, but what we are talking about is **professionalism**, a thorough knowledge not just gut reaction to things, a willingness to provide the appropriate backup information on the deals, the effective use of maps highlighted with all the appropriate data and so on that will enable the person who is distant from the deal opportunity but involved in its outcome to better understand. If it is appropriate and the need is there, the selling agent should go to toastmasters to improve his or her speaking skills, should identify the appropriate formats and contents of professional presentations and should take all the necessary steps to round out his or her preparedness.

Smith: Jim, your thoughts are very much appreciated, but before ending this interview could you sum up as succinctly as possible your advice and counsel to all brokers and selling agents? How can each individual separate himself or herself from the competition to gain your trust and that of people like you?

Freeman: *Just do a better job! Don't waste your bullets. Don't throw things at your target clients that are outside of their interests. Be accurate and don't waste their time so that they get tired of hearing from you. But be there. Do not let long lapses of time go by without the client hearing from you. The client needs to know that you are active in the market. Leave accurate and detailed information in your messages. If the telephone contact is not possible, send a personal note on some topic that is germane to the principal. This will go much farther on your behalf than some type of mass mailer that has been sent to many other principals. And, finally, remember that inaccurate information, loose talk and crossing the line between persistence and being a pain can permanently sink any hopes of a quality client relationship.*

Smith: Jim, thank you very much. It's been a pleasure.

CHAPTER
15

The Commercial Real Estate Selling Agent's Favorite Whipping Boy, the Real Estate Lawyer

One of the finest and potentially most productive relationships that you should cultivate is that of the commercial real estate attorney. The only other person whose counsel your client/principal will equally depend on, provided you have established **preeminent client service** with **professional selling excellence,** is that of the real estate lawyer. The real estate lawyer *must ensure* that all the necessary documentation on any deal opportunity is legally correct, *must act* in the best interests of his or her client to limit all aspects of client liability as much as possible within the framework of the potential deal, and *must seek* every possible monetary as well as business advantage. The lawyer also must understand the principles, motivations and spirit of the negotiations that affect all elements of the negotiating process and all forms of documentation. The real estate lawyer must be creative and well versed in all elements of deal making from understanding current real estate liability laws and pending legislation to maintaining a firm grasp of real estate finance and its myriad of perplexing and sometimes very one-sided (for the benefit of the lender, of course) loan documents. The real estate lawyer generally is very active during the due-diligence process and usually provides the last word or at the least the last recommendation on the content of everything from preliminary title reports and ALTA insurance policies to issues concerning surveys, Universal Commercial Code (UCC) searches, permits and licenses, regulatory matters (zoning and building-code compliance), environmental impact (toxic waste and asbestos), soil reports (composition and ground water), existing leases and existing notes and deeds of trust and every other pertinent issue imaginable.

The perception of the real estate lawyer that many brokers and selling agents carry with them like unnecessary baggage is that of someone who gets paid just for picking up the telephone whether or not he or she provides meaningful conversation, who many times has no clue about the principal motivations for making the deal work and who barely conceals contempt for what he or she views as the overpaid yet underproductive salesperson. The unfortunate truth is that in some cases this is exactly the attitude of many lawyers toward the commercial selling agent. The lawyer who often is called on to spend as many hours working nonstop as are necessary to close a deal opportunity looks up from his or her pile of documents and sees the selling agent or broker breeze in to pick them up to simply deliver these vital links for signatures. Maybe the lawyer will hear from the selling agent calling in a distressed and panicked posture at some point during the deal's evolution trying to get what the lawyer feels are impossible or inappropriate concessions for the other side of the transaction. The next time that our friend, the counselor, sees his or her deal mate, the selling agent, is typically at the closing when his or her nemesis comes in to collect some outrageous, or so he or she thinks, commission check. After looking down at the closing statement and spotting the commission amount, the lawyer packs up his or her briefcase, smolders on leaving the closing, returns to the office and kicks the cat.

And what about the selling agent? The selling agent's view is that if it were not for his or her lightning-fast mental reflexes, unfathomable depths of knowledge and most creative deal-saving suggestions, the lawyer would have blown the deal opportunity at least three times during the escrow period or maybe even before. These are hardly attitudes on which to build mutually supportive relationships or, for that matter, lawyer/commercial agent understanding.

Deal Maker or Deal Breaker?

I hope that you can see the levity that I have tried to inject into this very important but sometimes fragile and destructive professional-relationship component of successful deal making. The fact of the matter is that both sides do not always take the time to understand the merits of each other's efforts. The selling agent who often has spent months creating and developing one specific deal opportunity is not always willing to grasp the significance of the liability issue that the lawyer sometimes raises. Because these issues can become deal-opportunity killers, the selling agent first should try to develop a reasonable alternative that will protect the principal and yet still meet the request of the other side. Unfortunately, the selling agent's first response often is panic and unreasonable or ill-informed comments and suggestions to the lawyer. The lawyer who has been estranged from the agent during the negotiating process cannot believe the inane suggestions that he or she is hearing. Often, however, the lawyer overreacts in his or her zealousness to protect the perceived interests of the client. Certainly at times the lawyer may not understand the motivations and desires of his or her client to close the deal and thus may miss opportunities for compromise with parties from the other side of the transaction.

A Personal Point of View

I am quite pleased to say that my professional experiences with real estate lawyers during my entire career were very positive. In fact, I cannot recall one single time when an overly protective attitude or posture on the part of a client/principal's counsel led to the destruction of a deal. At certain times my point of view may have differed from the lawyers, on one or even both sides of the transaction, but in every case that I can recall we never let our individual egos or personal attitudes adversely affect the deal opportunity or the principals on either side.

In fact, one of my fondest memories in my brokerage career is that of my experiences with the many real estate lawyers with whom I came in contact while vigorously pursuing some deal opportunity. I found that most real estate attorneys are bright, well informed about the needs of the client/principal, willing to listen to reasonable alternative viewpoints, anxious to better understand additional elements of the evolution of the deal opportunity, very dedicated, hard working and tenacious in their willingness to make a deal work. Of course, there were one or two exceptions to this profile. I can recall one lawyer who went on vacation and left no forwarding telephone number during an extremely sensitive period of a $14,000,000 transaction. My principal was unwilling to take any additional steps toward solving a problem that had arisen until his lawyer could be contacted. Although the deal was not blown, it made for some exciting moments.

Who Said Anything about Playing Hide the _____?

You should be aware that sometimes the lawyer at the direction of his or her client/principal and perhaps your own, without your knowledge, will play hide and seek. Attorneys may take turns hiding while you are seeking to find out what is going on. Therefore, you must be aware of the signals that indicate this, such as your telephone calls left unreturned or returned without urgency, crucial documents not prepared on time, unreasonable delays in responding to the other side of the deal opportunity, lack of due diligence and so forth. Always remember that the attorney works for the principal, his or her client, and as good as your relationship might be with each of them, the interests of the potential deal as well as your own always will place and show.

Deal-Opportunity Ally and Confidant

As I have stated throughout this book, your ability to build quality relationships with other professionals related to the commercial real estate industry will pay large dividends. The competent and active real estate lawyer can be a tremendous source of information and a willing and helpful ally in closing your deal opportunities. Your willingness to take the time to meet with counsel on one or both sides of the transaction before and during the deal opportunity's evolution will go a long way toward smoothing the road of potential disagreements. Once you have identified the legal counsel of your client relationships, set up a meeting to introduce yourself and take the time to share your professional qualifications and directions with him or her. You do not need to have a specific deal opportunity in negotiation to do this. Make sure that the lawyer understands that this is a free meeting and does not assume that you are there at the request of his or her client. Establish this relationship based on the same rules previously established in the Big Bang Selling context. Many real estate lawyers are frustrated developers or syndicators and love to hear what is going on in the marketplace. Try to become a source of information for these people and to develop referrals from them to build new client relationships of your own.

I can recall many instances when the two principals on each side of the deal were about to go for each other's throats and chaos was about to reign, yet I was able to keep my sanity, composure and perspective because of the interaction with one or both of the deal-making lawyers involved in the process. The most valuable thing that you can do to foster a good relationship with any real estate lawyer is to demonstrate your knowledge of the deal opportunity itself in terms of price, terms, structure, timing and major deal points. Additionally, when you are willing to understand the legal components of the documents as well as you can and are willing to question those areas where you are unclear, the lawyer will see that you indeed are interested in more than just a commission. Always demonstrate your desire to first act in the interests of the client/principal. When you are disagreeing about some element of a deal opportunity and believe you are correct, do not get emotional but lay out a logical sequence of thought that illustrates to the legal counsel why you are right.

Ten Simple Ways To Build
Win/Win Relationships with Lawyers

You can establish great working relationships with attorneys in many ways, including the following:

1. Establish a meeting with relevant legal counsel to discuss the history, motivations, market influences, timing, personalities, etc., involved in the current deal opportunity. If it is a first meeting, take the time to share your professional background and qualifications. Let the lawyer know you are willing to support his or her efforts in any way possible to help the clients and further the potential deal. Offer to act as a sounding board to find the best available alternatives and solutions to any perceived or real problems.

2. Consistently demonstrate your knowledge of the deal opportunity particulars and the current desires and motivations of the principals. Keep the lawyer advised about the timing of due-diligence points and forewarn him or her of potential problems. Make sure that your principal complies with this arrangement.

3. Take an appropriate and active posture in all face-to-face or telephone negotiations involving your principals and their counsel. When you must remain silent, do so, and let the lawyers hammer out the legal points that are being disputed. Do not be intimidated, however, when negotiating deal or business points. No one should be as well versed as you regarding your own deal opportunity.

4. Make sure that your responsibilities are transacted with a strong sense of urgency and an appropriate direction.

5. Assist the lawyer whenever possible to track documents, principals, other counsel and all people and matters relevant to the success of the deal opportunity.

6. When you are unsure of any legal point of view, its perspective or its overall impact on the deal opportunity, question it

until you receive a satisfactory response. Make sure you do so in an unobtrusive manner and when appropriate.

7. Be aware of the advice that the lawyers are giving to your principals. Know how it impacts the negotiation or the deal opportunity itself. Keep informed.

8. Spend social time with the lawyers whom you respect. Share information, learn about their major challenges, their goals, their dreams. Do whatever you can to foster new business for their particular practices.

9. Be direct, candid and forthright when discussing critical issues germane to the negotiation and the deal opportunity itself.

10. Investigate current articles by various lawyers and judges that relate to all matters of commercial real estate. Identify various journals and brochures that discuss current issues influencing all areas of the business. Show that you want to know more than just what it takes to "collect a commission" and you will.

All Documents Are Not Created Equal

One of the greatest services that the commercial real estate lawyer renders is his or her review of all relevant documents. From letters of intent and contracts to purchase and final lease agreements and deeds of trust, these documents are the most critical components of making winning deals. It should come as no surprise that the majority of leases that are sent out for signature are prepared by the landlord. And it should be no surprise that these leases are in large part most favorable to the interests of the landlord. That is until the competent real estate lawyer representing a tenant gets involved. Your task as a selling agent is to understand the language and the components of the critical documents that are germane to your clients/principals and their deal opportunities.

The following items might be necessary to add to a pro-landlord lease when trying to protect and effectively represent your tenant/principal:

1. The tenant has the right to contest tax assessments and the landlord's income taxes are not to be paid by tenant.

2. The following categories of operating expenses are never to be passed on to the tenant: commissions, depreciation, interest and debt payments, capital improvements and tenant improvements.
3. The tenant shall have the right to review all itemized landlord operating expenses.
4. All advance payments of taxes and operating expenses are placed in interest-bearing accounts for which the tenant receives credit.
5. The tenant has a right to terminate the lease agreement if the premises are not available on time.
6. All parking rights shall be expressly indicated and identified.
7. All renewal options shall be expressly stated and clarified.
8. Stress option rights to adjacent space if relevant or needed.
9. The tenant has the right to perform any necessary maintenance functions and to deduct the cost involved if the landlord fails to adequately provide the maintenance.
10. All signage rights are to be expressly stated and agreed on.
11. The landlord is obligated to provide and maintain insurance.
12. The landlord is to indemnify the tenant for losses on common areas.
13. The tenant has the right to terminate the lease if the premises are damaged and cannot be properly restored.
14. The tenant shall have the right to a pro-rata share of condemnation proceeds.
15. Exercise of the landlord's rights shall not interfere with the tenant's business.
16. The tenant shall have the right to assign the lease.
17. No consents can be unreasonably withheld or delayed.
18. The tenant has the expressed right to use common areas.
19. The tenant has the right of quiet enjoyment.
20. The landlord must perform all obligations under the encumbrances to which the lease is subordinate.

The real estate lawyer performs a vital service to his or her client by altering the provisions in the lease document to the greatest benefit of the tenant. As a commercial selling agent, you must understand the issues and provisions from the points of view of both the landlord and the tenant. This is necessary not only to effectively execute your representation responsibilities but to provide you with the appropriate knowledge to effectively negotiate this type of deal opportunity.

The Lawyer versus the Lender
and Pertinent Observations for You To Make

Perhaps nothing is more vital than the creation, review and adjustment of loan documents. The wrong type of provisions from the point of view of your principal that might be contained in the loan documents can prove fatal to the success of either existing or future deal opportunities. Another hat that the skilled real estate lawyer wears is that of master loan negotiator. But once again, much of what he or she does to protect and benefit the client is not beyond the reach of understanding or involvement for the commercial real estate selling agent. You must remove the mystery from such matters and you must understand how every little part of something as innocent as a prepayment right can greatly influence the success or failure of your deal opportunity.

When your client/principal and his or her lawyer are reviewing the business points of any loan document as well as its various provisions, they must be very alert and astute. Under business points alone they must be aware of the exact amount of the principal, the interest rate, the amount of debt-service payment with specific due dates and provisions for late payments, the date of maturity, the prepayment rights, the rights of deficiency judgments (exculpation), the restraints on conveyance, the parameters for secondary financing, the security for the loan, the impound amounts and due dates, the rights to insurance proceeds when applicable and the conditions and terms of any necessary guarantees.

In addition to the business points of the loan document, the following provisions also must be stated to protect and comfort your principal: the conditions to the loan, the use of the property, due on-sale exceptions, insurance issues, specific components of the guarantees and the fees and expenses of the borrower. Here again, the lender in all likelihood will provide the basic documents; but, like most things in the business, certain points and provisions can be subject to interpretation, negotiation and change.

CHAPTER

16

The Resolution Trust Corporation (RTC) and Thee, or How To Work with the Feds To Sell Repossessed Commercial Real Estate

As I mentioned in the beginning of this book, the magnitude of the savings-and-loan problem has yet to be fully accounted for and understood. The current estimates in terms of the eventual total cost to the taxpayers of our country range from $150 billion to as high as $300 billion. Some more pessimistic observers estimate the total bill to be as high as a staggering $700 billion.

A sizable portion of this almost incomprehensible amount in financial losses in this country's S&Ls resulted not from bad real estate loans but from speculation in junk bonds. With the legalization of diversification and direct investments, many leaders of our now-troubled thrifts chose to offer above-market interest rates and thus returns to attract the deposits of large investors. In many cases, the chosen vehicles for doing so were Wall Street investment advisers or money brokers who placed the funds of their clients in these government-insured institutions. The thrifts then took a large part of those investments or deposits and purchased junk bonds that offered an even higher rate of return. They, of course, made a tidy profit on the spread between what they were paying out and what they were receiving. As the companies behind the issues of these junk bonds lagged or diminished in various aspects of their anticipated performance, the value in the investment marketplace for junk bonds greatly declined. To make matters worse for the S&Ls, new federal thrift rules, enacted to reign in nontraditional thrift investments, required that these junk bonds are sold no later than 1994. A final nail in this proverbial coffin is the demand in the new rules that these S&Ls devalue their bonds on their books to reflect the real market value.

To offset this major blow to the country's budget deficit, Congress created and passed the Financial Institutions Reform, Recovery and Enforcement Act of 1989. The key provisions of the act were taken from a White House press release dated August 8, 1989. It's important for any selling agent who portends to call himself or herself a professional or whose desire is to attain *professional selling excellence* to take the time not only to read but to understand the elements of this very important piece of legislation.

1. Strong Thrift Capital Requirements

The bill was designed to require thrifts to meet the same capital and accounting standards as do national banks. In addition to new, tougher, minimum capital requirements for thrifts, the bill provides other new standards that reflect national bank capital provisions.

The bill also creates a tangible capital requirement of at least three percent of assets. This will prevent the current situation in which institutions with enormous negative tangible net worths are able to comply with minimum capital rules and continue active expansion. All "supervisory goodwill" must be phased out by January 1, 1995. (This will very likely place many troubled S&Ls into insolvency unless a drastic positive impetus is created to drive up real estate asset values.)

Investments in thrift subsidiaries engaging in nontraditional activities must be deducted from capital. This will prevent the risk of sudden failure of insured institutions as a result of losses in subsidiary businesses.

Growth by undercapitalized firms will be strictly limited or prohibited.

Brokered deposits will not be permitted for undercapitalized thrifts.

2. Establishment of New Deposit Insurance Fund

Deposit insurance for thrifts will be provided by a new insurance fund called the Savings Association Insurance Fund (SAIF). SAIF will replace the current Federal Savings and Loan Insurance Corporation (FSLIC). The SAIF fund will be directed and administered by the Federal Deposit Insurance Corporation (FDIC), although it will be maintained separately from the existing bank insurance fund.

SAIF will continue to receive assessments paid by its members after 1991 and, should it become necessary, the Treasury will make payments to maintain the Fund's net worth at specified levels.

3. Resolution Trust Corporation (RTC) and the RTC Oversight Board

The RTC will be established to merge or liquidate all existing failed thrifts as well as any thrifts that fail prior to August of 1992.

The RTC will resolve all thrifts that have failed or will fail between January 1, 1989, and August 9, 1992, using $30 billion raised by the Resolution Funding Corporation (REFCORP) and $20 billion raised by the industry and the Treasury.

The FDIC will exclusively manage the RTC on a day-to-day basis subject to review by the Oversight Board to resolve failed thrifts.

The RTC will have employees of its own, although it may employ personnel from other agencies or private contractors.

The RTC will review and analyze all assistance agreements entered into by the FSLIC from January 1, 1988, to January 1, 1989, and will take appropriate steps to restructure these agreements if taxpayer savings can be achieved.

No later than April 30th of each year the RTC will provide an annual report of its operations, activities, budget receipts and expenditures for the preceding calendar year, as well as reports throughout the year.

The RTC will terminate on December 31, 1996.

The RTC Oversight Board will establish general policies for the RTC and oversee its activities. Members of the Oversight Board will be the Secretary of the Treasury (chairman), the Chairman of the Federal Reserve Board, the Secretary of Housing and Urban Development (HUD) and two public members appointed by the President.

4. Financing for Closing and Resolution of Failed Thrifts

The bill will establish the REFCORP to fund the case resolutions undertaken by the RTC. REFCORP will be headed by a three-member Directorate, which will be authorized to issue up to a $30-billion principal amount of long-term bonds to pay the costs of closing down or otherwise resolving insolvent thrifts.

For current cases, the bill provides $20 billion to pay for resolution activities in fiscal year 1989, including $18.8 billion from Treasury funds and $1.2 billion from the Federal Home Loan Bank System (FHLB). (At the behest of Congress to show rapid progress and to take pressure off the federal deficit in fiscal 1990, the $20 billion was spent in the resolution of some problem S&Ls or in closing others and paying off depositors.)

The bill provides $32 billion in public and private funds to resolve thrifts that fail from 1992 to 1999 and to capitalize the new SAIF.

The bill provides all necessary funds for FSLIC cases resolved before January 1, 1989.

5. Regulatory Restructuring

The FDIC will receive independent enforcement authority to take action against violations of safety and sound requirements by any insured thrift. This will enable the FDIC to protect the insurance fund against risks allowed by chartered or supervisory agencies.

Under the legislation, the FHLB Board will be abolished and its former activities will be divided into several functions. The primary function of examining and supervising both federally and state-chartered thrifts and their holding companies will be performed by a new agency, the Office of Thrift Supervision (OTS). Because the OTS will be an office of the Department of the Treasury, the interest of taxpayers and the general public will be more fully protected.

The FSLIC will be replaced by SAIF, which will be administered by the FDIC.

The Federal Housing Administration (FHA) Finance Board will supervise the credit activities of the 12 regional Federal Home Loan Banks.

The Federal Home Loan Mortgage Corporation (Freddie Mac) will become an independent government-sponsored enterprise.

6. Restrictions on Thrift Powers

The FDIC will have the authority to prohibit or limit the activities of state-chartered thrifts that it determines involve unacceptable risk levels.

Investments in junk bonds, either directly or through a subsidiary, will be prohibited, but may be placed in a separately capitalized affiliate where insured deposits will not be at risk.

Equity investments (such as direct real estate investments) will be prohibited within federally insured thrifts.

Loans to one borrower generally will be limited to the amount allowed for national banks.

7. Qualified Thrift Lender (QTL) Test

Thrifts must maintain 70 percent of their assets in housing-related loans and other qualified assets.

Thrifts that fail the QTL test must convert to a bank charter or become subject to certain restrictions.

8. Housing

The Federal Home Loan Banks will be required to contribute at least $100 million a year by 1995 to subsidize interest rates on advances to member institutions that make loans for low- and moderate-income housing.

The RTC must provide a three-month "first-look" period to qualified buyers of single-family homes held by the RTC and similar opportunities for qualified buyers of eligible multifamily housing extending up to 135 days.

9. Enforcement

Maximum sentences for major financial institution crimes, such as bribery and fraud, are increased to 20 years in prison. The maximum criminal fine for these violations is increased to $1 million.

The basis for civil penalties imposed by the regulators is expanded and current generally low penalties are increased to a maximum penalty of $1 million per day.

The Department of Justice will be authorized to receive substantial new appropriations to enable it to more than double the number of investigators and prosecutors working on financial fraud cases.

10. Studies

The Treasury, in consultation with the depository-institutions regulators and others, will conduct major studies on the federal-deposit insurance system as well as a study on the risk exposure to the federal government of government-sponsored enterprises.

Hopefully, a New Beginning

Well, one heck of a mess obviously took one heck of a bill (not without its own problems) to begin to rectify the mistakes and malfeasance that occurred during the early to late 1980s within our savings-and-loan industry and commercial real estate markets. But what does all of this mean to you, the selling agent or broker? It means great deal opportunities and exciting new relationships (see Figure 16.1 for the RTC decision-making process). It means the chance to work on some outstanding commercial properties that because of poor timing, mismanagement, poor marketing, misconception, overburdening debt, soft markets and many other contributing factors, some controllable and some not, has made these real estate assets revert to the very lenders who originally financed them.

Because one of the primary missions of the RTC is to sell these foreclosed assets, it definitely will need your help. Currently, more than 500 insolvent institutions are under the control of the FDIC. In addition, at least 400 more troubled thrifts have tangible capital between zero percent and three percent of their total assets and thus are bordering on insolvency. The total assets of the insolvent and seized thrifts are estimated to exceed $304 billion and $360 billion in the marginal institutions.

As stated in its resolution policies, "the primary goal of the FDIC in managing this problem is to resolve insolvent institutions in a manner that minimizes the long-term cost to the government." The next major goal is to maximize the recovery on failed institutions' assets while utilizing the private sector as much as possible. As for resolving the institutions themselves and its explanation, I shall leave that story for someone else's book, but let me simply say that "insolvent institutions will be

Figure 16.1   The RTC deal opportunity decision-making process.

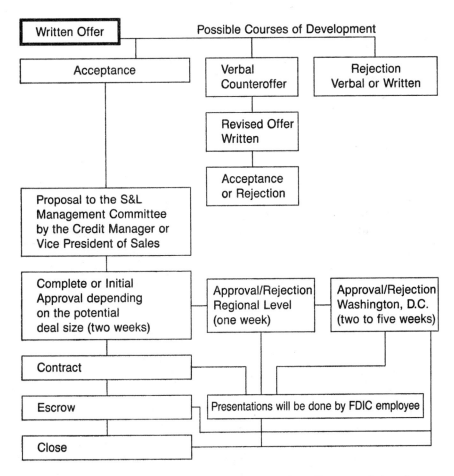

Author's note: It would be prudent at least to double all proposed time frames in order to avoid personal brain lock due to bureaucracy-induced frustration.

resolved subject to a competitive bidding process in which the acquirers of the restructured institutions will be expected to fully capitalize the institution at levels consistent with those required for national banks." Furthermore, the FDIC will evaluate the feasibility of arranging either whole institution solutions or those in which major problem assets are left behind with the RTC.

Your Opportunities in RTC Asset Disposition

"The FDIC will retain the flexibility to sell or otherwise dispose of a failed institution's problem assets before selling its franchise, hence bids will be welcome for assets without the franchise. Where markets are liquid and values can be readily ascertained, the FDIC would favor early sales of assets at appraised values."

The fear on the part of the citizenry, the economic-development agencies, the politicians and everyone else concerned with the viability and integrity in their commercial real estate markets is that the RTC will "dump" or sell at any price those assets that they deem necessary to unload. This is a very valid and important concern about the immediate and long-term health of many local and state economies in our more troubled commercial real estate markets. The fear is real because dumping real estate assets has a snowball or domino effect on all real estate values regarding healthy assets that are presently fiscally sound as well as those that are controlled by the RTC. The net effect of selling at any price with an "as soon as possible mandate" would be catastrophic not only to the assets themselves but to the holders of the debt, the clients/principals and their employees, the partners in the assets and the overall economic spinoffs to the individual communities in everything from declining tax revenues to the viability for locally held corporate expansion. It is my prayer that this scenario never will occur; however, my major concern with this nightmare coming to fruition rests not in the irresponsibility of the people managing the RTC but in the Congress. Already, some members of the House of Representatives are haranguing the Bush administration and the RTC for moving too slowly in selling off the thrifts and their troubled assets. If this vital economic issue is allowed to become a political and partisan issue, there undoubtedly will be undue pressure brought to bear on the RTC to "sell now and damn the values." Only the future holds whether logic and good business sense will prevail or whether a Congress that obviously was asleep during the creation of the ERTA bill, as well as during the relaxation of the regulatory requirements of the S&Ls, will try to save face by supposedly now "saving the nation billions." Let us hope that the clear minds of those leaders of sound business and moral judgment will prevail. *On the same note, however, let's hope a process is put in place that will move toward selling assets in an efficient and effective manner. As we go to press, this has yet to happen.*

A Word from a Voice at the RTC

To get a clearer perspective on the dumping question as well as to determine how a selling agent and his or her broker can become involved in the resolution of these problem real estate assets, I set out to identify and interview various employees of the FDIC who have been placed at the forefront of the nation's most challenging S&L failures. These were employees who had been brought in to act as credit specialists and marketing directors whose charter is to sell repossessed assets. These individuals have a unique perspective because their backgrounds were strong in private sector–related endeavors.

In regard to the dumping question and its potential to wreak havoc on the state and local economy, I found these individuals to be fully aware of that unnecessary potential. They certainly recognized the urgency of selling the assets and if necessary their entire thrifts; it is their belief, however, that they could do so in an orderly and value-added manner that would enable the RTC to realize the maximum potential market value for the assets. They reminded me that William L. Seidman, chairman of the FDIC, has gone on record as saying that there would be no fire sales or dumping. Because of their understanding of the dynamics and workings of the commercial real estate marketplace, it soon became obvious that if given the chance and the time they would accomplish their most difficult mission.

As a selling agent you must understand that these people do indeed want to sell their troubled assets. They further need your market input and considered understanding as to what the real and achievable market value actually is today and what it will be in the months to come. They invite your support in bringing qualified principals to the table to negotiate these challenging transactions; however, they will not suffer fools kindly nor should they. Their task is serious, their mission is critical: to get the assets sold and the thrifts back on solid ground.

The critical component of this entire process is whether or not the RTC staffs itself with people who understand deal making. Since the approval process is so extended, structuring and closing makable deals will face obstacles at each approval stopover.

One hopes that all RTC personnel who are part of the decision-making process are cognizant of the current realities in today's challenging markets with regard to values, prices, financing and timeliness.

Part of your challenge will be to stress to all RTC and thrift personnel who will listen the necessity for respecting the fluidity and changing dynamics of commercial real estate deals. You must help these people see the needs and appreciate the motivation and demands of today's sophisticated investment entities. They must understand that these investors *will not* suffer fools kindly either.

CHAPTER
17

Getting Hired: It Just Takes Selling Sense

If I could round up all the people who have tried unsuccessfully to get hired by various commercial real estate brokerage firms, including those who felt that they were personally slighted during the process, their numbers would be legion. Far too often, well-qualified and outstanding people are overlooked by the firms of their choice. Generally, this is because they are unable to get an interview with the hiring manager or if they do, they fail to gain that person's confidence and interest. When the rejection letters arrive thanking the candidates for their interest in a particular company but sweetly saying "thanks but no thanks," the forthcoming personal gloom could cover a desert sun. In many of these cases the prospective candidates just were not prepared to pursue a career in this challenging professional selling arena.

You must remember that people are making the decisions about whether or not you are qualified to be a success in this industry. Like everyone else, these people are not without flaws in judgment, perspective, understanding, tolerance, insight and so on. When you are applying for a selling position with your target brokerage company, the person in charge of hiring may not see the value of bringing you "on board." Never let the opinions of other individuals dissuade you from a goal that you genuinely believe is personally attainable.

After I decided to leave Xerox Corporation and relinquish my responsibilities as a sales manager who was in line or in Xerox personnel parlance "ready now" for a promotion to the next level, it became quickly apparent that I was destined to work for Coldwell Banker. The fact that some former associates managed to achieve great success at Grubb & Ellis, Cushman Wakefield and a host of other brokerage companies meant little to me at the time because I wanted to be a part of what I perceived as the best. Little did I know at the time that *one's success in commercial real estate selling is not primarily determined by whom he or she works for but by the breadth of his or her knowledge, the strength of his or her commitment and resolve and the overall quality and refinement of his or her service to clients.*

Anyway, for me it was to be more blue and white (the corporate colors of Xerox and Coldwell Banker). I certainly did not anticipate any problems in getting hired by CB or anyone else for that matter. I knew that some of my former associates had been hired by CB and I also knew that I could "outsell" them because I always had during our competition at Xerox. Well, the best-laid plans do not always work out immediately and overconfidence can breed failure as I was soon to find out. Because I was living and working in the San Diego area at that time, it seemed like a good idea to make my career transition in the same place. My first interview with the sales manager of the Coldwell Banker office went very well and after we finished he immediately ushered me into the office of the head man, the resident manager. After about 45 minutes of good-natured discussion on a variety of topics ranging from my time as Interfraternity Council Rush Chairman during my college days to the merits of the movie, *Animal House,* and finishing with why I wanted to work in the business for CB, the man in charge told me that he wanted me to meet with one of his top salespeople for whom a new position was opening as trainee/runner. By this time, I was surveying the office layout trying to decide which cubicle I wanted. My only concern was whether or not I would get a covered parking space with my name on the parking block. The very next day I received a call asking me to show up for a morning meeting with my new trainer, or so I thought, to review the available position. We had what seemed to me an interesting and informative discussion. I must say that I was a little concerned when he said he hoped to have his trainee remain in that capacity for two years. Because the normal training period at that time was one year, I think that my response left him somewhat less than exhilarated at my joining the firm. Anyway, that was the last time I ever saw that salesman or my target cubicle and soon thereafter it became next to impossible to get anyone at CB to take my calls. Finally after about one month, the resident manager agreed to see me but informed me that his gut told him not to hire me. That was it. His gut. I will never forget the humiliation that I felt at having just been rejected. My face burned. I was angry. I felt hurt, almost betrayed. Fortunately, I had stayed calm during the "gut rationale" and I told that man before leaving his office for the last time that someday I would be very successful in selling commercial real estate. As God and the fates would have it, I ended up in Phoenix with Coldwell Banker, became a trainee in apartment sales and experienced a great deal of enjoyment with some pretty exciting success.

Even my getting hired in Phoenix did not come without struggle. After taking the mandatory personality and aptitude tests, the results informed the hiring manager that although I possessed the necessary aptitude and skills, I really wanted a career as a writer or theater director.

Of course, I was not told these things initially. But after several successful interviews, my latest phone calls went unreturned. Refusing to accept defeat without a reason, I flew to Phoenix unannounced and uninvited and managed to get a meeting with the sales manager, who reluctantly shared his concerns and gave me the chance to refute the arm's-length analysis of the psychologist who interpreted the subjective test results. Fortunately for all concerned, I overcame the objections and concerns of the management and got a commitment to the only available opening.

The lesson for the reader is never to quit until you have exhausted all of your efforts. Flying over without an invitation was risky and potentially embarrassing to me and to my employer at the time. So follow your vision and refuse to lose or be intimidated.

I am glad to say that today my relationship with the man in San Diego is terrific. His name is Bob Faucett and currently he is the Southwestern Regional Manager for Coldwell Banker. In fact, during a recent speech that I gave to the resident managers and sales managers for his region, I spent the first ten minutes of my talk lampooning Bob for not hiring me. He laughed the hardest of anyone and all went well with the talk.

The lesson that rests in my experience is twofold: First, never take anything for granted in your pursuit of a selling position. I went into my initial CB interviews with all guns loaded, an excellent selling and selling-management background, a great deal of leadership experience in college and professionally, a number of professional honors and awards and total confidence and yet initially this was not enough. I was prepared, however, to relocate to any city with a CB office in a dynamic marketplace, such was the strength of my target result (goal) to work for them. It just so happened that there was an opening in Phoenix and away I went. The second lesson is that if you want to work in the industry badly enough, are willing to let nothing and no one deter you and are willing to gather the necessary experience and preparation, you will succeed. As for placing all of your hopes with one company, that is a decision that you, and you alone, must make. I quickly learned that there are formidable competitive selling agents in every company, large or small, local or national; therefore, look for the environment and fit that seem right for you.

Before deciding if commercial real estate selling really is for you, you first must ask many questions about yourself, the industry, the various types of brokerage (selling and leasing) opportunities and the type and size of the commercial real estate companies themselves and then you must understand where the industry is heading in the decade of the 1990s and beyond.

What Are the Necessary Qualifications?

The one most common trait among all of the successful selling agents whom I have encountered in the business is that each has a pair of lips. The diversity in backgrounds ranges from former pilots and top-gun instructors to former Xerox and IBM sales reps to marketing reps for General Foods, Armstrong Tile and Berry's local nursery. There are former teachers, former lawyers, former airline employees, former professional athletes who did everything from playing on the PGA Tour to playing on championship NBA teams. Many selling agents in the business today were hired right out of college. The huge expansion of many national and regional commercial real estate brokerage firms during the early and mid-1980s established a trend that formerly was unknown in the business: hiring people either without prior real estate knowledge or with little or no actual selling experience.

The new hiring attitudes also gave new opportunity to women with and without experience and with and without college degrees. The mix of these diverse talents has not been without its client and management challenges; in each of these categories, however, some wonderful successes and long-term professional careers have been established. Some colossal failures also have taken a large toll in terms of employee morale and discipline, client-relationship depression and malfeasance in the marketplace. The industry has survived, however, and as the demands of the 1990s grow, the strong will continue to survive and thrive.

Following are the types of qualifications that I believe will contribute significantly to someone's selling success in the commercial real estate business. These are based strictly on my opinions after spending ten years in the trenches:

1. Previous professional career experience in the fields of selling and/or marketing with a strong track record of success, i.e., office products, advertising sales, public relations, pharmaceutical supplies sales, etc.;
2. Previous professional career experience in which the retainment and growth of client relationships are critical to one's success, i.e., law, advertising, insurance, etc.;
3. A willingness and enthusiasm for cold calling and confronting difficult personalities;
4. A thirst for knowledge and excellence;
5. Intensity and focus;
6. Excellent verbal and presentation skills;
7. Excellent listening skills, sensitivity to others and empathy;

8. A firm grasp of personal and professional goals;
9. A willingness and desire to be active in professional organizations and community activities such as Junior Achievement, Big Brothers, United Way, Certified Commercial Investment Member (CCIM) classes, local economic-development groups, etc.;
10. Excellent writing skills;
11. The willingness to work with and understand the numbers regarding pro forma considerations, value interpretations and relevant investment considerations;
12. An understanding of the importance of effective time-management skills and the discipline to use these skills;
13. A desire and willingness to give back to your clients and the organization;
14. An interest in the role of financing and various lending institutions and entities that bring the deal opportunity to fruition;
15. An interest in property management from the perspective of both tenant and landlord;
16. A desire to understand the roles of the appraiser, consultant, accountant, title officer and real estate lawyer and the willingness to work with each;
17. An interest in observing everything of significance that influences and trends the market and all its segments; and last but certainly first,
18. A tremendous love for the business and an equally vast belief in your abilities to be able to "make it happen."

What about Experience?

As I said earlier, professional experience in selling or a knowledge of commercial real estate at some level is almost mandatory. However, there are large and small companies that will give a young or inexperienced person an opportunity. Some will even provide a limited amount of training and development. Your ability to know why you want to enter the arena and your ability to articulate what it takes and how you stack up will help in the hiring process.

I strongly recommend to anyone without professional selling experience to seek a company with excellent training and then to learn to sell. Obviously, I believe if you can understand and implement Big Bang Selling in its entirety, you can make it without prior selling success. If, however, when you enter the business, you understand the selling process, time management, the peaks and valleys of emotion, the competitive nature of a sales organization, how to use the telephone and how to create and deliver a presentation, and you have developed a keen eye for what is going on in the marketplace, then you will have a giant head start.

Should You Choose a Large or a Small Company?

As I said earlier and cannot emphasize enough, where you work in the long run is of little consequence. The advantage of working for a large well-known organization is primarily that the people who work there will be your peers and associates. Perhaps the training might be a bit better as well. One major reason for being a part of an outstanding large company is the amount of deal opportunity that is generated and to which you can be exposed. The energy that exists in a large company can be quite exciting if the group is positive and well motivated.

Try to determine the type of people and the type of client relationships that are involved in your target companies. Are the selling agents respected in the real estate community? What is the reputation of the organization? Remember, just because a company is national in scope does not ensure a quality-run local organization. Many variables in hiring, management, market penetration and client focus can affect a company's performance.

The principals with whom you will want to establish long-term relationships really care little where you work. They are more interested in whether your company is part of the fabric of the community. Do your people know what is going on and why? Are the agents the best and the hardest working? And these principals care most about **representation, results** and **responsibility!**

Numerous local companies with only one location are some of the finest because their people are recognized as a significant part of the business community and their clients enjoy doing business with them. Indeed, they typically employ some of the finest and most-experienced selling agents for they tend to be quite selective in whom they hire.

The companies that are regional in nature also offer many fine opportunities. Some specialize as organizations in either industrial, office or retail segments. Some strictly deal with tenant representations, while others act as development entities and lease their own projects. In fact, many developers prefer to employ their own leasing or selling staff and to avoid the brokerage community in large part or altogether. Your options are remarkably broad. Just as when you decide what client relationships to pursue, do the same with the companies with whom you would like to work. *A well-directed rifle shot will find the heart of a target in the majority of cases and will not cause nearly the amount of damage of a shotgun approach.*

What Specialty Should You Choose?

In many companies the choice may not be yours. If, however, prior to beginning the interview process you take the necessary time to understand at least the broad framework of specialties and the subspecialties of product type, market segment, location in segment, tenant profiles, industry or company uses, current amount of development on line or being planned, existing base of square footage by type and occupancy levels and why certain types of businesses and people are located where they are, then you might have a pretty good story to share with the person considering you for employment. After you conduct this research, drive around the different types of projects; get a feel for the clients, the customers, the tenants, etc.; and identify the top-selling producers at your target companies and schedule a lunch meeting to discuss their views on getting hired and the market in general.

The majority of specialties offer the primary opportunity to lease space. In the specialties of land, apartments and investment sales you will not receive this opportunity. Many agents feel that conducting small lease transactions is too time consuming; however, the base of knowledge that can be gained throughout the entire lease-up process is invaluable and will provide the keys to how investment sales work, how development deals are made and how lenders qualify target loans and in general will let the agent keep his or her finger on the pulse of the community.

How Do You Get Started and, More Important, How Do You Get Hired?

The larger national brokerage companies probably receive 100 to 200 applications per month per office for selling-agent positions. Because the turnover rates of their selling agents tend to be quite low, you can understand why it may be very difficult to get a position. To add to this problem, many people are hired because of their friendships with current employees and/or recommendations from those who are influential with current management. Generally, this works well for these companies because in most cases talented people want to surround themselves with other talented people. This can pose a real danger to the organization, however, because it may become too inbred and its types of personalities and talent base may become too similar. If you do not have such an advantage, create one of your own. Frankly explain to the hiring manager why you can fit in with his or her people, but make sure you stress how you can bring in new talents and fresh perspectives to gear up the overall professionalism and performance in the company.

Take the time to identify ten major client relationships with your target firm. Contact each client and ask to meet with the lead principal or managing partner. Tell him or her of your interest and qualifications and solicit his or her ideas and support. Be courteous and appreciative. If all goes well, ask if he or she would make a telephone call on your behalf. You will find that many successful people in the business are quite understanding of your challenge in getting started and are more than willing to help.

How Long Does It Take To Get Hired?

The process will vary based on the current need to fill a position and the candidates with commitments in the pipeline. Do not be discouraged if others have commitments yet are still waiting for openings. You can demonstrate your competence through ongoing written and verbal communication with the hiring managers. The hiring process generally will begin with a screening of your résumé and application. This may occur prior to your face-to-face interview or during the meeting. Your greatest challenge might be in getting the appointment; therefore, you must measure how you use the telephone when trying to get an appointment. If you receive no response, camp out in the office until the appropriate manager either can see you or is willing to commit to an appointment.

The screening interview will be handled by either a sales manager or a senior selling agent. You must be crisply dressed in business attire (take a look around the office to determine the company's dress code) and must produce support documents (résumé, recommendations and interview outline). You must pre-plan your questions on the company, the clients, the deals, the commission opportunities, the training and the standards of performance and as many relevant topics as you can think of. Take notes and listen fully before responding to questions. If you do not understand a question, ask for clarification. Some managers will be more interested in your current sports pursuits than in your past business success so make sure your answers are appropriate. This type of manager may feel that he or she can judge talent based strictly on one's interests. Do whatever works, I guess, but be prepared and be honest.

It always is helpful to ask the manager about his or her thoughts on the business, his or her background, deals and clients and how he or she would approach getting hired if in your position.

Ask for feedback and confirmation during the interview without being overbearing or pushy. Show your enthusiasm for the job and let the manager know of your commitment to succeed. Afterward, follow up with a typewritten letter summarizing the content and results of the meeting. If you and the manager have agreed on a follow-up action, then confirm it. If you have not yet received a follow-up meeting commitment, then you must continue to monitor the manager's attitudes and opinions. Try to get a follow-up meeting. Send the manager something relevant about the market or about one of his or her interests that might have been discussed during the interview process.

The second or follow-up interview will likely take place with additional managers of various authority. You may have to interview with several people of equal rank prior to seeing the final authority. Do your best to build relationships and demonstrate your interests and desire with meaningful respect. *Refuse to be intimidated or taken lightly.* If your interviews are without serious content and you are rejected, try to set up a meeting to discover why.

If you get past this process, you might be asked to take an aptitude and/or personality test that highlights some basic skills in math, English, logic, reasoning and so on. Do not let the test intimidate you. I realize that it may have been years since you had to figure out a square root, but taking the test will not be that bad. Companies use personality tests to determine applicants' predicted selling capabilities and success. Proponents of these tests claim that they can determine whether or not someone really wants to sell and has the interpersonal strengths to do so effectively. If you end up rejected because of a questionable test score, do your best to find out what areas hurt you. (Remember my experience.) I know of selling agents who failed miserably on these tests yet still were hired and went on to achieve great success.

At Least It's Easier than Proposing Marriage: Some Tips for Successful Interviews

Following are some suggestions for successfully completing hiring interviews:

1. Be on time.
2. Be prepared physically and mentally; look sharp and speak clearly and effectively.

3. Be respectful and courteous.
4. Ask meaningful questions and give thoughtful answers.
5. State your goals and target results within one year, three years, five years and beyond.
6. Know why you want to sell commercial real estate (not because you like people, please).
7. Take notes and summarize; ask for feedback and gain support for your ideas.
8. Ask your interviewer about his or her thoughts on the business.
9. Ask for a job at the end of the meeting; it's no secret why you are there, so let the manager know you care.
10. Follow up with creative letters and packages.
11. Refuse to give up until all alternatives are exhausted.

Good luck, good selling and remember, refuse to lose.

CHAPTER
18

New Issues, New Challenges, New Rewards— Big Bang Selling in the 1990s

As this book goes to press early in 1990, a variety of new challenges already are at work to greet the commercial real estate selling agents and brokers of the 1990s. Two of the biggest challenges will be the broker- and agent-liability issues, namely the risks of dual agency and the necessity of complete disclosure relating to all matters of toxic waste, ground-water contamination and asbestos infestation. Various rulings in federal and state courts have demonstrated that the commercial real estate broker and his or her selling agents will have to become well schooled in the particular laws, regulations and policies of their individual states concerning these critical issues.

The advent of increased exposure and legal liability in these areas will make it mandatory for the broker and/or agent to ensure that he or she has taken every step possible to inform all the parties to any deal opportunity or transaction of all relevant matters concerning the potential deal. The broker/agent must be able to demonstrate that he or she has taken every reasonable and prudent step to ensure full disclosure of all pertinent and material facts.

But My Company Always Has Represented Both Sides

Without question, many brokerage companies, individual brokers and their selling agents have on many occasions worked both sides of a commercial real estate deal. In fact, I would venture to guess that in the majority of these cases there was full disclosure about the nature of the legal representation and that this was properly acknowledged. In other cases, selling agents probably felt in earnest that they actually were representing the noncommission-paying side of the transaction even in those cases where written consent was not obtained by all parties. In their minds and actions, they had made both sides of the deal aware of who they were representing; however, they did not realize how critical it was to acknowledge this issue in writing. Although the practice of representing both sides of any deal opportunity is thorny at best and contrary to some state and local real estate regulation at worst, the fact remains that this practice occurs quite frequently. When the selling agent secures a much-sought-after listing from a client relationship, he or she does so in part because of his or her ability to sell or lease the deal opportunity. The agent knows who to take the potential deal or deals to in order to bring in the right type of tenants or buyers. When the selling agent acts to negotiate the deal opportunity on behalf of both principals, however, he or she can be construed as acting illegally or in violation of his or her fiduciary responsibility. Remember that the fiduciary responsibility of the broker and the agent rests with the principal who is paying the commission or who has acknowledged such representation in writing. If a selling agent acts on behalf of a particular buyer or tenant, he or she must ensure that all parties to the transaction are informed of this and acknowledge it in writing. In today's market with its peaks of success and valleys of foreclosure, many distressed principals are looking for a means to recover lost venture dollars and lost opportunity costs that went down the drain with deals that did not work out. Regardless of the intent of the broker or the selling agent in these cases of dual agency, the courts in some cases are ruling that it is the absolute responsibility of the broker and agent to ensure that all sides of representation are properly acknowledged in writing by all relevant principals and parties. In cases where this was not properly executed or was never mentioned, the potential for the broker and selling agent to be sued never has been higher. Simply stated, in some cases those disgruntled or ill-informed parties are entitled to monetary recourse on grounds of misrepresentation from those brokers and in some cases their selling agents.

The lesson for any broker or selling agent today is to absolutely ensure that in every deal opportunity you obtain full consent and acknowledgment of all principal understanding as it relates to all forms of brokerage representation and agency. In those cases where you are representing the nonpaying commission side of the deal opportunity, make sure that all sides know on whose behalf you are working to create the best deal. If you have been acting in a dual-agency capacity without problems and without written acknowledgment, immediately change your procedure. This could very likely become one of the major areas of litigation in the next decade so by all means protect yourself. (For a more detailed explanation of the laws and definitions of agency, dual agency and agent, please refer to John W. Reilly's *The Language of Real Estate*, published by Real Estate Education Company, Chicago, Illinois.)

Sure I Support Greenpeace, but What's That Got To Do with My Deal Opportunities?

One of your major responsibilities as a selling agent during the last decade of this century is to take every measure possible to ensure that all principals are aware of their responsibilities toward the deal opportunity and its parties in all issues concerning environmental matters. These matters range from buildings contaminated with asbestos to sites contaminated with various forms of toxic waste. At the very least, you should know that every credible lender will want to know the full extent of the existence of all negative environmental issues concerning any particular project for which he or she is considering making a loan. In fact, if it cannot be determined that these issues are not threats or liabilities or that they cannot be adequately repaired or cleaned up, then the chances are almost certain that the lender will withdraw the loan commitment and the deal opportunity will die a painful death. Therefore, you cannot leave this critical issue and responsibility solely in the hands of your clients/principals. You must take a proactive position in the investigation of these matters and document your involvement while doing so. Problems in these areas usually are viewed by many selling agents as uncontrollable deal breakers; it is my view, however, that if these issues are identified and disclosed early in the deal-opportunity development cycle, then they often can be repaired and overcome. Thus when you are meeting with owners whose properties or projects might be faced with negative environmental issues, take an aggressive role to ensure that everything possible is done to understand the extent of the problem and find the appropriate solutions. Do not make the mistake of the real estate ostrich by burying your head in the sand and hoping that the problem miraculously will go away.

If you are representing a buyer, you must make him or her realize that, although many existing laws impose strict liability on landowners and other property owners, it is imperative that the buyer make "all appropriate inquiry into the previous ownership and use of the property consistent with good commercial or customary practice." You must encourage your buyer to employ an independent engineer to conduct building or soil studies to determine the existence of hazardous-related materials and you must question the seller about his or her material knowledge of all pertinent environmental facts. The existence of these substances does not always mean that your deal opportunity will not close; however, you must make every effort to ensure that all parties are involved in rectifying the problems to move the deal opportunity forward.

You Can Be Unique

Your willingness to take an active and responsible role in recognizing the urgency and importance of such critical issues as dual agency and environmental hazards will demonstrate to all parties in any deal opportunity that you are in fact the most professional selling agent or broker in your marketplace and specialty. The fact that you go the extra mile to disclose to the principals all relevant facts and material issues will help you build both quality client relationships and your professional reputation. This conduct will put you in a position of acting in total concert with the *integrity* tenet of Big Bang Selling and will further solidify your *purpose* of rendering *preeminent client service*.

Strategies for Thriving in the Next Decade

The selling agents and brokers who will survive and prosper in the next decade will be the ones who are willing to take very broad and very finite perspectives on the commercial real industry in whole and in part. You must understand the simple and complex client relationships, the principal deal makers and their motivations, the creation and evolution of deal opportunities and closed deals, both in the international and domestic arenas and in your local markets and their segments. Selling success in the 1990s will be achieved by understanding the attractiveness and influences of all forms of commercial real estate, their interaction with U.S. and international economic growth, and the influences of the myriad of government monetary and trade policies that greatly support or detract from the overall health and vitality of this great industry.

Critical strategies for you to achieve your target results and *purpose* in the next decade will come through systematically understanding and analyzing your market share as well as your client-relationship deal-penetration levels. You must know how many and what types of deals and deal opportunities exist within your specialty and within your niches of focus. You must understand their price/value relationships and the principal motivations behind their being created and closed, as well as their impact on the marketplace generally and on the segment specifically. After you identify those active principals, you must take the necessary steps to develop those client relationships that you can best personally and professionally support, nurture and control. You must understand the total potential that exists in each of these target client relationships to determine your level of client penetration. In other words, how many actual and potential deals are you personally involved with or closing out of the total deals that the client relationship is creating and closing?

Earlier in this book, I mentioned that it is important to see yourself as your own individual sales or selling manager. One of your most important strategies will be to conduct, on an ongoing and predesignated basis, a formal sales-operations review for yourself and your client relationships. To effectively monitor your progress and results you must establish a format and time to review all your strategies and activities in every crucial area of your business to measure your overall or macro progress toward your *purpose* and target results. When conducting your own sales-operations review you should look at each area of Big Bang Selling from knowledge and client relationships to activities and selling skills to determine just how effective you are in your day-to-day and month-to-month activities. You should conduct these reviews at least once a quarter and more effectively once a month. Learn to break down your strategies and target results to ensure that the manner in which you are spending your time will produce the results that you desire. This is the ultimate time to use the process of **review, reflect** and **revise** to stay on track and to improve your pace and results.

In the development of the client relationship, this review is without question one of the most important things that you can do to build the principal's trust, confidence and faith in you. This is the time to inform the principal about the nature of your activities in the development of particular deal opportunities to meet his or her requirements. Whether in the case of the listing that you are representing for him or her or simply in some component of a request for information on the marketplace, take the time to professionally present in a review format exactly the steps that you are taking to succeed. In some cases this review should be presented on a weekly basis to update lease or sale activity; in the case of the overall relationship, it should be performed at least twice a year. Often the client/principal may avoid telling you directly that he or she is unhappy with your efforts as well as your results and thus you may be replaced by another agent. Therefore, develop a review format that not only discusses and provides information on your representation results but invites the client/principal to give you direction, constructive criticism and advice on how you can provide better service and thus satisfy his or her requirements.

Your ability to manage your selling calendar to maximize your time in face-to-face contact with these clients/principals then will enable you to effectively create, alter and revise the implementation and results of any particular selling strategy. Your overall **belief** in the pursuit of developing **the most genuine voice in deal making** will result directly from your willingness to embrace and implement Big Bang Selling. For when you genuinely act in the interests of your client relationships first and foremost, everything else, from target results to all forms of large and small *purpose*, will come to you beyond all of your personal and professional expectations. Good selling and God bless you!

APPENDIX

1

Explode into the Big Bang Theory of Professional Selling Excellence

Your immediate challenge is to implement the elements of "The Big Bang Theory of Professional Selling Excellence" in the following important areas.

Develop and maintain both macro and micro points of view as they relate to your selling strategies and to your individual road map for success.

Commit to structuring your day in the following manner whenever possible:

8:00–9:30 a.m.: Cold calls.

9:45–11:45 a.m.: Calls by appointment.

11:46–12:45 p.m.: Follow-up telephone calls, lunch and strategic plans regarding afternoon calls and activities.

1:00–2:00 p.m.: Cold calls.

2:15–3:45 p.m.: Calls by appointment.

4:00–6:00 p.m.: Follow-up telephone calls, preparation of documents, creation and practice of presentations, and appropriate research.

Remember that cold calls should be focused from the standpoints of who you call on to what you say at various stages when you are in the door.

Select your industries and then prioritize the companies or firms within those industries on which to call.

After you make the initial calls, you then will have those potential client relationships with which to fill your projected "calls by appointment" areas in your daily calendar.

Integrate the three steps to positive relationship building: *acknowledgment, respect* and *recognition.*

When calling on a client/principal, you should show the person at the front desk the same respect, acknowledgment and recognition as you show the CEO of the company.

Remember the elements and value of the *review, reflect* and *revise* concept.

It's important to recall the power that you will realize by gaining expertise in the knowledge of specific industries and their particular real estate needs as well as the strength that will come to your relationships by understanding the individual companies and their principals.

Get on top of all major deals happening within your marketplace, within your client's business and within the companies in your specialty. Find out:

1. What are the motivations behind the deal?
2. Who made the decisions?
3. What was driving those decisions?
4. Where were those antecedents set in motion?
5. When and why did it happen?
6. How was it done and by whom?

To gain expertise within a market segment or industry, develop a specific market profile. Determine the:

1. Number of companies or firms,
2. Type of products or services rendered,
3. Specialties within the industry,
4. Major customers/clients by specific company,
5. Financing or banking relationships,

6. Legal relationships,
7. Specific profiles of the industry's and the companies' clients,
8. Types of existing facilities,
9. Likes and dislikes of present facilities,
10. Decision-making criteria for existing location or relocation,
11. Deal structures for the past 12 months by market segment,
12. Number of deals by company during past 12 months with specific deal profile
13. Number of deals by industry during past 12 months with emphasis on economic factors and locations chosen.
14. Geographic areas or existing locations for each profiled company,
15. Competitive challenges from other industries,
16. Characteristics of the existing space/building/tenant improvements that are unique to that firm and why,
17. Revenues by company,
18. Number of employees by company,
19. Standing within their industry,
20. Current real estate representation and why, and
21. National/regional/local political/socioeconomic influences.

Remember that to establish new relationships you must know more than just when the client's lease expires, how many square feet he or she has and where he or she is looking.

You must establish a base of interest in the client, in the client's business and in the client's industry that will set you apart from your competition.

Try to be involved (worst case) in every decision regarding opportunities in your specialty.

Remember the value of activity: number of calls; number of meetings; number of presentations; number of trips to showings; number of social meetings; number of phone calls; number of cold calls; and the quality thereof.

In summary, develop a road map. Ask "Do I know more about this deal than anyone," "Did I do everything possible to make it happen" and "Did I ask the "What if?" question?"

Employ the who, what, where, when, why and how of deal making.

Ask "Am I a heat-seeking missile toward deal opportunity?" Then define your **purpose** from why you are in the commercial real estate business to why you are making the next sales call.

Remember, a strong sense of *purpose* will enable you to persevere and to overcome any obstacles. Next enjoin **knowledge, relationships, communication, creativity, competitive spirit, focus, integrity, attitude** and **commitment** to form a block of **belief** that always will give your efforts that essence of winning.

Finally, surround these with a powerful selling **process** that is qualitative and quantitative in approach and context. Remember the cookie dough theory.

The time is now, the walrus said, to think of many things:

1. The new decade of the 1990s,
2. Your market and client relationships,
3. The number of new deal opportunities,
4. Your depth of knowledge and skills,
5. Your spirit and commitment,
6. Your specific earning goals,
7. Your specific career goals,
8. Your peer and industry relationships,
9. Balancing your goals throughout your life,
10. Why you are the best,
11. Why you are the best,
12. Why you are the best.

APPENDIX

2

The Big Bang Selling Agent 30-Day and Forward-Action Plan

Week One:

Organize cubicle per Chapter 8, Setting Up for Selling.

Pull all available source material on specialty and review, organize and summarize and keep at hand.

Review available data on current market by all specialties to get a broad perspective of market.

Identify all weekly and monthly newsletters, magazines and periodicals relating to your specialty and overall market and subscribe or put your name on distribution list.

Meet with administrative manager to review all support expectations and procedures.

Meet with sales manager and/or resident manager/owner to review their game plan for your development and progress.

Identify top performers by specialty and set up meetings for breakfast, lunch or in the office to initiate relationships.

Identify and review all company support mechanisms that will further your selling efforts.

Prepare an outline for personal introduction of you and your professional qualifications for prospective client and support relationships.

Investigate the type of leave-behind packages (if any) that other selling agents in your office are using. If the content and format are well done, ask the agents for their support and permission to use a similar approach. If denied, create your own with input from your management team.

Identify and study current market and client strategies to gain the broad picture and approach.

Identify those active client relationships that your office currently is not working. Initially do this through questioning your associates and managers.

Identify concentration within market segments of your specialty by project/product location and begin to organize information on aerials.

Investigate past closed-deal structures completed within your specialty and review in-house deal opportunities, especially listings within your specialty.

Prepare a compilation and summary of closed deals in your specialty over the preceding 12-month period that were transacted by your associates if data is available.

Week Two:

Continue all uncompleted activities from week one.

Identify and visit all listings and known deal opportunities within your specialty by market segment.

Identify and begin to visit all recently closed deals to assess price/value and market relationships by specialty.

Identify municipal planning staffs and establish appointments to ascertain attitudes toward growth, employment, development, developers, etc.

Identify and drive through most active market segments for closed and proposed deals by product type within specialty.

Review total base of existing projects and square footage, units, land, etc., to begin measuring existing absorption, projects in the pipeline and ability of the market segment to absorb new activity.

Week Three:

Continue target activities from week two.

Begin to focus on those areas or segments where there seems to be the most activity or most potential.

Determine what is driving the activity in terms of company or firm movements, job growth, speculative development, user demand, etc.

Begin to identify the developers and the tenants (by industry type and company profile) who are most active.

Begin to choose the market segments and the type of projects within your specialty with which you would like to work.

Identify ownership of projects within specialty by quality, location, market appeal, occupancy, tenant profiles, etc.

Outline and develop your initial presentation formats for meeting with principals and practice its execution and delivery.

Week Four:

Continue target activities from week three.

Segment ownerships and research telephone numbers and locations.

Contact owners, developers, tenants, etc., with whom you would like to meet.

Determine key principals.

Establish meetings with key principals.

Cold call target owners, developers and tenants if you are unable to secure appointments.

Complete your professional qualification and company leave-behind package.

Review your outline of what to say after "Hello" (in other words, once you are in the door, what to say and do).

Begin to establish your micro and macro target results and never take your eye off the Big Bang Selling **purpose.**

Set an income goal, deal goal, deal-opportunity goal, client-relationship goal, number-of-calls-per-day goal, number-of-presentations-for-commitments goal and goals to gain knowledge and skills in all areas. Make sure that when you add in a realistic success ratio that your numbers do in fact balance and will yield your projected results.

What To Do after the First Month?

Secure your mission mentality, continue to study your market specialty by the products and people who inhabit it, refine your presentations and focus on developing client relationships.

After first month:
Drive and travel to review your specialty's various modes.
Begin to understand value in terms of comparable deals.
Learn why the deals are being done.
Determine who is doing the deals.
Determine what the deal structures are giving to each side and why.
Begin to identify all key principals within your specialty.
Begin to identify key lenders and lawyers within your specialty and get to know them.
Schedule at least four predetermined meetings per day with at least three of these meetings with principals on either the buy or sell, lessee or landlord side of deal making.
Spend the balance of your time traveling and studying your specialty and the market segments.
Work in the field between 9:00 a.m. and 4:00 p.m. every day.
Schedule meetings and return telephone calls while out in the field or before 9:00 a.m. and after 4:00 p.m.
Do all in-office letter writing, research, meeting attendance, administrative functions and so on before 9:00 a.m. and after 4:00 p.m.
Review the number of meetings and the number of deal opportunities that you control and/or are developing each week.
Analyze the content and quality of your professional presentations as well as your ability to get in the door, be heard and gain commitments.
Be open and honest with everyone that you deal with and do not try to avoid any issue with which you are not familiar.
Cooperate with other agents and brokers but protect your special strategies and client relationships.

APPENDIX
3

What Do You Say after You Say "Hello"?

Remember not to personalize seemingly aloof or disinterested attitudes.

You must use different approaches for different types of calls; your initial approach, however, always should be to let the client/principal and members of the organization know that you want to investigate a proper foundation for doing business together.

Your challenge is to motivate the client/principal to spend time with you so if you sound like every other broker and agent (i.e., "when does your lease expire?"), and if you do not try some other method, chances are you never will become aware of those deal opportunities that await you.

Always begin by asking the potential client about himself or herself, his or her role in the company, the condition of the company, its products, its clients/customers, its competitors, its challenges, its future, its past and its present. Determine the grand vision of the client and his or her company. Determine how he or she sees the industry.

Begin to weave into the presentation the significant elements of your special market focus and knowledge. Share what is happening in the real estate market and how it applies to the client. Explain your perception of trends in the market, actual deals made, motivations behind those deals, etc. Share relevant thoughts about his or her business or industry that you have discovered and ask for verification. Question the client about subsidiary departments and decision makers and their needs in regard to all commercial real estate requirements.

Learn about their families, education, childhood, clubs, interests and honors and those of their associates and peers. Determine where you can build alliances that will substantiate your role as their voice of professional real estate counsel.

Always be grateful for the opportunities that the client is sharing.

Stand your ground on tough points when you know it is in the best interests of the client and the deal opportunity. Refuse to be intimidated. *If you know more about your deal opportunity and the purpose behind any particular meeting than anyone else, you never will be intimidated!*

Always leave the meeting with a commitment for a follow-up action or meeting of some kind that will further the development of the client relationships and/or the deal opportunity.

Selling Business Plan Format and Operations Review

The following items are needed to implement a successful deal-opportunity plan of action:

1. Three-ringed binder,
2. Dividers by category,
3. 90/180-day working time frame,
4. Aerials/photographs by building by segment,
5. Current listings,
6. Current listings by competitor,
7. Monthly deal summary by market segment or building,
8. Current client list by industry by segment,

9. Competitive client list by industry by segment,
10. Target clients by month,
11. Top ten deal opportunities by client by segment,
12. Target activities for month, quarter, and full year,
13. Target skill improvement areas,
14. Target knowledge improvement areas,
15. Market segment profile: tenants, products, buildings, industries and
16. Outline of specific presentation elements.

APPENDIX
4

The Big Bang Selling
Workbook

The purpose of this working notebook is to provide a method for an ongoing process of *review, reflection* and *revision.*

You must maintain constant visual contact with your existing and prospective client relationships and the deal opportunities that they represent.

Rather than using deal files, old messages, a legal pad or your memory to keep track of current deal opportunities (under development or creation, qualification, out for signature, escrow, contract, etc.), use the selling working notebook as a foundation from which to plan your days, weeks and months.

This working notebook will enable you to recognize the various stages in which your client relationships exist. Furthermore, it will provide you with an up-to-date profile of the status and relative stages of your active deal opportunities.

The more you focus on a given set of client relationships and the specific current and future deal opportunities that they represent, the more clearly you will understand the merits of your particular concentration on these clients and these deal opportunities.

Because deal-opportunity development involves many steps or building blocks, you must monitor on a daily basis the progress that you are making with specific deal opportunities.

Client relationships should be reviewed bimonthly to ensure appropriate implementation of specific strategies to further the relationships.

The working selling notebook also will serve as a positive frame of reference to help prepare critical and ongoing client operations' reviews regarding deal-opportunity progress and specific broker actions.

Divider Areas/Topics

Industry Profile

Description of products and services by various types
Gross revenues of local firms, regional and national
Current fiscal and overall business health and outlook
Specific types of companies/firms within industry
Top 25 companies
Major competitive industries
Significant landmarks within industry
Significant players within industry
Types and modes of real estate holdings
Fee versus leasehold
Centralized or decentralized facilities and decision making
Approximate number of real estate deals made annually
Approximate commission dollars generated by these deals

Company or Firm Profile

Standing or rank in industry
Specific types of products or services
Annual revenues
Customer/client profile
Major competitors

Number of employees
Type of ownership
Company/firm officers or partners
Number of locations
Real estate held and how
Profile of locations, tenant improvements, etc.
Square footage by location
Decision-making criteria and process
Lease or ownership structure
Decision-maker and support-staff data
Real estate deals closed during past 12 months
Structure or model of deal structure
Current financing relationships
Real estate needs next 24 to 36 months
Opportunity for new firm creations (potential new clients)
Current real estate brokerage relationships
Projected deal opportunities balance 1989–1990
Current deal opportunities in progress
Potential deal opportunities and requirements
Competitive broker deal opportunities
Professional/personal background of principals
Professional/personal background of support staff

Deal Opportunities by Client Relationship

Representation and requirement
Stage or block of development
Call history
Showings
Presentations by type and date
Market segment focus
Potential commission dollars
Proposed close date and lease execution
Next stage of deal opportunity
Decision maker and criteria
Time frames of client
Competitive presence
Call/contact history

Summary of Active Deal Opportunities/Closed Deals Year to Date

Deal Opportunities at a Glance

Requirement
Company/firm
Decision maker
Secretary
Telephone number
Last contact
Type of contact
Next contact
Type of contact
Commission dollars
Personal split

Industry Profile

1. Industry selected: _____

2. Description of products and/or services: _____

_____

_____

_____

3. Description of clientele or customers: _____

_____

_____

_____

4. Gross revenues of local industry elements: _____

_____

5. Gross revenues of national industry: _____

6. Current fiscal and overall business health and outlook: ___

_____

_____

_____

7. Specific types of companies/firms within industry: _____

_____

_____

_____

8. Top 25 companies within industry by gross sales, number of employees, number of locations, square footage and activity in marketplace:

1. _____	14. _____
2. _____	15. _____
3. _____	16. _____
4. _____	17. _____
5. _____	18. _____
6. _____	19. _____
7. _____	20. _____
8. _____	21. _____
9. _____	22. _____
10. _____	23. _____
11. _____	24. _____
12. _____	25. _____
13. _____	

9. Major competitive industries: _____

_____

_____

10. Top five companies in competitive industries:

1. _____   1. _____
2. _____   2. _____
3. _____   3. _____
4. _____   4. _____
5. _____   5. _____

11. Significant landmarks within industry: _____

_____

_____

_____

12. Significant people (by company and title) in industry: _____

_____

_____

_____

13. Typical types of real estate holdings (fee versus leasehold, multiple facilities or locations, preferred locations, etc.): _____

_____

_____

_____

14. Approximate number of real estate deal opportunities closed within past 12 months: _____

_____

15. Approximate total commission dollars generated from those closed deal opportunities: _____

Selling Agent Selling Update Format

Office specialist
Major industry focus:

1. _____

2. _____

3. _____

Top 30 (ten per industry) client relationships:

Industry: _____

	Company	Principal	Telephone
1.			
2.			
3.			
4.			
5.			
6.			
7.			
8.			
9.			
10.			

Deal opportunities in development:

    Tenant: _____

    Requirement: _____

    Time frame: _____

    Lease expiration: _____

Current status: _____

_____

Gross commission: _____

Broker split: _____

Agent split: _____

Proposed execution date representation: _____

Proposed lease execution: _____

Purpose and next contact date: _____

_____

Selling Agent Deal Opportunity Summary
90-Day Outlook

	Client Relationship	Requirement	Commission	Date
1.				
2.				
3.				
4.				
5.				
6.				
7.				
8.				
9.				
10.				
11.				
12.				
13.				
14.				

15. _____

16. _____

17. _____

18. _____

19. _____

20. _____

Specific partner-needed assistance: _____

Client Relationship Profile

Company/firm name: _____

Standing or rank in industry: _____

Specific types of products or services: _____

Annual revenues: _____

Number of employees: _____

Net earnings: _____

Stock-price profile (past 12 months): _____

Type of ownership: _____

Names of critical principals, titles and responsibilities, direct telephone numbers:

Name/Title	Duties	Telephone Number

Names of key secretaries and receptionist: _____

_____

_____

Name of primary contact: _____

Professional background: _____

Family/personal information: _____

Company/firm customer/client profile: _____

Major competitors of company/firm: _____

Number of locations by city, state, building address: _____

Current real estate held and/or leased by square footage, by city, by state, by building: _____

Top five elements of decision-making criteria for real estate needs and considerations: _____

Description of decision-making process (including specific individuals) regarding the fulfillment of real estate needs: _____

Names of key support-staff personnel with personal backgrounds: _____

Real estate deal opportunities closed during past 12 months by location, square footage, deal structure, deal price, competitive brokerage presence and company/firm motivation: _____

Current professional associations and relationships (lenders, lawyers, architects, engineers, space planners, real estate brokers, etc.): _____

Projected real estate requirements for next 12 months: _____

Projected real estate requirements for next 24 to 36 months: __

Motivations/influences behind these requirements: _____

Specific existing lease data (location, square footage, user/department, expiration date, reason for being there): _____

Future prospects for expansion, relocation or reduction in space requirement: _____

Who brokered: _____

Are they still a factor: _____

Specific existing lease data (location, square footage, user/department, expiration date, reason for being there): _____

Deal Opportunities by Client Relationship

Company/firm: _____

Representation/position: _____

Decision maker and motivation: _____

_____

Requirement/time frames: _____

_____

Stage or block of opportunity development: _____

_____

Call history: _____

_____

Presentations by type and date: _____

_____

Market segment focus: _____

_____

Potential commission dollars (gross and net to you): _____

_____

Projected close date, lease execution, move-in date: _____

_____

Summary of Active and Closed Deals

Company/firm: _____

Requirement: _____

Decision maker/secretary: _____

Telephone numbers: _____

Commission dollars gross and your split: _____

Last contact/type: _____

Next contact/type: _____

Projected close date and payday: _____

A P P E N D I X

5

Sample Letters

Follow-up Letter to First Meeting

January 2, 1990

Mr. Robert B. Farmer
President
Young and Creative Development
300 La Jolla Boulevard
San Diego, California 92110

Dear Mr. Farmer:

It was a pleasure to speak with you today concerning the history of your company, your investment and development goals for 1990 and your specific methods for formulating opportunities. Although you indicated you were satisfied with your current brokerage arrangements and representation, I want you to know that I am committed to outworking my competition in regard to creating and targeting specific deal opportunities for your organization.

As mentioned during our meeting, it is my hope and intention to develop a positive working relationship with you and your subordinates by submitting only those deal opportunities that are relevant to your requirements. Furthermore, I would like to remind you that any specific market data that I can share that might support your efforts will be a part of my services during the course of our relationship. It is my belief that my awareness of the current state of the market is more than competitive with your current brokerage services and it would be my hope that you will take advantage of this opportunity to further your knowledge base.

Pursuant to your comments at the end of our meeting, I shall follow up on the Woodhills areas to provide you with all current information concerning development activity in progress and currently in various stages of planning. Once again, thank you very much for your consideration and time.

Respectfully submitted,

Presentation/Package Letter

January 2, 1990

Mr. Richard Brenann
Senior Vice President
Eammon, Strasser and Weeks
225 North Michigan Avenue
22nd Floor
Chicago, Illinois 60601

Dear Richard:

The Thomas Arthur Company is pleased to have the opportunity to present our tenant representation and consulting proposal together with our supplementary corporate presentation to Eammon, Strasser and Weeks for your consideration.

Our presentation this afternoon will have highlighted much of the material contained in the enclosed submission and we are confident that at its conclusion you will be convinced that the Thomas Arthur Company's solutions have approached your facilities issues in a thoughtful, comprehensive and results-oriented manner.

Our tenant representation services philosophy emphasizes our commitment to your needs through excellent communication, creativity, responsiveness and an unequaled work ethic on our client's behalf.

The financial aspects of our proposal highlight a fee structure that is intended to demonstrate that the Thomas Arthur Company provides a higher level of service with the greatest amount of client value.

Thank you very much for giving us the opportunity to present our services and please be assured that we all look forward to the privilege of providing Eammon, Strasser and Weeks our finest tenant representation services.

Respectfully submitted,

A P P E N D I X
6

Sample Table of Contents for Packages

THE THOMAS ARTHUR COMPANY
COMPREHENSIVE REAL ESTATE SERVICES
JANUARY, 1990

TABLE OF CONTENTS (Package A)

Section I

1. Thomas Arthur Company corporate background
2. Summary of comprehensive services
3. Client-relationship summaries
4. Project-team organizational charts
5. Project-team résumés
6. Professional affiliations
7. Market information and data-base systems
8. Client financial considerations and alternatives

Section II

1. Program time function analysis
2. Client solutions and alternatives
3. Support data and specific market features
4. Space analysis and configurations
5. Sample letter of intent
6. Sample marketing plan for sublease considerations
7. Recommendations

TABLE OF CONTENTS (Package B)

Project summary
Market studies
Competitive projects
Demographics
Business plan
Operating information
Environmental reports and asbestos study
Title reports
Pro forma analysis with actual data
Pro forma analysis with assumptions
Summary of all debt information
Financial analysis
Alternative financial and debt structures

Index